AMERICA'S ELITE

US SPECIAL FORCES
FROM THE
AMERICAN REVOLUTION
TO THE PRESENT DAY

CHRIS McNAB

First published in Great Britain in 2012 by Osprey Publishing,
Midland House, West Way, Botley, Oxford, OX2 0PH, UK
4301 21st Street, Suite 22B, Long Island City, NY 11101, USA

E-mail: info@ospreypublishing.com

Osprey Publishing is part of the Osprey Group

© 2013 Osprey Publishing

A CIP catalogue record for this book is available from the British Library

ISBN: 978 1 78096 284 9
E-pub ISBN: 978 1 78200 316 8
PDF ISBN: 978 1 78200 317 5

Page layout by Myriam Bell Design, UK
Index by Zoe Ross
Typeset in Bembo and Trade Gothic
Originated by PDQ Digital Media Soultions, Suffolk, UK
Printed in China through Bookbuilders

13 14 15 16 17 18   10 9 8 7 6 5 4 3 2 1

Osprey Publishing is supporting the Woodland Trust, the UK's leading woodland conservation charity, by funding
the dedication of trees.

www.ospreypublishing.com

Front Cover: From left to right, top to bottom: Tom Laemlein, US Navy, Thomas Flanagan, Mir Bahmanyar,
NARA, Phil Stern, Phil Stern, Phil Stern, Phil Stern, Mir Bahmanyar and Chris Osman, NARA, Mir Bahmanyar,
Mir Bahmanyar and Chris Osman, MHI, Mir Bahmanyar and Chris Osman, John Galetzka, NARA, DOD, USASOC,
Mir Bahmanyar, Mir Bahmanyar, NARA, Mir Bahmanyar, John Galetzka, Justin Vienne, Phil Stern, DOD.

AMERICA'S
ELITE

OSPREY
PUBLISHING

CONTENTS

INTRODUCTION

LEFT: US SEAL team members participate in a tactical warfare training exercise in 1987. The SEAL in the foreground is carrying a field radio and is armed with a Colt Commando assault rifle equipped with an M203 grenade launcher. (NARA)

TO OUTSIDERS, THERE IS SOMETHING undoubtedly compelling about the world of US Special Operations Forces (SOF). The men and women who inhabit the half-seen world of "special ops" are lauded and often mythologized as an elite within an already expert military; individuals who represent the ultimate levels of professional soldiering. Their missions are spoken of with respect and fascination, not least because SOF operations often pit a handful of men against a numerically superior enemy, and frequently behind enemy lines where survivability is stacked against the infiltrated combat teams.

A good part of the respect afforded SOF also comes from the very difficulty of entering them in the first place. Out of a total US armed services of 1.5 million active personnel (plus the same in reserve), just 66,000 belong to the US Special Operations Command (SOCOM), and only a fraction of those are actual active frontline combatants. The demands placed upon the troops in the field, both physically and intellectually, mean that anyone wanting to enter SOF ranks has to pass through selection and assessment programs designed to test applicants virtually to destruction.

Take the US Navy's Basic Underwater Demolition/SEAL (BUD/S) course, as an example. All US Navy personnel, officer and enlisted alike, who desire to become naval commandos must attend BUD/S, conducted at the Naval Special Warfare Center, Coronado. Just to qualify to attend the course, candidates must swim 500yd (457m) using breast- and/or sidestroke in less than 12 minutes 30 seconds. They are allowed a ten-minute rest before having to perform a minimum of 42 push-ups in two minutes, before taking a two-minute break. Next comes at least 50 sit-ups in two minutes, again followed by a two-minute rest, and then a minimum of six pull-ups, with no time limit. After resting for ten minutes they have to tackle a 1½-mile (2.4km) run wearing boots and long pants, in under 11 minutes 30 seconds.

This is only the start. BUD/S proper then begins with an indoctrination program in which the students must meet the minimum physical requirements and learn rudimentary skills needed for the actual course. BUD/S has three distinct phases:

FIRST PHASE: BASIC CONDITIONING

First Phase is eight weeks long and emphasizes increased physical conditioning for students, including weekly 4-mile (6.4km) runs in boots as well as timed obstacle courses. The student will also take part in ocean swims of up to 2 miles (3.2km) while wearing fins. Rudimentary training also includes classes on basic small-boat skills. The initial four weeks of First Phase are preparation for the fifth week, commonly known as "Hell Week." Students undergo five and a half days of continuous training, with no more than four hours of sleep during the week. Hydrographic surveying and the preparation of hydrographic charts are taught over the remainder of the BUD/S First Phase.

SECOND PHASE: DIVING

Scuba (self-contained underwater breathing apparatus) training consists of two types – open circuit (compressed air) and closed circuit (100 percent oxygen). This is considered by many to be the SEALs' raison d'être, and accordingly lasts eight weeks.

THIRD PHASE: LAND WARFARE

This part lasts nine weeks and teaches basic field craft, demolition, reconnaissance, weapons, and tactics. BUD/S concludes with a practical tactical exercise at San Clemente Island, off the San Diego coast.

Additional training lasting from six months to a daunting one year is sometimes necessary before an officer is considered fully qualified. The practice has also been for BUD/S graduates to go on to complete a three-week course in standard airborne training at the US Army Airborne School at Fort Benning, Georgia. And this is still a long way from the end of the SEAL's training journey. Following graduation from BUD/S he will then undergo a 28-week SEAL Qualification Training program. In this he is given all manner of specialist instruction, including such elements as demolition, combat

Sergeant First Class John McIntosh, a member of the "High Altitude, Low Opening" (HALO) parachute team, jumps from a CH-47D Chinook as part of a change-of-command ceremony in 2009 for his unit, Charlie Company, 5th Battalion, 19th Special Forces Group (Airborne). (US Army)

engineering, advanced combat first aid (such as the 26-week Special Operations Combat Medic course), amphibious reconnaissance, advanced parachuting techniques, and much more. Note, however, that the recruit can still fail the program, and not make it into the SEALs. In fact, during the year-long complete training program, around 80–85 percent of those who attempt to join the SEALs do not make it to an operational unit.

On account of such in-built adversity, SOF training programs alone therefore attract our admiration, plus the focus of those individuals who want to test themselves to the utmost by joining a force held in admiration by the rest of the armed services. It is in the world of operations, however, that SOF truly make their mark. This book, which charts a history of special forces from the days of colonial America through to operations in present-day Afghanistan and Iraq, will explore both the successes and the failures of SOF, from the Rangers of the 18th century through to the SEAL operation against Osama bin Laden in 2011. In doing so, we will see how SOF produce exceptional individuals capable of the most astonishing feats of endurance and tactical skill.

An early question that has to be answered, however, is what constitutes "special forces?" The answer is not as simple might be supposed. If we classify SOF as those who have received advanced training beyond the standards of regular infantry soldiers, including specialist tactical or technical skills, then we could include not only all paratroopers and Marines (who receive airborne and amphibious training respectively), but also almost any specialist soldier, such as a weapons technician and communications officer. For this reason, the US military community has indeed often resisted the very notion of an "elite," feeling that giving the title to some groups of soldiers downgrades the professionalism and expertise possessed by the general armed services. Such is a valid complaint, yet the fact remains that with the creation of overarching SOF organizations such as SOCOM, the notion of a specialist soldiery purpose-designed to perform unusual high-risk *combat* operations is now ingrained in US military culture. Indeed, perhaps the best way to define SOF is to list the "Five SOF Truths" stated by SOCOM itself:

1. Humans are more important than hardware. People – not equipment – make the critical difference. The right people, highly trained and working as a team, will accomplish the mission with the equipment available. On the other hand, the best equipment in the world cannot compensate for a lack of the right people.

2. Quality is better than quantity. A small number of people, carefully selected, well trained and well led, are preferable to larger numbers of troops, some of whom may not be up to the task.

3. Special operations forces (SOF) cannot be mass-produced. It takes years to train operational units to the level of proficiency needed to accomplish difficult and specialized

SOF missions. Intense training – both in SOF schools and units – is required to integrate competent individuals into fully capable units. This process cannot be hastened without degrading ultimate capability.

4. Competent special operations forces cannot be created after emergencies occur. Creation of competent, fully mission-capable units takes time. Employment of fully capable special operations capability on short notice requires highly trained and constantly available SOF units in peacetime.

5. Most special operations require non-SOF assistance. The operational effectiveness of deployed forces cannot be, and never has been, achieved without being enabled by joint service partners. The support of Air Force, Army, Marine, and Navy engineers, technicians, intelligence analysts, and the numerous other professions who contribute to SOF have substantially increased SOF capabilities and effectiveness throughout the world.

– http://www.socom.mil

The progressive "truths" here encapsulate the essence of the SOF warrior: trained to an exceptionally high level; integrated into small units of equal professionalism; tasked with missions beyond the capabilities of large-scale forces; and fully integrated into the general operational support of the wider armed services.

In this book we will see how these principles have emerged and been refined over the centuries. As much as an explanation of the evolution of elite combat units, it also provides a practical illustration of how SOF are indeed warranted in the US armed forces, at both conceptual and practical levels. In today's complex conflicts, more than ever, the ability to deliver precision strikes against high-value targets, while negotiating the social and political complexities of the world around those targets, is at a premium. SOF are there to do precisely that.

COLONIAL
AND CIVIL WAR
WARRIORS

THE BRITISH NORTH AMERICAN COLONIES evolved in the face of hostile fortune from the first settlements in Virginia and Massachusetts in the early 17th century. The development and success of the various colonies set up along the North Atlantic coastline was truly extraordinary. Within a few decades, after usually difficult beginnings, the population and wealth of the communities grew rapidly. Some of the small coastal settlements grew into important port cities such as Boston, New York (originally founded by the Dutch), Baltimore, and Philadelphia. By the middle of the 18th century the colonial populations of European origin were reckoned to total over a million and a half souls.

Unlike those implanted by other European powers, the early settlers of these English colonies in North America were often refugees from their own native land, usually for religious reasons. They were soon joined in the New World by individuals from all walks of life who were seeking a better future than they could hope for in Europe. Thus, for example, the Puritans in Massachusetts and the Quakers in Pennsylvania were eventually outnumbered by later immigrants inspired by more material motives; but the special character of the first settlements was never quite lost, and continued to be influential in the social and political lives of these colonies. The settlers in Virginia and further to the south were not as rigid in their religious beliefs, being for the most part adventurers who wished to establish rich plantation domains; they were especially successful in Virginia and South Carolina.

The colonies were not established without many struggles – first against the Indians, who periodically resisted the arrival of the settlers by waging ferocious wars, and later against the Spanish in Florida to the south and especially against the French to the north and west. The Spanish remained somewhat contained in Florida and, while worrisome to the British settlers in the Carolinas and Georgia, did not constitute a major or consistent menace. The French were another matter. Due to their extensive explorations in the interior of North America, they had established colonies and outposts that formed an arc from the Gulf of Mexico to the Gulf of the St Lawrence by the early 18th century. The French colonies were far smaller in population but were militarily very powerful, largely due to their many Indian alliances. They were governed by a largely autocratic and military authority; apart from regular garrisons they also had well-organized and well-led militias which became intimately familiar with long-range movement through the wilderness and with the tactics of woodlands warfare.

Here, if anywhere, lie the roots of the future development of US Special Forces. The soldiery of the emergent colonies was a varied tapestry of improvised and formalized units, a mix of regular and provincial militias, the latter of frequently uneven quality. Yet the challenges of fighting in the American wilderness meant that those who combined field craft with the ability to handle a musket and knife were soon in demand.

OPPOSITE: A "Minuteman" of the Revolutionary War, as depicted in an engraving from *Harper's Weekly* from July 15, 1876. The Minutemen were a militia force geared up for rapid deployment at a moment's notice. (NARA)

One of the earliest formal expressions of such an ethos was the "Ranger," especially those associated with a certain Robert Rogers.

THE RANGER WARRIOR

Along the frontiers of the northern American colonies, where most of the battles of the French and Indian War (1754–63) took place, "Rangers" proved indispensable adjuncts to the main regular and provincial armies, both as partisan warriors and as scouts. They were essentially backwoodsmen – hunters, trappers, militiamen, and Indian fighters – used to operating independently rather than in regimented ranks of soldiery, living off the land and relying on their knowledge of terrain and gun to keep them alive. The very qualities that many commanders despised in the Rangers – field attire that often resembled that of "savage" Indians; unconventional tactics; their occasional obstreperousness; their democratic recruiting standards that allowed blacks and Indians into their ranks – are what helped make them uniquely adroit at fighting their formidable Canadian and Indian wilderness foes, in all kinds of weather conditions and environments.

Battles with Native American warriors in the early 17th century had demonstrated the virtual uselessness of European armor, pikes, cavalry, and maneuvers in the dense

LEFT: RANGERS' KIT, EQUIPMENT, WEAPONS, AND SPECIAL CLOTHING, 18TH CENTURY
1) A c.1735–50, .75-cal "Long Land Pattern" Brown Bess musket, sawed down from its overall length of 61 34in (157cm) to a lighter, more maneuverable 50 38in (128cm), with its sight repositioned. 2) An English-made, .65-cal carbine with a rifled barrel and socket bayonet. 3) Field officer's fusil, a short, streamlined musket generally weighing several pounds less than a Brown Bess. 4) Belt hatchet or tomahawk. 5) A pair of silver-mounted Queen Anne style screw-barrel (or "cannon-barrel") pistols, favorites of many officers and civilians. 6) An American-made cutlass with a cylindrical wooden grip and iron hilt, its blade 26½in (67cm) long. 7) Folding clasp knives such as this bone-handled, brass-ended one were favored by Rangers over sheath knives, and for obvious reasons were dubbed "scalping knives." 8) Small "spying-glasses," or "prospective glasses," often closing to only 4in (10cm) in length (such as this all-brass type), were carried by Rogers and his officers on scouts. 9) Rangers preferred shooting with loose ball and powder horn rather than with fixed cartridges. 10) A typical Ranger round, as noted by Captain Knox, consisting of "a smaller shot, of the size of full-grown peas: six or seven of which, with a ball, they generally load." 11) An iron ice creeper, worn under the instep and held in place by thongs or buckled straps. 12) A type of ice skate common to the 18th century, with straps, small iron peg for the heel of the thick moccasin or shoe, and three smaller points for the sole. 13) Detail of a decorated leather legging, or "Indian stocking." Leather leggings, however, were not as common among the Rangers as were those made of such coarse woolen materials as frieze, stroud, or rateen, generally green in color, as in 14), or dark blue. A ribbon or binding trims the edges of the cloth, and straps for belt and feet keep the legging from sagging. 15) A snowshoe of a shape common to the 18th-century New England frontier. Hide strings, and sinew of deer, moose, or horse, made the netting. 16) A typically wide-brimmed, civilian Scotch bonnet, most often blue, although some colonial merchants sold them in "various colors." 17) A simply made leather jockey cap, its upturned visor left unfaced. 18) Mitten made of blanket material. Others were made of knitted wool, or of beaver or other skins. 19) A hat with its brim cut down to enable the Ranger or soldier to move more easily through the woods. 20) A pair of "Snow Moggisons," as they were called in a list of clothing for a planned winter drive against Crown Point in 1756. (Gary Zaboly © Osprey Publishing)

New World forests. Although New England militia units had proven themselves courageous and adaptable during the horrific baptism of fire with local tribes known as King Philip's War (1676–77), it was not until the early 1700s that the colonists could produce frontiersmen capable of penetrating deep into uncharted Indian territory. In 1709, for instance, Captain Benjamin Wright took 14 Rangers on a 400-mile (640km) round trip by canoe, up the Connecticut River, across the Green Mountains, and to the northern end of Lake Champlain, along the way fighting four skirmishes with Indians.

The "Indian hunters" under Massachusetts' Captain John Lovewell were among the most effective of the early Rangers. Their long, hard-fought battle at Lovewell's Pond on May 9, 1725, against Pigwacket Abenakis under the bearskin-robed war chief Paugus, became a watershed event in New England frontier history. Its story was told around hearths and campfires for decades, and its example informed future Rangers that Indian warriors were not always invincible in the woods.

When the third war for control of North America broke out in 1744 (commonly called King George's War, after George II), several veterans of Lovewell's fight raised their own Ranger companies and passed on their valuable field knowledge. Among the recruits who joined one company assigned to scout the upper Merrimack River valley around Rumford (later Concord), New Hampshire, was the teenager Robert Rogers.

Incessant French and Indian inroads turned the war of 1744–48 into a largely defensive one for the northern colonies. Log stockades and blockhouses protected refugee frontier families; Rumford itself had 12 such "garrison houses." When not on patrol or pursuing enemy raiders, Rangers acted as armed guards for workers in the field. Bells and cannon from the forts sounded warnings when the enemy was detected in the vicinity.

At the beginning of the last French and Indian War, each newly raised provincial regiment generally included one or two Ranger companies: men lightly dressed and equipped to serve as quick-reaction strike forces as well as scouts and intelligence gatherers. The Duke of Cumberland, Captain General of the British Army, not only encouraged their raising but also advised that some regular troops would have to reinvent themselves along Ranger lines before wilderness campaigns could be won.

Nevertheless, it was not until after the shocking 1757 fall of Fort William Henry that plans were finally accelerated to counterbalance the large numbers of Canadian and Indian partisans. Enlightened redcoat generals such as Brigadier George Augustus Howe, older brother of William, recognized that the forest war could not be won without Rangers. Howe was so firmly convinced of this that in 1758 he persuaded Major-General James Abercromby to revamp his entire army into the image of the Rangers, dress-wise, arms-wise, and drill-wise. Major-General Jeffrey Amherst, who would orchestrate the eventual conquest of Canada, championed Major Robert Rogers and the formation of a Ranger corps as soon as he became the new commander-in-chief in late 1758. "I shall always cheerfully receive Your opinion in relation to the Service you are Engaged in," he promised Rogers. In the summer of 1759, Amherst's faith in the Rangers was rewarded when, in the process of laying siege to Fort Carillon at Ticonderoga, they again proved themselves the only unit in the army sufficiently skilled to deal with the enemy's bushfighters. Even the general's vaunted Louisbourg light infantry received Amherst's wrath after two night attacks by Indians had resulted in 18 of their number killed and wounded, mostly from friendly fire.

Before the year was out, Rogers had burned the Abenaki village of Odanak, on the distant St Francis River, its warriors the long-time scourge of the New England frontier. In 1760, after the Rangers had spearheaded the expulsion of French troops from the Richelieu River valley, Amherst sent Rogers and his men to carry the news of Montreal's surrender to the French outposts lying nearly 1,000 miles (1,600km) to the west. He sent them because they were the only soldiers in his 17,000-man army able to accomplish the task.

The final phase of the battle of Bunker Hill demonstrated the inherent weakness of the militia. Once the British regulars overcame the fortifications, the bayonet broke colonial resistance. British generals avoided further daylight attacks on entrenched rebels. (Courtesy Army Art Collection, US Army Center of Military History)

A depiction of Rogers' Rangers, as they would have been seen c.1760. The green uniforms in themselves were something of a revolution, as they constituted an early form of camouflage and were an indication of the value the Rangers placed on concealability. (NARA)

Captain Robert Rogers' Ranger corps became the primary model for the eventual transformation of the regular and provincial army in that region. Colonial irregulars aside from Rogers' men also contributed to the success of British arms during the war: provincial units such as Israel Putnam's Connecticut Rangers, companies of Stockbridge Mahican and Connecticut Mohegan Indians, Joseph Gorham's and George Scott's Nova Scotia Rangers, and home-based companies such as Captain Hezekiah Dunn's, on the New Jersey frontier. During Pontiac's War (1763–64), Ranger companies led by such captains as Thomas Cresap and James Smith mustered to defend Maryland and Pennsylvania border towns and valleys.

RECRUITMENT, TRAINING, AND ENLISTMENT

Rogers' Rangers, the most famous, active, and influential colonial partisan body of the French and Indian War, never enjoyed the long-term establishment of a British regular regiment, with its permanent officer cadre, nor were they classed as a regiment or a battalion as the annually raised provincial troops were. In fact, at its peak Rogers' command was merely a collection, or corps, of short-term, independently raised Ranger companies. Technically, "Rogers' Rangers" were the men serving in the single company he commanded. By courtesy, the title was extended to the other Ranger companies (excepting provincial units) with the Hudson valley/Lake George army, since he was the senior Ranger officer there.

Rogers first captained Ranger Company Number One of Colonel Joseph Blanchard's New Hampshire Regiment in the 1755 Lake George campaign. Thirty-two hardy souls volunteered to remain with him at Fort William Henry that winter to continue scouting and raiding the enemy forts in the north, despite the lack of bounty or salary money.

Near the beginning of the spring of 1756, reports of Rogers' success in the field prompted Massachusetts' Governor-General William Shirley (then temporary commander of British forces) to award him "the command of an independent company of Rangers," to consist of 60 privates, three sergeants, an ensign, and two lieutenants. Robert's brother, Richard, would be his first lieutenant. No longer on a provincial footing, Rogers' Rangers would be paid and fed out of the royal war chest and answerable to British commanders. Although not on a permanent establishment, Ranger officers would receive almost the same pay as redcoat officers, while Ranger privates would earn twice as much as their provincial counterparts, who were themselves paid higher wages than the regulars. (Captain Joseph Gorham's older Ranger company, based in Nova Scotia, enjoyed a royal commission, and thus a permanency denied those units serving in the Hudson valley.) Rogers was ordered by Shirley "to enlist none but such as were used to travelling and hunting, and in whose courage and fidelity I could confide."

Because the men of Rogers' own company, and of those additional companies his veteran officers were assigned to raise, were generally frontier-bred, the amount of basic training they had to undergo was not as protracted as that endured by the average redcoat recruit. A typical Derryfield farmer, for instance, would have entered the Ranger service as an already proficient tracker and hunter. He was probably able to construct a bark or brush lean-to in less than an hour, find direction in the darkest woods, make rope from the inner bark of certain trees, and survive for days on a scanty trail diet.

The typical New Hampshire recruit could also "shoot amazingly well," as Captain Henry Pringle of the 27th Foot observed. Based at Fort Edward and a volunteer in one of Rogers' biggest scouting excursions, Pringle wrote in December 1757 of one Ranger officer who, "the other day, at four shots with four balls, killed a brace of Deer, a Pheasant, and a pair of wild ducks – the latter he killed at one Shot." In fact, many New England troops, according to an eyewitness in Nova Scotia, could "load their firelocks upon their back, and then turn upon their bellies, and take aim at their enemies: there are no better marksmen in the world, for their whole delight is shooting at marks for wages."

The heavy emphasis on marksmanship in Rogers' corps, and the issuance of rifled carbines to many of the men, paid off in their frequent success against the Canadians

Detail from Captain Thomas Davies' *A South View of ... Crown Point.* "Hutts of Rangers & Indians Wigwams" are shown, according to the key. Bark lodges can be seen near the log huts in several forms: wigwam, tent, and lean-to. (Thomas Davies, National Archives of Canada /C-013314)

and Indians. (Marksmanship remains among the most important of all Ranger legacies, one that continues to be stressed in the training of today's high-tech special forces.) Even in Rogers' only large-scale defeat, the battle on Snowshoes of March 13, 1758, the sharpshooting of his heavily outnumbered Rangers held off the encircling enemy for 90 minutes. Over two dozen Indians alone were killed and wounded, among the dead one of their war chiefs. This was an unusually high casualty rate for the stealthy Native Americans ("who are not accustomed to lose," said Montcalm of the battle). So enraged were the Indians that they summarily executed a like number of Rangers who had surrendered on the promise of good quarter.

Learning how to operate watercraft on the northern lakes and streams was another crucial skill for every Ranger. Birchbark canoes and bateaux (rowing vessels made for transporting goods) were used in Rogers' earliest forays on Lake George. In 1756, these were swapped for newly arrived whaleboats made of light cedar planking. Designed for speed, they had keels, round bottoms, and sharp ends, allowing for a quick change of direction and agile handling even on choppy waters. Blankets could be rigged as improvised sails.

Additional things the new recruit had to learn, or at least to perfect, included: how to build a raft; how to ford a rapid river without a raft or boat; how to portage a whaleboat over a mountain range; how to "log" a position in the forest as a makeshift breastwork; how to design and sew a pair of moccasins; how to utter bird and animal calls as "private signals" in the woods; and sometimes how to light and hurl a grenade.

TACTICS AND CAMPAIGNING

Because the *modus operandi* of Rangers remained unknown to the bulk of the regular army, Rogers was ordered in 1757 to pen a compendium of "rules, or plan of discipline," for those "Gentlemen Officers" who wanted to learn Ranger methods. To ensure that the lessons were properly understood, 50 regular volunteers from eight regiments formed a special company to fall under Rogers' tutelage. His job was to instruct them in "our methods of marching, retreating, ambushing, fighting, &c." Many of these rules, totaling 28 in number, were essentially derived from old Indian tactics and techniques, and were well known to New England frontiersmen.

Rule II, for instance, specified that if your scouting party was small, "march in a single file, keeping at such a distance from each other as to prevent one shot from killing two men." Rule V recommended that a party leaving enemy country should return home by a different route, to avoid being ambushed on its own tracks. Rule X warned that if the enemy was about to overwhelm you, "let the whole body disperse, and every one take a different road to the place of rendezvous appointed for the evening."

Other rules required that even the most proficient recruit had to undergo special training in bush-fighting tactics. If 300–400 Rangers were marching "with a design to attack the enemy," noted Rule VI, "divide your party into three columns … and let the columns march in single files, the columns to the right and left keeping at twenty yards [20m] distance or more from that of the center," with proper guards in front, rear, and on the flanks. If attacked in front, "form a front of your three columns or main body with the advanced guard, keeping out your flanking parties … to prevent the enemy from pursuing hard on either of your wings, or surrounding you, which is the usual method of the savages."

Rule VII advised the Rangers to "fall, or squat down," if forced to take the enemy's first fire, and "then rise and discharge at them." Rule IX suggested that "if you are obliged to retreat, let the front of your whole party fire and fall back, till the rear hath done the same, making for the best ground you can, by this means you will oblige the enemy to pursue you, if they do it at all, in the face of a constant fire."

Most of Rogers' activities during the war consisted not of battles and skirmishes but of lightning raids, pursuits, and other special operations. As General Shirley's 1756 orders stated, Rogers was "to use my best endeavours to distress the French and their allies, by sacking, burning, and destroying their houses, barns, barracks, canoes, battoes, &c." The "&c" included slaughtering the enemy's herds of cattle and horses, ambushing and destroying his provision sleighs, setting fire to his fields of grain and piles of cordwood, sneaking into the ditches of his forts to make observations, and seizing prisoners for interrogation.

When the big armies under Johnson, Abercromby, Forbes, Wolfe, Amherst, Bouquet, and others marched into enemy territory, Rangers acted as advanced and flank guards, often engaging and repulsing the kind of partisan attacks that had destroyed Braddock's force. One imperative in bush fighting was camouflage; for Rogers' men, green attire was a constant throughout the war. Other Anglo-American irregulars, like Gage's 80th Light Infantry and Putnam's Connecticut Rangers, wore brown. Some, like Bradstreet's armed bateau men and Dunn's New Jersey Rangers, wore gray. A few Ranger companies in Nova Scotia wore dark blue or black.

Green may have been their color of choice, but Rogers' men never enjoyed a consistent uniform pattern throughout their five-year career, as the regulars and some provincial regiments did. On campaign with Rogers in Nova Scotia in July 1757, a Derryfield farmer-turned-Ranger would have been dressed in "no particular uniform," according to observer Captain John Knox of the 46th, who added that each Ranger wore his "cloaths short." This probably signified a variety of coats, jackets, waistcoats, or just shirts, all deliberately trimmed to make them lighter. In the field, the Rangers often resembled Indians, exhibiting a "cut-throat, savage appearance," as one writer at Louisbourg recorded in 1758.

Rangers conduct a perimeter defense, La Barbue Creek, 1757. The Indian tactic of two men defending a tree, with one of them firing while the other reloads, had been sensibly adopted by many white frontier soldiers. One of the foreground Rangers spits a musket ball into the barrel of his musket, which speeded up the loading process (as many as six to eight bullets could be held in the mouth). (Gary Zaboly © Osprey Publishing)

Among the many perils facing a Ranger assigned to a winter scout in the Adirondack Mountains were temperatures sometimes reaching 40 degrees below zero, snowblindness, bleeding feet, hypothermia, frostbite, gangrene, and lost fingers, toes, and noses. Deep slush often layered the frozen lakes, and sometimes a man would fall through a hole in the ice. Rogers routinely sent back those who began limping or complaining during the first days on the trail. Things only got more onerous as they neared the enemy forts: fireless camps had to be endured, unless they found a depression on a high ridge where a deep hole could be scooped out with snowshoes to accommodate a small fire. Around this were arrayed shelters of pine boughs, each containing "mattresses" of evergreen branches overlaid with bearskins. Wrapped in their blankets like human cocoons, the Rangers would dangle their feet over the flames or coals to spend a tolerably comfortable night.

Guarding the Ranger camp in no-man's land or enemy country required sentry parties numbering six men each, "two of whom must be constantly alert," noted Rogers, "and when relieved by their fellows, it should be done without noise." When dawn broke, the entire detachment was awakened, "that being the time when the savages chuse to fall upon their enemies." Before setting out again, the area around the campsite was probed for enemy tracks.

Drawing provisions, bedding, and extra clothing on hand-sleds prevented the men from burning too many calories and exuding dangerously excessive sweat. Expert snowshoers, they could nimbly climb "over several large mountains" in one day, as provincial Jeduthan Baldwin did on a trek with Rogers in March 1756. Aside from additional warm wear such as flannel under jackets, woolen socks, shoepack liners, fur caps, and thick mittens, the marching winter Rangers wore their blankets wrapped, belted, and sometimes hooded around them, much as the Indians did.

Battling the French and Indians in snow that was often chest-deep could be lethal for a Ranger with a broken snowshoe. Ironically, the green clothing worn by Rogers' men proved a liability when they had a white slope of snow behind them. According to Captain Pringle, during the 1758 battle on Snowshoes, Rogers' servant was forced to lay "aside his green jacket in the field, as I did likewise my furred Cap, which became a mark to the enemy, and probably was the cause of a slight wound in my face." Pringle, "unaccustomed to Snow-Shoes," found himself unable to join the surviving Rangers in their retreat at battle's end. He and two other men endured seven days of wandering the white forest before surrendering to the French.

Given the nature of their operations, the Rangers had to be particularly disciplined with their rations. On a winter trek in 1759, Ranger sutler James Gordon wrote, "I had a pound or two of bread, a dozen crackers, about two [pounds of] fresh pork and a quart of brandy." Henry Pringle survived his post-battle ordeal in the forest by subsisting on "a small Bologna sausage, and a little ginger … water, & the bark & berries of trees." Also eaten was the Indians' favorite trail food, parched corn – corn that had been parched and then pounded into flour. It was in effect an appetite suppressant: a spoonful of it, followed by a drink of water, expanded in the stomach, making the traveler feel as though he had consumed a large meal.

Obtaining food from the enemy helped sustain Rangers on their return home. Slaughtered cattle herds at Ticonderoga and Crown Point provided tongues ("a very great refreshment," noted Rogers). David Perry and several other Rangers of Captain Moses Hazen's company raided a French house near Quebec in 1759, finding "plenty of pickled Salmon, which was quite a rarity to most of us." In another house they dined on "hasty-pudding." At St Francis, Rogers' men packed corn for the long march back, but after eight days, he wrote, their "provisions grew scarce." For some reason game was also scarce in the northern New England wilderness during the fall of 1759, and the Rangers' survival skills underwent severe tests even as they were being pursued by a vengeful enemy. Now and then they found an owl, partridge, or muskrat to shoot, but much of the time they dined on amphibians, mushrooms, beech leaves, and tree bark. Volunteer Robert Kirk of the 77th Highland Regiment wrote that "we were obliged

The conventional picture of American infantrymen, lined up in ranks to present a coordinated wall of bayonet and shot. Skirmishers, sharpshooters, and Rangers broke away from this tactical model, in favor of small-unit maneuver. (Courtesy Army Art Collection, US Army Center of Military History)

to scrape under the snow for acorns, and even to eat our shoes and belts, and broil our powder-horns and thought it delicious eating."

Things grew so desperate that some Rangers roasted Abenaki bounty scalps for the little circles of flesh they held. One small party of Rangers and light infantry was ambushed and almost entirely destroyed by the French and Indians. When other Rangers discovered the bodies, "on them, accordingly, they fell like Cannibals, and devoured part of them raw," stuffing the remaining flesh, including heads, into their packs. One Ranger later confessed that he and his starving comrades "hardly deserved the name of human beings."

Excellent marksmanship, aside from scoutcraft and daring, is what made the best Rangers. Former hunters and trappers most of them, they understood how a single well-aimed shot might alter the course of a skirmish or battle in the forest. Robert Rogers instructed his companies to practice firing at marks so frequently that at least one British commander, Lieutenant-Colonel William Haviland, scolded him, considering it an "extravagance in Ammunition." (Gary Zaboly © Osprey Publishing)

A private in Captain John Lovewell's New England Ranger Company, 1725. In his clothing and equipment, this private exemplifies the hybrid European/Indian composition of Lovewell's men. Note the Indian toboggan, usually made of two planks of green spruce, birch, or elm wood that were lashed together with rawhide. (Gary Zaboly © Osprey Publishing)

OTHER CAMPAIGN CHALLENGES

"We are in a most damnable country," wrote a lieutenant of the 55th Foot at Lake George in 1758, "fit only for wolves, and its native savages." In such a demanding environment the Rangers were constantly being pushed to their physical and psychological limits, especially when captives of the enemy. Teenager Thomas Brown, bleeding profusely from three bullet holes after Rogers' January 1757 battle near Ticonderoga, "concluded, if possible, to crawl into the Woods and there die of my Wounds." Taken prisoner by Indians, who often threatened his life, he was forced to dance around a fellow Ranger who was being slowly tortured at a stake. Recovering from his wounds, Brown was later traded to a Canadian merchant, with whom he "fared no better than a Slave," before making his escape. Captain Israel Putnam himself was once saved from a burning stake by the last-minute intervention of a Canadian officer. Ranger William Moore had the heart of a slain comrade forced into his mouth. Later, he had some 200 pine splints stuck into his body, each one about to be set afire by his captors, when a woman of the tribe announced she would adopt him. Two captured Indian Rangers were shackled with irons and shipped to France, where they were sold into "extreme hard labor."

Tasks that might appear Herculean to others were strictly routine for the Rangers. In July 1756, Rogers and his men chopped open a 6-mile (10km) path across the forested mountains between Lake George and Wood Creek, then hauled five armed whaleboats over it to make a raid on French shipping on Lake Champlain. On their march to St Francis, the Rangers sloshed for nine days through a bog in which they "could scarcely get a Dry Place to sleep on." Rogers himself is said to have escaped pursuing Indians after his March 1758 battle by sliding down a smooth mountain slope nearly 700ft (210m) long. His four-month mission to Detroit and back in 1760 covered over 1,600 miles (2,500km), one of the most remarkable expeditions in all American history.

At campaign's end, of course, there were rewards to be enjoyed. In late August 1758, Rogers gave his company "a barrell of Wine treat," and after a large bonfire was lit, the men "played round it" in celebration of recent British victories. As the Richelieu Valley was being swept of French troops in 1760, provincial captain Samuel Jenks wrote with delight, "Our Rangers … inform us the ladys are very kind in the neighbourhood, which seems we shall fare better when we git into the thick setled parts of the country." Natural wonders previously unseen by any British soldiers, including Niagara Falls, awaited the 200 Rangers who followed Rogers that year to lay claim to Canada's Great Lakes country for England, and to win the friendship of some of the very tribes they had so often fought.

OPPOSITE: An engraving of the illustrious Robert Rogers. Rogers left a lasting military legacy – his "Rules of Ranging" are still to be found in the US Army Rangers handbook. (NARA)

LIGHT INFANTRY AND SHARPSHOOTERS

By clearly demonstrating how useless machine-like linear tactics were in the shaggy northern forests, the Rangers also inspired reforms in the regular army, including the creation of its first light infantry companies. Light infantry warrant a place in this book, if only for the fact that the emphasis on mobile sharpshooters laid the conceptual foundations for future scout-reconnaissance units. Americans have long made their ability with rifles, something required on a frontier where most of one's food came from what one hunted, a matter of national pride. In the mid-18th century the short, large-bored hunting rifles of German forests became long, slender, small-bored rifles used on the frontiers by men who were keen shots. When the American Revolution (1775–83) broke out it was natural that men used to these weapons would disdain the smoothbore, inaccurate musket, and pin their faith on the Pennsylvania rifle.

In 1775 frontiersmen in Pennsylvania flocked to join Edward Hand's Rifle Regiment of the Continental Army, then besieging the British at Boston. Other rifle units were quickly raised, including one from Virginia, about which George Washington wrote, "These are all chosen men, selected from the army at large, well acquainted with the use of the rifle and with that mode of fighting, which is necessary to make them a good counterpoise to the Indians… I expect the most eminent services from them."

While these riflemen concerned British officers at first, in action their weapons were slow to load and, lacking the ability to be mounted with the bayonet, riflemen made easy prey to quick-moving British light infantry. Still, some rifle units stayed in

A rare eyewitness glimpse of a French and Indian War army on the move: Captain Thomas Davies' 1760 watercolor of Amherst's troops advancing toward Montreal down the La Chine rapids of the St Lawrence River. Two companies of Rangers (Waite's and Ogden's) accompanied the expedition in whaleboats. (Thomas Davies, National Archives of Canada/ C-000577)

Rangers shunned living in tents; if no log hut was available, they would erect a "half-faced" shelter of bark or brush (much like a modern lean-to). One of their non-scouting duties was to go out to shoot bear, deer, and smaller game to supplement both their own larder and that of the redcoats. Animal hides were cleaned and dried: bearskins made excellent mattresses and rugs, deerskins were cut into moccasins, leggings, gun cases, and snowshoe netting. (Gary Zaboly © Osprey Publishing)

the American service throughout the war. Washington even requested them at Yorktown to pick off enemy cannoneers in their fortifications. Although riflemen did little to win the Revolutionary War, they entered American mythology thereafter. Indeed, US military authorities created a military version of the Pennsylvania with the army's M1803 rifle, a .54-cal, half-stocked, flintlock rifle. In 1808, on threat of war, the army established its first regular army rifle regiment. The regiment did well during the War of 1812, with the official report of the taking of York, Canada, noting, "Too much credit cannot be given to Forsyth's [Rifle] Corps for their conduct in this affair. They displayed great coolness and undaunted bravery." In 1814 Congress authorized three additional

PREVIOUS PAGE: Light infantry seen in action at the battle of Lexington, 1775. Men armed with smoothbore weapons were lucky to hit a single human at 100yd, while those with rifles could accurately engage targets at twice that range and beyond. (NARA)

rifle regiments for the army, which were reduced to one regiment after the war. In 1821 a government more concerned with saving money than with military preparedness folded the 1st US Rifle Regiment.

The Mexican War (1846–48) had no special sharpshooter units, although rifles using percussion locks had been made by US armories starting in 1841. The Mississippi Volunteer Regiment, commanded by later Confederate President Jefferson Davis, managed to receive these weapons and use them to great advantage at the battle of Buena Vista during the Mexican War. However, most troops used smoothbored muskets, many of them still flintlock. It would not be until 1855 that a long-barreled rifled musket would be authorized for general use. In theory such a weapon, accurate to at least 500yd (457m) although capable of killing far beyond that, would enable every soldier to be a sharpshooter. However, very little target practice was allowed, and the average soldier was little better a shot with an M1855 rifled musket than his Revolutionary War ancestor was with a smoothbore musket.

Therefore, when the Civil War broke out, experts on both sides decided that specialized sharpshooter units would be required in the field. During the American Civil War both sides raised special sharpshooter units, although the Union got off to a much earlier start than the Confederacy. The men on both sides often considered themselves, with some reason, as elite units, marked by special uniforms and insignia, armed with special weapons, and receiving special training in marksmanship and related topics. However, they were used not as modern sniper units, although from time to time individuals from their ranks were designated for this job. Most reports of individuals such as generals being hit by "sharpshooters" are incorrect; the individual concerned was usually hit by either a stray shot or a lucky shot by a line infantryman.

Instead, Civil War sharpshooter units were largely used as skirmishers, an elite shock force of the kind that in the late days of World War I the Germans would call storm troops. It was largely their job to attack strong enemy positions and defend weak friendly ones. They fought, not in two lines shoulder to shoulder as line infantry, but consistently as light infantry in open order, taking cover wherever possible. Confederate sharpshooter John D. Young later described the Civil War sharpshooter unit's function as acting "as Kinglake aptly puts it, as 'the spike-head of the division,' being used either to push in, or else to ward off attack."

UNION SHARPSHOOTERS

On the war's opening, an expert shot, Hiram Berdan, proposed raising a special unit of US Sharpshooters in the north. Born in New York in 1823, Berdan was a noted wealthy inventor, most of whose work had been with firearms. He was known as the top amateur rifle shot in the United States. Moreover, he had a special flare for marketing, although he totally lacked military experience.

Berdan proposed a unit in which each potential recruit would have to pass a shooting test to become a member. A correspondent of the *New York Times* noted in August 1861:

> Some idea of the rigidity of the text may be gathered from the fact that no man is admitted who does not shoot, at 600 feet distance, ten consecutive shots at an average of five inches from the bull's-eye. That is, the aggregate distance of the whole ten shots must not exceed fifty inches. Not a man is accepted under any circumstances who varies a hair-breadth from the mark. Remarkable though it may seem, many of the men exceeded this proficiency. Colonel Berdan himself has, on a windy day, with a strange rifle, put ten balls within an average distance of one inch and one-tenth each from the bull's-eye, at 600 feet. At 1000 feet the Colonel made a string of 22 inches. Sergeant-Major Brown, under more unfavorable circumstances, made a string of 33 inches, with a strange rifle. In testing the applicants at Albany, about two-thirds were found unfitted, and indeed the general average of incompetent applicants is more than that. The American riflemen prove generally superior, especially in the hunters of New England and the West…
>
> It is the design of the Colonel to have the regiment detached in squads on the field of battle to do duty in picking off officers and gunners on the European plan, by which they take the risk of being cut off by cavalry, or executed, as they certainly would be, if taken. It is the first regiment of rifles ever formed worthy of the name − i.e., that subjected each member to the rifle-shooting test.

Berdan's suggestion was approved by the Secretary of War on June 15, 1861, and testing ranges were set up across the north. In fact, this regiment would be different from the average volunteer unit in that different companies would come from different states and serve together in one unit. As it turned out, enough expert shots were found to raise two regiments of US Sharpshooters (USSS). In the 1st USSS, Companies A, B, D, and H came from New York; Companies C, I, and K came from Michigan; Company E came from New Hampshire; Company F from Vermont; and Company G from Wisconsin. In the 2nd USSS, Company A came from Minnesota; Company B from Michigan; and Company C from Pennsylvania; Companies E and H came from Vermont; while Companies F and G came from New Hampshire.

From the beginning recruits regarded themselves as being the elite of the army. As First Sergeant Wyman White, Company F, 2nd USSS, later recalled, when his company was first gathered together at a local hotel, none of them knowing each

These two sketches were made by Daniel Nicholas Chodowiecki (1726–1801), a German painter, shortly after the Revolution and based on the notes of a German officer recently returned from America. They show an American sharpshooter on the left, and a regular Pennsylvania infantryman on the right. (NARA)

other, "it was no trouble at all to tell which of the guests were sharpshooters, as most of them acted as though they felt the safety of the Union was hanging on their shoulders. And that company of one hundred men seemed to give a considerable number of the men a feeling of strength and power which ought to be acknowledged by all outsiders present."

The USSS went on to serve with the Army of the Potomac in all its campaigns. Specific companies began to be mustered out at the end of their service in August 1864, and companies were consolidated thereafter. On December 31, 1864, the 1st and 2nd USSS were consolidated into one battalion. The 2nd was officially discontinued on February 20, 1865, and the remaining companies were transferred back to line regiments of their home states. In the meantime, other units were also recruited as sharpshooter battalions, including Yates' Sharpshooters in Illinois in December 1861, the 1st Maine Sharpshooter Battalion in late 1864, and Andrews' Sharpshooters in Massachusetts in September 1861.

In terms of training, at first Berdan figured his men were such good shots that they could go immediately into action. Accordingly he sent his first companies to be armed into Virginia shortly after arriving in Washington. However, they got the worst of a small skirmish, losing two men in the process. Captain Rudolph Aschmann, 1st USSS, wrote, "This experiment showed very clearly that courage alone does not make a soldier and that competent elementary training is a necessary preparation for active service."

Training for the sharpshooters was more specialized than for line infantry, which basically drilled to maneuver as two lines of soldiers in combat. The average infantryman received very little practice in firing his musket at all; indeed many only fired the rounds they had loaded their weapons with when they went on guard duty as they came off that duty.

On the other hand, Captain C. A. Stevens, 1st USSS, wrote:

The time was occupied in [the unit's first] camp [of instruction] in target practice, learning the company drill and battalion movements, guard, patrol, and camp duties; and, under the instruction of Lieut. Mears, U.S.A., lieutenant-colonel of the regiment, they were soon able to execute the most difficult regimental drills, and were probably unexcelled therein by any regiment, particularly in skirmishing, a service they were destined to perform at the front, in all the great battles of the Army of the Potomac, up to the time of their expiration of service.

In the target practice, a matter of the greatest importance, many excellent scores were made, and under the supervision of Col. Berdan, great improvement was made in their marksmanship.

A group of men, dressed in civilian clothes, show off their shooting abilities as officers of the US Sharpshooters watch, on the lookout for talent in markmanship. Special shooting ability examinations were held in most of the Northern states to find the best shots for the US Sharpshooters. (Stephen Walsh © Osprey Publishing)

OPPOSITE: An unidentified soldier of the 2nd United States Sharpshooters in Union uniform with target rifle, bowie knife, and Colt '49 pocket revolver in front of a painted backdrop showing a landscape with lake and fort. (LOC)

The unit could call on a US Army manual published by the War Department, *A System of Target Practice*, which had been translated from a French Army manual. The manual called for the soldier to first aim his weapon, which was placed on a rest. An officer standing behind him could then point out any errors in his aiming methods. Each soldier was required to take his weapon apart and put it back together and to practice estimating distances. For bayonet drill they used a *Manual of Bayonet Exercises*, another translation of a French Army manual, this done by George McClellan who would soon command the Army of the Potomac. Since they would be used more as skirmishers than snipers, skirmish drill was one of the most important aspects of their training. Skirmish drill was covered in a 42-page section in the most common manual of the period, William Hardee's *Rifle and Light Infantry Tactics*.

First Sergeant Wyman White later recalled how much his company enjoyed skirmish drill:

Skirmish drill is an open order drill. Men form line in two ranks, then at the order deploy by fours, two files of both ranks would take distances twenty feet apart. Then at the order deploy in line, each man on the left of the four would take distance five paces to the left of Number one in the front rank, he standing fast. Number one in the rear rank standing five paces to the left of the Number one in the front rank. Number two in the front rank being five paces to the left of Number one in the rear rank, and Number two in the rear rank taking distance five paces to the left of Number one in the front rank. The squads of fours taking distance still further to the left and deploying to the distance of five paces apart until the whole company or regiment was in a single line five paces space between each man.

Thus deployed, three hundred fifty men would make a line about a mile long. We took our orders from the call of the bugle as no man's voice could reach the length of the line. We had calls to advance, to commence firing, cease firing, by the right flank, by the left flank, lay down, rise, halt and retreat and finally every movement necessary to move the command.

There was a call to rally by fours which is a very pretty movement and the order to resist cavalry. Each man knew his place; Number one of the front rank stood fast, the other three faced to the right and double quick their step, Number one of the rear rank taking his place in the rear of Number one in the front rank and facing the rear, Number two of the front rank taking his place on the left of Number one of the front rank and Number two of the rear rank taking his place to the left of Number two of the rear rank. All face out with bayonet fixed; each man bracing his left foot and his left shoulder solid against his comrade on the opposite corner making a solid group of four. And four cool men drilled in bayonet exercise need have no fear of cavalry.

There were also movements and bugle calls to rally by sections, rally by platoon, and rally by company and regiment. Our regiments generally were engaged in skirmish line all throughout the war. Of course, we were drilled in bayonet exercise and infantry drill and when the army moved in the spring our regiment was quite a well drilled command.

Berdan and his officers recognized that men who took long marches across battlefields to fight battles in strictly skirmish order would have to be in top-notch physical condition. Therefore, they set up organized football games and jumping, racing, wrestling, boxing, and fencing matches. In the winter they also organized snowball contests between units.

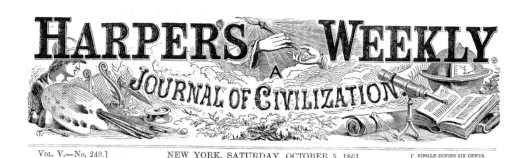

HARPER'S WEEKLY

A JOURNAL OF CIVILIZATION.

Vol. V.—No. 249.]   NEW YORK, SATURDAY, OCTOBER 5, 1861.   [SINGLE COPIES SIX CENTS.
[$2 50 PER YEAR IN ADVANCE.

Entered according to Act of Congress, in the Year 1861, by Harper & Brothers, in the Clerk's Office of the District Court for the Southern District of New York.

THE BERDAN SHARPSHOOTERS AT WEEHAWKEN.

CAPT. A.B. JONES, N. HAMPSHIRE SHARPSHOOTERS.

THE LOADING STAND.

THE FIRING STAND.

THE MARKER & THE TARGET.

TARGET FIRING — DISTANCE 35 RODS.

THE TELESCOPIC RIFLE — Weight 32 lbs.— Diameter of barrel 2¼ inches.— 42 balls to the lb.

THE NEW HAMPSHIRE SHARP-SHOOTERS.—[SEE PAGE 638.]

A cover of *Harper's Weekly* shows US sharpshooters engaging in a shooting competition plus demonstrations for the members of the public in their marksmanship skills. Note the percussion cap rifle shown at the bottom, fitted with an early telescopic sight, which also features a "false muzzle" attachment to aid loading.

ON CAMPAIGN

Since sharpshooter skirmish work made the individual walk and run further and work harder than the average infantryman of the line, sharpshooters burned more calories in the field. Much marching was done in hot weather under a boiling sun and many men put wet leaves in their forage caps to cool them down during the march.

Sharpshooters, whenever marching through potentially dangerous territory, tended to keep more alert than did line units. Greene wrote home from northern Virginia on July 27, 1862, that his unit's line of march halted for the night:

Skirmish drill was a standard system used by both sharpshooters and line infantry. It called for a company to be broken into small groups of four men, who then spread out two in front and two some five paces to the rear. The pairs would leapfrog forward on the advance and backward in the retreat. The diagram taken from a period infantry tactics manual uses a black square for each individual soldier and shows how in breaking down into skirmish drill the men operate in groups of four. (Stephen Walsh © Osprey Publishing)

And all of them were making coffee with their guns stacked and belts off, all except our company's. The Col. would not let them take them off, but made them stay within reach of their rifles.

Thus they were (the 2nd Wis. washing their feet, a part of them) when the spy, or rather scout, of Gen. Gibon's [sic] came dashing down the road with the news that a body of cavalry was coming down on them. But he was not quick enough for scarcely had he told it when down out of the woods came a large body of rebel, or Ashby cavalry. All was in confusion.

The major of the 2nd Wis. ordered his men to run for the woods but the sharp shooters, like men, grasped their rifles and not waiting for orders, poured a most deadly fire into them killing 5 men and wounding the officer commanding. Upon receiving this volley, the enemy wheeled and dropped on to their horses necks. Another volley started them on a retreat with the Indiana cavalry (now mounted) at their heels.

In battle the sharpshooters were generally used as Berdan originally planned, in small groups no larger than one or two companies. New commander Charles Mattocks wrote home in March 1864, on taking command of the 1st USSS, to say their function was to "go ahead and 'kick up the muss.'"

Their Confederate opponents were well aware of the sharpshooters' abilities, and treated them with great respect. Private Alexander Hunder, 17th Virginia Infantry, recalled their being across the lines from their defenses at Williamsburg in 1862. "Some of these sharpshooters had holes dug in the ground close to our trenches, within which they had every comfort, while they kept a close and constant watch over us. We used to place a hat on a stick and lift it above the embankment just to see them put a bullet in it," he wrote. "We lost in the Seventeenth, by these sharpshooters during our occupancy of the trenches, a sergeant killed, one private killed, and two wounded."

Still, two killed and two wounded is not a great number of casualties out of an entire regiment, leaving one to wonder how effective the sharpshooters were in battle. Some evidence suggests that they were not as effective as originally believed. For example, on the second day of the battle of Gettysburg the 1st USSS ran into remainders of the 10th and 11th Alabama Regiments. At a distance of some 300yd (274m), the 11th Alabama took cover behind a rail fence in an open field – hardly fully protective cover. Even so, the regiment lost only one officer and 17 men wounded at this range to the sharpshooters' bullets. In fact, in that fight some 66 Federals and 56 Confederates were reported killed, wounded, and missing.

The two regiments of US sharpshooters suffered from another problem at the highest command level. Berdan himself, while an excellent manager and organizer, quickly earned the dislike of all ranks. Totally without military knowledge, he was forced to bring in a regular army officer to train his troops in basic drill. Moreover, he was arrogant, temperamental, and dictatorial. Above all, he appeared to be cowardly, in an age when bravery was considered vital to a man. In heavy fighting in the Peninsula Campaign he often found excuses for going to the rear to "protect the sick," or "procure ammunition." Despite this, his official reports exaggerated his own role greatly.

On July 4, 1862 five company-grade officers sent a petition to Berdan's superior asking for his relief. Although he managed to avoid this, he was placed under arrest on March 2, 1863 by his divisional commander and court-martialed. Berdan again escaped a guilty finding. On the other hand, the 1st Regiment's commander, Caspar Trepp, a professional Swiss soldier who had seen action in the Crimean War and Garibaldi's Italian campaign, was an excellent officer. The two were bound not to get along, and Berdan eventually arrested Trepp on a trumped-up charge. The court martial found Trepp not guilty and he returned to do excellent service.

On August 7, 1863 Berdan was placed on medical leave for a relapse of a minor wound that he had received at the Second Battle of Bull Run, when he was struck in the chest by a stray shell fragment while in the rear, as usual. He would never return to active duty and was honorably discharged on January 2, 1864. Trepp continued in action, only to be killed by a shot through his red corps cap badge at Mine Run in November 1863.

CONFEDERATE SHARPSHOOTERS

"Probably the most effective troops in the late civil war," wrote Captain John Laughton, Jr., a member of the sharpshooter battalion of Mahone's Brigade of the Army of Northern Virginia, "for the number of men engaged, were the sharpshooters. The value of this branch of the service became so apparent that companies and battalions were organized in most of the brigades of infantry."

At first no provisions were made in the Confederate Army for sharpshooter units. However, troops soon saw the value of such units, and in April 1862 the Confederate Congress passed an act to organize battalions of sharpshooters:

SECTION 1. The Congress of the Confederate States of America do enact, That the Secretary of War may secure to be organized a battalion of sharpshooters for each brigade, consisting of not less than three nor more than six companies, to be composed of men selected from the brigade or otherwise, and armed with long-range muskets or rifles, said companies to be organized, and the commissioned officers therefore appointed by the President, by and with the advice, and consent of the Senate. Such battalions shall constitute parts of the brigades to which they belong, and shall have such field and staff officers as are authorized by law for similar battalions, to be appointed by the President, by and with the advice and consent of the Senate.

Irregular warfare required constant riding, quickly wearing out horses, and guerrillas and raiders routinely helped themselves to local stock in disputed territory during the Civil War. (LOC)

SECTION 2. Be it further enacted, That for the purpose of arming the said battalions, the long-range muskets and rifles in the hands of the troops, may be taken for that purpose: Provided, The Government has not at its command a sufficient number of approved long-range rifles or muskets wherewith to arm said corps.

II. Gen.'s commanding military departments may cause to be organized within their commands battalions of sharpshooters, as provided in this act, in such numbers as they may deem necessary, not exceeding one such battalion for each brigade, and will report to the Department the organization of such corps, recommending for appointment the commissioned officers allowed by law.

III. In organizing such battalions generals commanding may cause such details or transfers to be made as will not reduce any company or corps below the minimum number required by law, taking the men for each such battalion so far as possible from the particular brigade of which it is to form a part.

IV. Requisitions will be made upon the Ordnance Department for the arms for such battalions, and until the said requisitions can be filled the generals commanding may cause such exchanges and transfers of long-range muskets and rifles to be made as may be necessary to arm the said battalions, returning surplus arms when such requisitions are filled to the Ordnance Department.

At Gettysburg a company of the 2nd USSS ended up on the far left of the Union forces and ambushed an attempt to turn up the Union left by Confederates on the second day of battle. They distracted the Confederate commander, who did not know their numbers, and greatly aided the eventual Union victory. (Stephen Walsh © Osprey Publishing)

RIGHT: SHARPSHOOTER SERGEANT

A sergeant of the US Sharpshooters, in his unique green coat and trousers, with his special issue knapsack, cartridge box, and Sharps rifle. The first uniforms had a trim that was so dark that it was almost impossible to pick it out from the rest of the coat. Since the Quartermaster Department did not have any green cloth on hand initially, the first uniforms were made by dyeing dark blue dress coats dark green, the resulting clothing being so dark as to be almost black. Caps were made from a different cloth from coats, and the manufacturer used yellow cloth, already on hand, dyed green for the first caps. Eventually the army's Philadelphia Depot received "wool dyed, fast color green kersey" from Elk Mills, near Newark, Delaware, for the unique first issue "Tilson" coat (2) and trousers. The sharpshooter would carry his cartridges in two tins within a leather cartridge box (1a) which was worn on the waist belt (1b). Also shown is the hair-covered cowskin knapsack (3); this was lined with linen except for the sides which were made using heavy composition board. This artwork also depicts the special knapsack (4a) and mess kit issued to the 1st and 2nd US Sharpshooters; here we see the mess kit attached to the back of the pack, and standing alone next to the pack (4b). (Stephen Walsh © Osprey Publishing)

1a

1b

2

3

4a

4b

These units were further defined when on May 22 it was ordered that each sharpshooter battalion should consist of men strictly from a single state, rather than being mixed companies as was the case with the 1st and 2nd USSS. The men, however, were not recruited from civilian life into sharpshooter units but rather were transferred for specific campaigns from regular line infantry units. Such companies were formed in the western theater fairly early, and were in the field by the 1862 campaign.

Since Confederate sharpshooters were already veterans by the time they were transferred into sharpshooter companies, they already knew company and battalion drill, as well as the basics of soldiering. This saved a great deal of time in preparing them for active service. However, sharpshooter service required more than basic infantry knowledge, and the new units were quickly trained in additional skills.

Irving Buck of Cleburne's Brigade of the Army of Tennessee noted that in early 1862, when a sharpshooter company was first raised in the brigade, Major Calhoun Benham, of the division staff, instructed them first in the exact working of every part of the rifle, then in marksmanship, and to judge distance by the eye (no range finders were in use) by marching them to ground of different topographical features. An object would be pointed out, and distance to it estimated, after which the actual distance would be measured. By constant practice the men became quite expert in doing this, over hills and across ravines or level ground.

Benham, who had been an attorney before the war, became the Army of Tennessee's expert in training potential sharpshooters, and in 1863 was sent to Richmond to have a manual he had written published on the subject. The manual, largely drawn from the British Army's Regulations for Conducting the Musketry Instruction, consisted of a section on the weapon, noting effects of sun, wind, powder charge, etc. on firing; a section on how to actually fire the weapon, including blank firing; and one on judging distances. What it did not include was a section on actual live firing target practice, Benham noting that, "The situation of our armies, and the economy necessary in ammunition, render it impossible to practice at the target to any great extent." The manual was finally published in September 1863.

While Benham's manual was used in the Army of Tennessee, it was not apparently the manual of choice in the Army of Northern Virginia. The Confederate sharpshooter officer John Young wrote that the men in the Army of Northern Virginia battalions were trained from "a brochure, translated from the French by General C.M. Wilcox, and comprised the skirmish drill, the bayonet exercise, and practical instruction in estimating distances."

One Confederate sharpshooter, Sergeant Barry Benson, recalled that "On the 6th of April [1864], the Battalion of Sharpshooters were officially organized, and inspection held. After that we used to practice shooting at a target. We practiced judging distances also, for it is essential for a soldier to know how far his enemy is from him, in order to adjust his sights properly."

John Laughton, Jr. wrote that the early spring of 1864 was spent:

in perfecting ourselves in the skirmish drill by signals and in rifle-target practice at different ranges – from fifty yards to 1,000 yards – and so proficient did the men become in estimating distances that, although the chain was used to confirm their calculations, its use was finally discontinued as being unnecessary. Every day these practices were kept up under strict discipline, and systematic regulation and improvement in marksmanship noted, and such men as failed to make satisfactory progress were returned to their companies and others substituted.

Getting hold of the right weapons complicated firearms training. Lacking an adequate industrial base, the Confederate Ordnance Department was unable to supply weapons as sophisticated as the Union's Sharps or Colt rifles to their sharpshooters. There were some Whitworth rifles already in service in the Confederate Army, but these were expensive and had to be imported through a blockade that was growing increasingly effective. Still, they were the weapon of choice for snipers, and, as they were essentially the same weight and size as the standard infantry rifled musket, they were easier to use

Confederate sharpshooters – Cobb's and Kershaw's troops take cover and open fire from behind a stone wall at Fredericksburg in December 1862. The priority targets for the sharpshooters would be enemy officers and NCOs. (LOC)

and transport than the heavy target rifles that Federal snipers used. In fact, the .45-cal Whitworth ammunition weighed less than the .577-cal Enfield ammunition carried by line infantrymen.

The vast majority of Whitworth rifles, moreover, were made for the British Army and were therefore unavailable to the Confederate government. Instead the Confederates had to accept essentially civilian models, such as had been made for sale to British rifle volunteers. As an indication of the quality of these weapons, some had been stamped on the trigger guards "2d quality." Most of them were made prior to the spring of 1862, and therefore before serious organizing of sharpshooter battalions. An arms and ammunition report dated June 25, 1864 from General Johnston's command of the Army of Mississippi indicates there were 32 Whitworth rifles in that command,

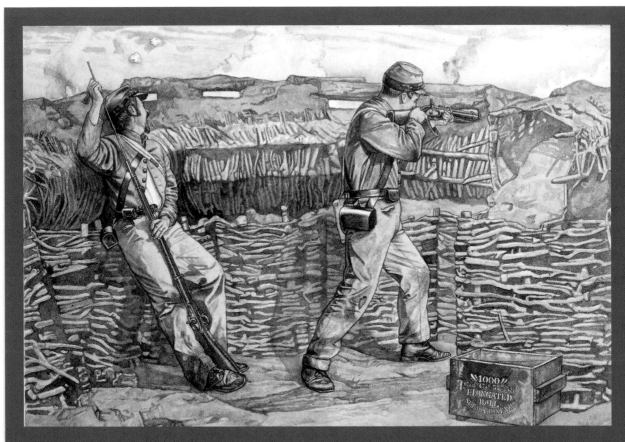

Skirmishers were used in the trenches in sieges such as Knoxville, Atlanta, Petersburg, and Nashville, to pick off enemy troops as they became exposed for a short time. These sorts of redoubts were made of wicker round gabions, filled with earth, topped with horizontal gabions with logs and earth and firing holes placed above that. (Stephen Walsh © Osprey Publishing)

and these were later assigned to the Army of Tennessee. A report dated July 13, 1863 indicates that 13 Whitworth rifles with telescopic sights were sent from the arsenal in Augusta, Georgia, to Charleston, South Carolina.

Confederates also pressed some civilian "country rifles" and target rifles into service, often reboring them to .54 and .58 calibers to use standard issue ammunition. Eleven sharpshooters in the Kentucky Orphan Brigade received British-made Kerr rifles. One of these brigade sharpshooters, Edward Thompson, recalled, "The Kerr rifle was a long range muzzle loading rifle that would kill out the distance of a mile or more, requiring a peculiar powder; and there was some difficulty in charging it, so that it was not likely to be effective except in the hands of a cool composed man. The use of ordinary powder made it necessary to swab out the barrel after every forth or fifth shot."

The Kerr rifle, made by the London Armoury Company and invented by the company's superintendent, James Kerr, was a 0.44-cal rifle that used a novel ratchet form of rifling and a quick twist. The problems Confederates found with the Kerr were

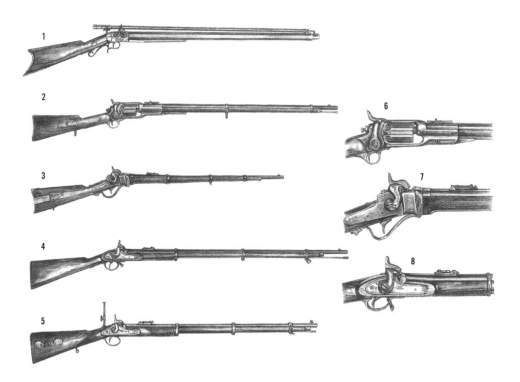

This plate shows the various weapons that sharpshooters used or trained with. The Colt percussion revolving rifle, M1855 (2) and detail (6) was prone to exploding. The Sharps breechloading percussion rifle (3) and detail (7) was used by Union forces: the model shown is the full-length rifle (there was also a cavalry issue carbine). The Whitworth rifle (5) and an Enfield rifled musket, M1853 (4) and detail (8) were used by Confederate forces. The Target Rifle is also shown (1). (Stephen Walsh © Osprey Publishing)

that it fouled more rapidly than the standard rifled musket and was somewhat inaccurate at long ranges with its issue ammunition. To solve this problem, Confederate sharpshooters acting as snipers appear to have used Whitworth ammunition with their Kerr rifles. In the spring of 1863 Major General Patrick Cleburne of the Army of Tennessee organized a sharpshooter company that was issued with 20 Whitworth rifles, fitted with telescopic sights, and ten Kerr rifles, "more than was given to any other division," Cleburne's staff officer Irving Buck later boasted. Kerr rifles were not made to accept a bayonet.

However, few Confederate sharpshooters served as snipers; instead their units were given the role of brigade skirmish battalion. Confederate sharpshooters were usually the first to go into action when a battle began. "The duty expected of the sharpshooters was to establish and occupy the skirmish line, while the enemy was in front," noted John Laughton, Jr., of Mahone's Brigade's sharpshooter battalion, "and to serve on the picket line in all day duty – being relieved at night by one of the regiments of the brigade and to serve as rear guard when on retreat. Its officers were also required to serve as scouts when the opportunity was presented."

According to Captain W.S. Dunlop, who led a sharpshooter battalion, "When the opposing armies met upon the field it became their [skirmishers'] duty to open and bring on the fight, or to stand like ushers on the vestibule of battle and receive and welcome our friends in blue whenever they choose to visit our lines." D. Augustus Dickert, a veteran of the sharpshooter battalion of Kershaw's Brigade in the Army of Northern Virginia, recalled moving to the attack at Cedar Creek in 1864: "The James' or Third Battalion having some months before been organized into brigade sharpshooters, adding two companies to it, preceded the brigade, and was to charge the fords and capture the pickets." This was dangerous work, and Dickert paid the price at that battle when he was ordered to take the survivors of his company and head to a point on the extreme left of the division as the Federals counter-attacked:

When I arrived at the point designated, which was in thick woods, to my horror I found the place literally alive with yankees. I had double-quicked right into the midst of the "blue bellies." "Surrender," came in tones of thunder. I stood amazed, astonished beyond conception. "Surrender," again came the command. There was absolutely no alternative. There was no chance to fight and less chance to run. My brave boys and I were prisoners of war.

Other sharpshooter fights were more fierce. George Bernard, commander of a sharpshooter company at the battle of the Crater, later wrote:

OPPOSITE: Colonel John Singleton Mosby led one of the only partisan Ranger units not to be disbanded by the repeal of the Partisan Ranger Act in February 1864. His record of success and firm discipline over his troops meant that he was more valuable in independent command than within the depleted Confederate Army. (LOC)

I was desperately wounded in three places when within thirty feet of the breastworks, and at the first volley from a concentrated fire of several lines massed for a forward movement. The fire was not only from a direct front, but was also an enfilading fire, which came from those of the enemy in the crater, this being to our right. The proportion of wounded and killed in the sharpshooters was exceedingly large, probably without a parallel. The battalion went into the fight with 104 men and officers, and of these ninety-four men and officers were killed and wounded; of the nine officers present eight were shot through the breast.

Captain Wallace Broadbent, commander of the sharpshooter battalion of Mahone's Brigade, was found after the Crater fight with 12 to 15 bayonet wounds through his body.

Sharpshooters were sometimes used to gather intelligence by taking prisoners. The commander of Lane's Brigade of the Army of the Potomac, for example, was once asked, "Can't you catch a Yankee tonight for General Lee? Some of the enemy are moving, and he wants to know what command it is." General Lane sent for his sharpshooter battalion's commander, who took some of his men out that night towards the enemy's rifle pits. As Lane described it, "the men had to crawl towards the enemy in the moonlight, but finally commander Major J. T. Wooton leaped up and shouted out, 'Boys, we have got them.' Away they went, at a run, in double ranks, and wheeling right and left, just as you would open the lids of a book, they came back, bringing their prisoners with them."

Sharpshooters delighted in this sort of operation. Major Dunlop wrote: "There existed an active spirit of rivalry between the different battalions of sharpshooters, as to which should perform the greatest number and the most daring feats in the line of legitimate duty, to the annoyance and damage of their opponents operating in their respective neighborhoods; and each kept a sharp lookout for opportunities to make a dash into the enemy's lines, stampede their pickets, or capture their men."

Confederate high command sometimes massed their sharpshooters for special efforts. For example on March 27, 1865 Barry Benson recalled all the sharpshooter battalions of his divisions being gathered together, some 400 men. They were sent in a line into some woods and told not to make any noise until discovered. Eventually a Federal picket called for some of them in his front to halt. "In the same instant a wild Confederate yell split the air," Benson remembered. "A solid rush, and we leaped over the works amongst the half awakened foe, who barely fired a score of shots as they fled in confusion. To the right and left we swept, clearing the line as we went. A few scattering shots, and our surprise and victory were complete." No effort was made to capitalize on this victory with a reinforcing column, and after holding the line all day

A typical Confederate sharpshooter of 1863 in the western theater wears the standard uniform issued through Georgia depots without any special markings. Also shown in this plate is the flag of the 2nd Battalion, and the soldier's various load-carrying items. (Stephen Walsh © Osprey Publishing)

the sharpshooters were retired that night and line infantry regiments came to take their place.

After the battle, many sharpshooters took advantage of their posts in the front to search the dead. "I do not think there was much robbing of the dead in the beginning of the war," Barry Benson wrote, "but as time went on and the men became hardened, and their necessities greater, the pillage of the fields extended not only to the taking of articles of value, such as money, watches, and rings, but even to coats and trousers. Blackwood says that he has seen dead men stripped entirely naked, but this I am sure I have never seen."

Such frontline work always cost men, but high commands made sure their sharpshooter battalions were constantly at full strength. As John Laughton recalled, "when the casualties of battle decimated the ranks, other details were made up from the regiment in which the loss occurred, thereby keeping up the full maximum of strength."

At the same time, as the war continued to go against the south, line regiments began to suffer heavy losses from desertion. John Young, however, believed that, "There were, I am glad to say, no deserters from the sharpshooters, as was natural; for they were the elite of the army."

Apache Indian Scouts, of the US Army, with the 6th Cavalry, c.1895. The Apache Scouts added a form of special forces expertise to regular American units, particularly in their use for tracking and reconnaissance. (NARA)

Young's sentiments were accurate. In an age of mass soldiery, much of it poorly trained or inadequately armed, the sharpshooters represented both a new way of tactical thinking, and superior training and fieldcraft. The concept of a separate elite amongst the US military was still a long way from being accepted amongst highest ranks of the post-1865 high command, however. It would take a world war more than 70 years later to embed that concept more firmly in the American military psyche.

"Bloody Knife," Custer's Indian Scout, who was killed alongside Custer at the battle of Little Big Horn in 1876. He is seen here with a Henry repeating rifle. (NARA)

ELITE TROOPS
OF WORLD WAR II

LEFT: A Native American "Code Talker" in a foxhole on Saipan, June 27, 1944. About 400 Code Talkers were employed by US forces in the Pacific, using their native languages to provide secure communications. (NARA)

THE FIRST HALF OF THE 20TH CENTURY saw profound transformation in the US armed forces, the catalyst being two world wars. In 1917, when the United States entered World War I, the US Army made a rapid change in its course of development. What had been a small professional force, functioning for the most part as a constabulary, blossomed into an army of continental European scale – a nation at arms, drawing manpower from all strata of society. It assumed a new role as well, for this army was intended to fight total war on foreign soil.

At the time of Pancho Villa's raid on Columbus, New Mexico in 1916, the US Army only numbered around 125,000 men, not counting the National Guard. During the course of World War I, however, 4,734,991 served, of whom two million went to France with the American Expeditionary Force (AEF). It was a great expansion indeed. The army was initially divided into three forces: the Regular Army, the National Guard, and the National Army, this last force to be composed of conscripts. Yet due to the manpower needs of modern war the three were combined into one Army of the United States, with all divisions containing some conscripts.

As with all armies of what the British labeled the "Great War," the US Army and also the Marine Corps experienced a dramatic increase in specialization amongst their ranks. The demands of artillery, logistics, communications, combat engineering, military aviation, and numerous other factors meant that the roles of the soldiery became far more diverse. Amongst combat troops, however, there are few that we can identify specifically as "special forces" in the strict sense of the word. The US "doughboys" certainly developed skilled units, men who were highly competent in shock trench assaults using grenades, rifles, and machine guns. In many ways, such men laid the groundwork for the elite assault troops of the next world war, demonstrating that maneuver, guile, and total mastery of small arms and explosives could be decisive. Yet such men were more extensions of the common soldiery, rather than dedicated elites trained and purposed in a specialized manner.

World War II, by contrast, saw the true birth of US Special Forces, even if they hadn't collectively acquired such a title. Why this war gave rise to SOF reflects the complexity and scale of the global conflict, not only on a military level but also in terms of political and ideological warfare. From one angle, technology itself was a driver. The 1930s and subsequent war years were one of the most technologically creative periods in human history, not least regarding transportation and weaponry. Monoplane military aircraft and improved on-road/off-road vehicles gave soldiers unprecedented mobility across borders and battlefields, adding new dimensions of maneuver and deployment. The latest generations of transport and supply aircraft not only meant that troops could be maintained (to varying degrees) by an air bridge to the frontline, but they also enabled troops to be deployed *behind* enemy lines, either in mass formations as airborne troops or as secretive units purposed for clandestine warfare. Being deployed in enemy territory by necessity demanded troops trained to exceptional levels of expertise if they were to survive at all.

Another factor in the rise of SOF during World War II is the geographical scale of the conflict, and the political and social implications therein. By mid-1942, huge swathes of both Europe and Asia lay directly under German or Japanese occupation respectively. The Allies quickly realized that dislodging these occupations was going to be a long and bloody process, a slog of years rather than months, and with uncertain outcomes. Time and geography therefore meant that covert actions and small-unit raids were often the only way in which to prosecute the ground war in lieu of a major campaign. Such missions demanded men (and some women) of exceptional nerve and training, with roles and objectives kept strictly secret from the outside world – public exposure usually meant death for, say, an Office of Strategic Service (OSS) operative working covertly in a small town in southern France. The remit of these operations was exceptionally broad, from training insurgent groups in the Burmese jungles through to reporting on

A US infantry team in the trenches of World War I. Note that one of their number has a grenade-launching attachment fitted to the muzzle of his rifle. Although World War I did not see the United States use special forces in the modern sense, the skills of fast assault were nevertheless advanced during this conflict. (NARA)

General Dwight D. Eisenhower talks with men of the 101st Airborne on June 6, 1944, just before they board their airplanes to participate in the first assault in the invasion of German-occupied Europe. (NARA)

German unit strength in occupied France. The soldiers, and civilians, who served in these roles were invested with specialized training, not only in the use of small arms and demolitions, but also in communications, sabotage, subversive warfare, foreign languages, counterfeiting, and many other underworld skills.

While actual combat is the most high-profile aspect of elite forces, it should be remembered that many SOF actions in World War II were purposely tasked to avoid such encounters. For World War II was a true total war, each side dedicated to the social, political, and military destruction of the other, and in this environment information was

RIGHT: A TYPICAL US RANGER RECRUIT IN 1942 AT ACHNACARRY, SCOTLAND, THE COMMANDO TRAINING DEPOT
1) The 1st Ranger Battalion member holds an M1 Thompson submachine gun with a drum magazine; he still wears the old style M1917 helmet, soon to be replaced by the new M1 steel pot. 2) 60mm M2 mortar. 2a) Mortar rounds. 3) Boys .55 antitank rifle (British); this weapon was used only in training and at Dieppe by the Rangers. 4) M-1 rifle. 5) M1919 A4 light machine gun. 6) M1911 A1 automatic pistol. 7) M1903A1 rifle w/grenade (M9 antitank) on an M1 launcher. 8) M1918A2 Browning automatic rifle (BAR). 9) 81mm M1 mortar. 9a) Mortar rounds. 10) Fairbairn-Sykes fighting knife; this Commando knife was issued to / bought by members of the 1st Ranger Battalion upon graduation. 11) 4ft (1.3m) toggle rope; a series of them interlaced would make rope bridges for river crossings. 12) A Ranger is leaping off a 20ft (6m) obstacle course in the background. Though not airborne qualified, it certainly must have seemed so to some of the recruits undergoing training; they were in the best shape of their lives. 13) Achnacarry Castle – home of the Commandos and Rangers. (Michael Welply © Osprey Publishing)

king. A major role of elite troops in World War II was therefore reconnaissance and intelligence-gathering, by whatever means possible. Often at appalling risk to themselves, soldiers would put themselves in close proximity to the enemy, even mingle with them on occasions, and attempt to collect information that might give the Allies a critical advantage in forthcoming battles. Conversely, special agents might also attempt to sow disinformation among the enemy, leading them to make both strategic and tactical mistakes.

In this chapter, we will look at the broad spectrum of SOF troops established during World War II, from the publically visible forces to the highly secretive. As we shall see, while the rationale behind each unit was distinctive, the demands on the courage and talent of the individuals involved were uniform.

THE NEW RANGERS

By 1942, after over two years of combat, the world had been transformed into a maelstrom of death and destruction. Wherever Allied forces were fighting, they were pushed back by their better-trained and better-led German and Japanese counterparts. Unprepared for the war it was entering, the US Army still needed to gain the confidence of the people back home. Positive action was also needed to restore the morale of the citizens of the remaining and ever-shrinking free world, while simultaneously providing hope for millions of the oppressed living in conquered territories. Britain's answer to the

OPPOSITE: US Army Rangers ascend the coastal cliffs of Normandy to knock out German gun emplacements on June 6, 1944. The Ranger actions at Pointe-du-Hoc were classic models of special forces strikes against well-defined and important targets. (NARA)

LEFT: Members of the 2nd Rangers receive the Distinguished Service Cross (DSC) on July 8, 1944, for gallantry and heroism in action during the early battles to reclaim occupied Europe. (NARA)

same problems that she had encountered just a few years earlier was the creation of the Commandos as envisioned by Lieutenant-Colonel Dudley Clarke of the Imperial Staff and supported by Prime Minister Winston Churchill.

In the US, President Roosevelt sought to create commando-style units to do just the same – strike back at the enemy and restore the confidence of the American public in the military. In the spring of 1942, General George Marshall, Chief of Staff of the US Army, sent Colonel Lucian K. Truscott Jr. to England to liaise with the British General Staff and coordinate training between the inexperienced US troops and the battle-proven British Commandos. On May 26, 1942, Colonel Truscott submitted proposals to General Marshall for the creation of an American unit along the lines of the commando model. The War Department authorized Truscott and Major General Russell P. Hartle, commander of all army forces in Northern Ireland, to activate the US Army's 1st Ranger Battalion. The title, "RANGER," after the famous 18th-century Rangers of the French and Indian War, was selected by Truscott "because the name Commandos rightfully belonged to the British, and we sought a name more typically American." Initially and unbeknownst to most, the Ranger unit was formed for the specific purpose of training soldiers in commando skills and then reassigning them to other units, thus providing a well-trained and battle-hardened core for the new American units. On June 7, 1942, the 1st Ranger Battalion was formed and its camp established at Carrickfergus, Northern Ireland.

The original battalion consisted of a headquarters company of seven officers and 62 enlisted men, as well as six companies (A, B, C, D, E, F) of three officers and 59 enlisted men each. A Ranger battalion was significantly smaller than the traditional American infantry battalions, and the size of these companies was determined by the size of the small landing crafts used by the British Commandos.

VOLUNTEERING AND TRAINING

An official communiqué outlining the new Ranger unit stated on June 1, 1942:

Since we are starting late in the organization of the unit which will be operating alongside similar British Units, with much experience, it is of the utmost importance that personnel selected for this unit be fully trained soldiers of the highest possible type.

Officers and non-commissioned officers should possess qualities of leadership of a high order, with particular emphasis upon initiative, judgment and common sense. All officers and men should possess natural athletic ability, physical stamina, and should be without physical defects. While mental requirements demand only alertness and initiative, it is highly desirable that keen and intelligent personnel be selected; otherwise, much of the experience gained will not be utilized. No age limit is prescribed, but it is noteworthy that British Commandos average about twenty-five years of age.

It is to be noted that Commando training involves a number of specialties in addition to physical training and qualification in arms. Among the specialties not listed in the table of organization are: Demolition Personnel, Mechanics, Truck and Tractor Drivers, Maintenance Personnel and the like. Special attention should be given to selecting men with desired specialist qualifications, physical standards and a high degree of training in order to reduce to a minimum the necessary period of preliminary training.

In addition to the specialists indicated above, personnel with experience in the following are particularly desirable:

Judo

Scouts (men versed in woodcraft) – especially important

Men experienced in small boats – especially important

Mountaineers

Seamen

Engineers (Demolitions and Pioneers)

Men with knowledge of railway engines

Weapons specialists – especially important

Men with some knowledge of power plants, radio stations, etc. to facilitate demolitions.

Members of a Ranger unit utilize captured German cavalry horses for dispatch riding and reconnaissance, somewhere in France in June 1944. The man on the left is armed with an M1 carbine, a usefully light weapon for special forces, albeit one lacking power over long ranges. (NARA)

Rangers illustrate the vertical assault method they applied at Normandy in June 1944. The cliffs were scaled with a rather improvised mix of ropes and ladders, and covering fire was provided by naval forces offshore. (NARA)

Certainly, this was not an ordinary outfit. Men flocked to the call of adventure and mystique, or volunteered simply to get away from their current units. Approximately 700 of the 2,500 volunteers survived two weeks of testing and training. The rest were RTU'd (returned to unit of origin). The survivors formed a battalion, and on June 28, Darby's 1st Ranger Battalion moved to the Commando Training Depot at Achnacarry Castle, Scotland. The surplus 200 were RTU'd at the Commando Depot. The 1st Ranger Battalion comprised 26 officers and 488 men ready for commando training.

The two most influential American officers that molded the 1st Ranger Battalion into a sharp spearhead unit were the battalion commander, Major Darby, and his executive officer, Captain Herman Dammer. Darby Ranger Warren Evans who received a battlefield commission with the Rangers recalls:

Dammer was Darby's right hand man, a detail man. He did not have the flair that Darby had but was probably the better planner. With Dammer, everything was thought through carefully. Darby was a more emotional and inspirational-type leader… After we had an action, Darby's after-battle-report would be very colorful. Dammer's report, on the other hand, was dry and to the point, very sterile. They were completely different men. Darby followed the book on how to be a good leader, although he was somewhat carelessly flamboyant at times. He was not demanding but we knew he meant what he said. We admired him even more because he was in on all the action with us.

At Achnacarry the Americans were also introduced to the man tasked with guiding the training of the Rangers – Lieutenant-Colonel Charles Vaughan, a ruddy-cheeked, husky British officer who radiated enthusiasm and goodwill. Darby recalls his impressions of the task master:

The tremendous personality of Colonel Vaughan pervaded the atmosphere of the Commando Depot. A former Guards drill sergeant and an officer in World War I with later experience in commando raids in World War II, he was highly qualified for his job. He had served with distinction during the commando raids against Vaagso and the Lofoten Islands in Norway. A burly man, about six feet two, strongly built and of ruddy complexion, he

Lieutenant-Colonel William Darby (right) chats with a French field officer in North Africa. Darby organized the Ranger battalions and became a lieutenant-colonel after the heroic but troubled raid on Dieppe in 1942. (NARA)

had a face which at times showed storm clouds and at other times, warm sunniness. A man of about 50 years of age, he was in excellent physical condition and was remarkably agile. He was constantly in the field, participating in, observing, and criticizing the training of the men. During it all he was highly enthusiastic. Observing a mistake he would jump in and personally demonstrate how to correct it. He insisted on rigid discipline, and officers and men alike respected him. He was quick to think up means of harassing the poor weary Rangers, and as he put it, "To give all members the full benefit of the course." The British Commandos did all in their power to test us to find out what sort of men we were. Then,

William "El Darbo" Darby and the rough and tough Chuck Shunstrom manning a 37mm antitank gun in the port city of Gela during an Italian tank counterattack. Following the assaults on Gela, the Italians and Germans threw several counterattacks at the Americans. Rangers fought with bazookas, TNT charges, and plain old guts, stopping the armored counter-thrusts repeatedly. In one case, Darby and Shunstrom bumped into one of the few antitank guns available and engaged a "black" Renault tank. (Michael Welply © Osprey Publishing)

apparently liking us, they did all in their power to prepare us for battle. There were British veterans who had raided Norway at Vaagso and at the Lofoten Islands, men who had escaped from Singapore, and others who had slipped from the Italians in Somaliland. As instructors at the depot, these men were a constant source of inspiration to my Rangers and, at the same time, a vivid reminder of the difficulties of the job ahead. At the beginning of the training, in the presence of the commanding officer of the Commando Depot, I told the Ranger officers that they would receive the same training as their men. Furthermore, the ranking officer present was to be the first to tackle every new obstacle, no matter what its difficulty. I included myself in this rule, believing deeply that no American soldier will refuse to go as far forward in combat as his officer.

Training for the Rangers was threefold. It included physical fitness, weapons familiarity, and small-unit tactics. Speed marches at 5mph (8km/h), log drills, borrowed from ancient Scottish games, and hand-to-hand combat were a main staple. Obstacle courses required stamina, shooting ability, and finally, when completely exhausted, ferocious bayonet drills. The two-man buddy system was perfected. One Ranger would move forward while another would provide covering fire. Live fire exercises with "enemy rounds" striking around the Rangers provided realistic training. Innovative training equipment included bullets made of soap. This type of training was far superior to anything American men were taught during basic training.

The Rangers who completed commando training represented all types of Americans. The youngest was 17 and the oldest 35, with an average age of 25. Sixty percent of the Rangers came from the 34th Division, 30 percent from the 1st Armored Division, and the remaining 10 percent were from medical, quartermaster, and signal troops of V Corps. The Ranger officers did not field one regular Army officer with the notable exception of West Pointer William Darby. All were guardsmen or reservists. Although the enlisted personnel had come from regular army units, the majority of them were draftees who had volunteered for the new Ranger unit.

THE CABANATUAN RAID

A detailed study of all the dozens of Ranger operations in World War II, in Italy, Africa, Europe, and the Pacific is impossible here, but one action in particular represents the fundamental connection of the Rangers to the SOF ethos. In January 1945 the 6th Ranger Infantry Battalion was given a high-risk mission – rescue 500 American, British, and Dutch prisoners-of-war held at a brutal camp near Cabanatuan in the Philippines. The operation also included other elements of the US Army's burgeoning special forces community.

Early on January 26, an American wearing an old-style campaign hat appeared on horseback at Sixth Army HQ at Dagupan just inland from Lingayen Gulf. He had ridden 40 miles (64km) overnight, a hard cross-country ride under any circumstances, let alone through a war zone. Colonel Horton V. White, Sixth Army G2, received the rider. He was Major Robert Lapham, a reserve officer originally assigned to the 45th Infantry (Philippine Scouts) as a second lieutenant. After the surrender of Bataan, Lapham formed a 10,000-man guerrilla group in central Luzon called Luzon Guerrilla Armed Forces or "Lapham's Raiders." This soft-spoken officer had a 1-million peso bounty on his head. He had been part of a desperate 36-man mission striking out from Bataan with the aim of destroying Japanese aircraft at distant Clark Field. They had infiltrated almost to the field when they received word of the surrender. Rather than comply with the order, they went into the hills to form guerrilla bands.

Lapham was not unknown to the G2, which was familiar with his radioed reports long before the American landing at Luzon. He reported that his units had kept the Cabanatuan POW Camp under surveillance, which was some 60 miles (96km) from Sixth Army HQ in Nueva Ecija Province. Nearby Cabanatuan City ("Place of the Rocks") was the province's capital. The camp's population fluctuated, but in past months many of the prisoners had been sent away, as the Japanese command had ordered that all POWs be evacuated from the Philippines to be employed as labor. Only about 500 remained and they were in bad shape. Lapham possessed details of the camp's layout, guard dispositions, and defenses. The guerrillas sensed that the guards would murder the prisoners en masse if their liberation appeared imminent. It was reasoned that as defeat appeared more apparent the guards would react suddenly and violently. But Lapham assured White that his guerrillas could assist in a rescue attempt.

A strange occurrence had taken place at the camp on January 6, three days before the American landing. Most of the guards hastily departed, leaving only a few ill men. The Japanese command was aware of the approach of the American invasion fleet and was forming ad hoc units. Virtually unguarded, the prisoners considered escaping, but half of them could not walk any distance. It was considered that a smaller, fitter group might escape, but it was feared that as they had no idea of the lie of the land beyond the camp, or the location of friendly forces, they would be swiftly hunted down. They were also reluctant to leave the helpless prisoners to the mercy of the guards. Understanding that there was a chance the guards might massacre them, the prisoners were making clubs and knives, determined that they would not go down without a fight. The guerrillas had no time to react, as over the next two days replacement guards trickled in. After the American landing on January 9, most of the guards again left, leaving just 20 to watch over the POWs. Nearing starvation, the prisoners took the chance of raiding the livestock pens right under the guards' noses. Slaughtering two carabaos, they served them out.

After scrounging a great deal of the food the guards had left, the men were strengthened enough that if rescue came many could at least walk a short distance. Soon, additional guards arrived and a stricter regime was once again enforced.

After a meeting at 1500hrs, Colonel White, recognizing the volatility of the situation and the need to act quickly, notified General Walter Krueger. I Corps were expected to reach Cabanatuan City in about five days – January 31 or February 1 at the latest. White estimated that if they did not make a rescue attempt by the 29th the prisoners were doomed or would be moved on foot, which could prove just as fatal. There was no time for a lengthy study of the situation, detailed planning, and a leisurely decision. Instead, the decision would have to be made immediately and executed with all haste. The rescue force would have to infiltrate at least 30 miles (48km) of enemy territory. That alone would require two days. Extreme precautions had to be taken to ensure the rescuers were not detected, not only by the Japanese, but also by Filipino collaborators in villages who could inform on them. There were also communist People's Anti-Japanese Army (Hukbalahap or Huks) guerrillas in the area, who, although often fighting alongside US-supported guerrillas, were vehemently anti-American and could impede the progress of the raiders. If the Japanese were alerted they might move the prisoners or massacre them on the spot. They could also ambush the rescuers or launch an immediate counterattack as the would-be rescuers charged into the camp. Even more appalling would be the prospect of a successful liberation followed by a relentless pursuit, with the Japanese harassing a strung-out column of sick and frail men. No reaction force could respond quickly enough to save them if this occurred. Besides the camp guards, there were large numbers of troops from the 105th Division moving through the area, reinforced by tanks, although, for the most part, the Japanese stayed on the roads and did not actively patrol the countryside.

"Sounds risky," was Krueger's comment. The Texan general was indeed risking not only the lives of the prisoners and their rescuers, but his own reputation. The mission would have to be highly classified, with only select individuals informed of the final objective, to ensure any hope of success.

Krueger had to consider the motivations for the mission before making this crucial decision. Was it an emotional issue of rescuing the survivors of Bataan and Corregidor or was there a true military benefit? Krueger, having come up through the ranks, had a soft spot for the troops. Was it worth the risk of losing the rescue force and the prisoners? If anything went wrong there would be few survivors. There might also be retaliations against civilians and on villages en route if they were suspected of aiding the Americans. Did the risks justify the objective? Ultimately, Krueger felt the humanitarian mission warranted the risk. If successful, and his staff believed there was a 50/50 chance of it being so, it would have a great effect on morale among his troops and on the home front.

Lieutenant General Walter Krueger, Commanding General, Sixth Army. Krueger had the foresight to organize the 6th Ranger Battalion and the Alamo Scouts, which performed the Cabanatuan rescue. (US Army)

Some on the staff felt that the presence of Lapham's guerrillas improved the odds. They would provide guides and security, clear the way through villages, establish roadblocks to halt Japanese reinforcements and counterattacks, and assist the reconnaissance party that would first place the camp under surveillance. They would also provide unarmed auxiliaries to carry weakened prisoners by litter and carabao cart, as well as supplying food and water during the return to US lines.

In 1942 some of the fledgling guerrilla bands had attempted to conduct attacks on the Japanese, but, lacking adequate weapons, ammunition, supplies, training, command and control, and experience, they were often defeated. General MacArthur ordered them to go to ground in order to preserve their forces, receive weapons, stockpile supplies, and train. Formal communication links and liaison teams were established between US forces and the guerrillas. Their most valuable role was to collect and report intelligence. Thanks to them, American forces were well informed on Japanese activities by the time they launched their assault on the Philippines. In September 1944 the guerrillas were finally given the orders they had long awaited – they were to actively attack Japanese lines of communications, destroying and harassing supply and troop movements.

Throughout 1944, Lapham's guerrillas proposed several times to raid the camp and release the 2,000 or so prisoners that were then held there. They would have to get them to the east coast over 40 miles (64km) away across the open valley and then through the Sierra Madre Mountains – a most difficult task since the Japanese could devote their full resources to hunting them down. The Navy could not marshal the 20–30 submarines required to rescue the weakened and injured POWs, and so any rescue attempt would have to wait until the Americans had landed and the invasion begun in earnest.

In September, Lapham's Squadron 201A chopped down and collapsed both the temporary and new permanent bridges the Japanese had built over the Cabu River just a mile east of the camp. The temporary bridge was on a spur 300yd (274m) northwest of the highway, which had served as the main transport link in the area. It had been constructed as the Japanese rebuilt the original 75ft (22.8m) bridge, which had been destroyed by retreating US-Filipino forces in 1941. A second new bridge was not completed until mid-November 1944, also requiring a new temporary bridge.

Alamo Scout members of Nellist and Rounsaville Teams after the Cabanatuan POW camp raid. (Left to right top row) Private First Class Gilbert Cox, Private First Class Wilbur Wismer, Sergeant Harold Hard, Private First Class Andrew Smith, and Private First Class Francis Laquier. (Left to right bottom row) Private First Class Galen Kittleson, Private First Class Rufo Vaquilar, First Lieutenant William Nellist, First Lieutenant Thomas Rounsaville, and Private First Class Franklin Fox. Not pictured are First Lieutenant John Dove, Private First Class Thomas Siason, Private First Class Sabas Asis, and Private First Class Alfred Alfonso. (US Army)

The US Army Rangers who participated in the POW rescue traveled with the minimum of kit and equipment. 1) This Ranger wears a typical fatigue uniform with white identification strip, M1944 combat boots, and a field cap. He carries two ammunition bandoliers (48 rounds in each), a first-aid pouch, a 1qt canteen (on the right hip), and a M1918 Mk 1 trench knife. He is armed with a .30-cal M1 rifle. 2) The Cabanatuan POW camp sentries donned only minimal equipment when standing guard in the towers, fighting positions, and at the gates. Many only wore one cartridge belt rather than the usual two. This camp guard is shown wearing the usual tropical uniform with field cap, puttees, and boots. He carries a 30-round cartridge pouch, a canteen on his right hip and a Type 30 (1897) bayonet. He is armed with a Type 38 (1905) rifle. (Howard Gerard © Osprey Publishing)

The next question facing Krueger was what unit he would select for this dangerous mission. Sixth Army's 47 infantry battalions had been fighting and marching for almost three weeks. They were far from exhausted, but combat was taking its toll. Additionally every unit was needed on the broad front and its flanks as they advanced south. The rescue force would have to cover 30 miles (48km) over moderately rough terrain, overrun a guarded camp, possibly fight off counterattacks, then march back with 500 weakened prisoners, and could well be engaged on the return. The 1st Cavalry Division (serving as dismounted infantry) was landing on Luzon the next day and could not possibly be ready on such short notice. The separate 503rd Parachute Infantry Regiment (PIR) had just stood down after a grueling month-long fight on Mindoro, while the 11th Airborne Division on Leyte was preparing for an amphibious and parachute assault on southern Luzon in five days. Fortunately, Krueger had foresight and had previously created two special units ideal for this mission. He first considered other units, as he wished to preserve these special units for rapidly emerging critical missions. This was certainly the situation he now faced.

In November 1943 Krueger had directed the formation of a special reconnaissance training organization, the Alamo Scouts Training Center (ASTC) on New Guinea. It had a twofold mission. First was to train selected individuals from Sixth Army infantry units in jungle and amphibious reconnaissance skills. Most would return to their units and pass on their skills. The six-week course taught physical conditioning, hand-to-hand combat, jungle survival, intelligence collection, scouting and patrolling, navigation, communications, Allied and enemy weapons, infiltration and exfiltration techniques, and rubber-boat handling. Candidates were required to have combat experience, be able to swim, be in excellent physical condition, and have 20/20 vision.

Second, some graduates were selected for assignment to the Sixth Army Special Reconnaissance Unit – referred to simply as the Alamo Scouts. Many were paratroopers or from the 1st Filipino Infantry Regiment, a US Army unit organized in the States. Uniquely, peer evaluation was used to select men for what can be called the US Army's first long-range reconnaissance patrol (LRRP) unit. Enlisted graduates gave the names of three enlisted men and three officers they would prefer to serve with on a team. Selected officers named the three enlisted men they desired on their team and the teams bore the names of each commanding officer. (Similar peer evaluation is used in today's Ranger Course.)

The Alamo Scouts operated in teams of one officer and between five and seven enlisted men, conducting covert scouting missions behind enemy lines. These were most often landing beach reconnaissance missions, but the Scouts also operated inland and occasionally snatched a prisoner for interrogation. The previous October, two teams, Rounsaville (six men) and Nellist (seven men) had liberated 78 Dutch, Japanese, and

French civilian internees at Cape Oransbari, Netherlands New Guinea. The two teams were accompanied by a Dutch Army interpreter and three native guides, and were landed on the north side of the cape by PT boats, along with a four-man contact team that remained with the boats. The teams followed a 5-mile (8km) path through the jungle and at 0200hrs arrived at the inland village where the internees were held. The guides made contact with villagers and learned there were 25 Japanese soldiers plus five Kempeitai (military police) in another hut holding the village chief hostage. Two-and-a-half miles away, on the south side of the cape, was a Japanese beach outpost of four men with machine guns. A plan was quickly developed and the Scouts split into three groups to be in position before dawn. Rounsaville Team with two men from Nellist Team would attack the two Japanese groups in the village while the rest of Nellist Team hit the beach outpost. All three Japanese positions were struck by lightning-fast attacks and most of the enemy were killed in less than four minutes, with no friendly casualties. The internees were collected and led to the beach position where they were picked up by two PT boats at 0700hrs. The mission's success was credited to close teamwork, flexibility, and the ability to make quick decisions to meet the situation.

Having approved the Cabanatuan operation, Colonel White contacted Lieutenant Colonel Frank Rawolle of the Sixth Army Special Intelligence Subsection, which was responsible for the control of the Alamo Scouts and liaising with the guerrillas. Much to his delight, White found that both Nellist and Rounsaville Teams were available. Other Alamo Scout teams had already infiltrated into the Japanese rear area to conduct reconnaissance and contact cooperative guerrillas (not all guerrillas cooperated with US forces, some having their own political agendas). The Scout teams were organizing ammunition and supplies for the guerrillas, confirming their often-inflated intelligence reports, and coordinating joint operations.

The muscle for the raid would come from another unit created by Krueger. Five Ranger battalions had operated in the Mediterranean and Europe, but none had been raised in the Pacific. The 6th Ranger Infantry Battalion was of unusual origin. It began life as 2nd Battalion, 99th Field Artillery Regiment (75mm Howitzer, Pack) in July 1940. In January 1941 it was redesignated 98th Field Artillery Battalion (75mm Howitzer, Pack). After training in the mountains of Fort Carson, Colorado, it arrived in Australia in January 1943 for projected deployment on New Guinea. However, Australian authorities would not allow its 800 mules ashore for fear of their carrying some disease dangerous to livestock. The following month the unit moved to New Guinea for a year's training. Even though there were still operations being conducted on New Guinea, there was no requirement for the mule-borne artillery battalion and, in April 1944, 33-year-old Lieutenant Colonel Henry A. Mucci was assigned as the battalion commander with the task of converting the unit to a Ranger battalion, as it was found that a pack howitzer battalion employed on Guadalcanal was more of a hindrance than a help. The mules and some of the artillerymen were shipped to Burma to serve with Merrill's Marauders and, later, the MARS Task Force in the opening of the Burma Road.

Of the 900 artillerymen in the battalion, only 300 enlisted men and 12 of the 31 officers volunteered for the Rangers. Over 200 additional men were selected from volunteers in replacement depots. The remaining gunners were a tough bunch. They had had to be able to handle the howitzers and deal with stubborn mules. They had a minimum height requirement of 5ft 10in (1.8m) and many were farm boys already

Rangers en route to Cabanatuan POW camp on January 29, 1944. They traveled very light, not even taking backpacks or sleeping gear. (US Army)

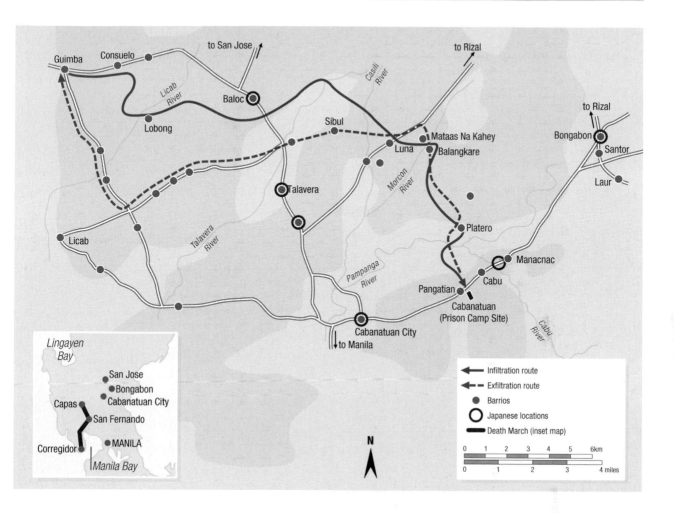

Ranger infiltration and exfiltration routes. (© Osprey Publishing)

familiar with the character of cantankerous animals. Magazine articles described the Rangers and former muleskinners as the biggest, toughest men in the army. Mucci drove the battalion hard, conducting 5-mile (8km) runs, 20-mile (32km) forced marches with full equipment, obstacle courses, organized athletics, swimming, weapons-handling, patrolling, small unit and raid tactics, and rubber boat training. He created a physically tough unit and emphasized flexibility. One of the most valuable doctrines he fostered was independent thinking on the part of leaders when operating on their own. Although the unit commenced Ranger training soon after Mucci took over, it was not redesignated the 6th Ranger Infantry Battalion until September 24, 1944. The unit kept a low profile and wore no insignia or rank. They referred to one another by nicknames in an effort to develop close-knit teamwork.

The battalion's début mission was to secure three small islands at the entrance to Leyte Gulf for the mid-October 1944 first landing of the re-conquest of the

Philippines. They installed beacon lights to guide the invasion fleet through the channel and raided a small Japanese installation to obtain intelligence. One company returned to one of the islands to wipe out the remaining Japanese. They reconnoitered other Leyte Gulf islands and secured Sixth Army HQ on Leyte.

The battalion landed on the second day of the January 1945 Luzon invasion. It was given no assignment, instead being held in readiness for special missions. In the meantime, it guarded Sixth Army HQ and conducted patrols where the Rangers saw some action. But Mucci was hoping that Headquarters would grant the Rangers a mission more suitable to their highly trained status, and, as yet, under-used skills.

Mucci was summoned to G2 on January 27 and briefed on the situation. This was exactly what his battalion had trained for. The Sixth Army Special Intelligence Subsection under Lieutenant Colonel Rawolle would conduct overall mission planning and coordination. The mission was planned with minimal need for external support. The 6th Infantry Division, which was in the frontline sector nearest to Cabanatuan, was tasked to provide transportation, rations, and medical support for 500 arriving personnel, but they had no idea as to who they would be and from where they were coming.

Rawolle quickly hammered out a simple plan immediately after his January 26 (Friday) meeting with Robert Lapham. He submitted it to Colonel White who briefed General Krueger and approved it after asking some questions. The Alamo Scouts would first infiltrate to place the camp under surveillance and make contact with the guerrillas who would play a major role in the raid. Even though Sixth Army had been ashore for less than three weeks, Rawolle was familiar with and had confidence in the guerrillas, especially after his meeting with Lapham. The Rangers would infiltrate cross-country, attack the camp, free the prisoners, and make the long and dangerous exfiltration back to friendly lines. Guerrilla forces would block Japanese reinforcements and cover the withdrawal and exfiltration. Major Lapham was disappointed not to be accompanying the Rangers, having been deemed more valuable coordinating guerrilla activities at the launch site.

Thus began one of the most daring raids of the Pacific War. Some 14 Scouts set off behind enemy lines on January 27 to make an advance observation of the camp and link up with guerrilla forces, led by Captain Juan Pajota, at the village of Platero, with 120 Rangers moving up the next day to make the 30-mile (48km) infiltration to their target. All forces made a difficult and tense journey to the meet-up point just a few miles from the camp, where they decided to postpone the operation for 24 hours on account of major Japanese Army units moving through the area nearby. One of the greatest challenges to the operation was how to approach the camp, as the Japanese had cleared the ground around it to improve observation. Pajota suggested that a US Army Air Force (USAAF) aircraft could buzz the camp at an agreed moment, distracting the Japanese attention skywards while the Rangers crossed the open ground. Mucci agreed to the proposal. In terms of the camp attack itself, 90 of the Rangers commanded by Captain Robert Prince would assault the main camp and free the prisoners, while the other 30 US soldiers, led by Lieutenant John Murphy, would assault the rear of the camp. Once liberated, the prisoners would be led to a meet-up point on the Pampanga River 1½ miles (2.4km) north of the camp, there to be met by 150 guerrillas who would use carts pulled by carabao to transport the POWs back to American lines.

Pajota's Filipino guerrillas wore old US khakis, work clothes, and even Japanese uniform components. Their armament and web gear was just as varied. (US Army)

The Northrop P-61A Black Widow was a twin-engine, twin-tailboom, radar-equipped night-fighter crewed by two men and armed with four 20mm cannons and four .50-cal machine guns, all forward-firing. However, "Hard to Get" lacked the .50-cal guns on its belly. (US Army)

At 1700hrs on January 30, 1945, the Rangers, Scouts, and their accompanying guerrillas quietly departed Platero. They tied strips of white cloth around their upper left arms for identification. Staying behind was the radio team; the SCR-694 could not be operated on the move so it was better off in the village. They would send a success message based on the flares fired from the camp.

There were just over 370 men in the column that worked its way through bamboo and cogon grass to the Pampanga. They waded across where a sandbar divided the river into two streams and provided a knee-deep crossing; it was much deeper elsewhere. The column separated into three groups with the Rangers heading for the camp and the guerrillas and Scouts splitting off to key support positions in the vicinity. A key role for the guerrillas, both Pajota's and those commanded by Captain Eduardo Joson, was to set up blocking positions to prevent the influx of nearby Japanese troops to the camp. Two hundred of Pajota's men established a roadblock around a wooden bridge over the Cabu River to the east of the camp (the bridge was also laid with demolitions), while 75 of Joson's men, plus a Ranger bazooka team, created a defense to the southwest of the camp to stop Japanese reinforcements from Cabanatuan itself.

At first the Rangers pushed through high grass, but it soon gave way to rice paddies. The 30-man Company F platoon turned off to the east, heading for the stream they would follow under the camp highway to their support positions on the east and south sides of the camp. Company C continued toward the camp until they saw the silhouettes of its guard towers. The Rangers went to ground and waited – complete darkness was still over an hour away.

At 1835hrs, the USAAF P-61A Black Widow "Hard to Get" screamed over the Japanese bivouac at 200ft (61m), scattering startled troops, guards all but leaping from the towers as she roared over. So low was the approach that the flyers could see the Rangers lying prone in the rice paddies. Throttling the aircraft back they climbed to 1,000ft (304m) and turned back to follow the highway over the bridge again. "Hard to Get" came directly over the camp with the guards crouching in the towers and the prisoners, scrambling out of the barracks, waving wildly. Unbeknown to the flyers, the POWs were arguing – was the strange plane American or Japanese? They had never seen a plane of the likes of this one – futuristic looking and completely black in color with no insignia. One prisoner swore he saw a naked woman painted on the nose … it had to be American! The black plane wheeled and made repeated passes for a further 20 minutes.

By 1915hrs, Company F's 2nd Platoon had successfully crawled through the drainage ditch and stream paralleling the camp's east side, approximately 200yd (182m) out. Reaching the south fence, some men crawled west through a ditch parallel with the fence to take up firing points covering the camp's southeast tower, fighting positions, and rear gate. The men in the stream-bed on the east side crawled in closer to their targets. A sentry in the northeast tower suddenly shouldered his rifle, aiming toward the Rangers. Again, everyone froze until he finally lowered his rifle. Remarkably, he had apparently convinced himself that whatever he had seen was nothing of consequence. Each team that had been assigned a tower or fighting position was soon in place between 6 and 25yd (5.5 and 23m) away. They were confident that the sudden burst of fire from their M1 rifles, BARs, and Thompsons would rip apart the sentries now engaged in quiet conversation and a shared cigarette. Sergeant Joe Youngblood's team was responsible for the southeast corner tower, which still appeared empty. They would fire on it anyway, taking no chances of overlooking a sentry. It was also his duty to cut the escape hole through the perimeter fences.

North of the camp, Company C's 1st Platoon, the break-in force, was in a ditch immediately across the highway and taking aim at unsuspecting guards while the 2nd Platoon was in a drainage ditch 10yd (9m) behind them. In the paddy another 10yd to the rear was the reserve of cameramen (official photographers were accompanying the mission), medics, and guerrillas. They were awaiting the first shot from First Lieutenant John Murphy with the Company F platoon on the east and south sides of the camp. Meanwhile, guerrillas shimmied up nearby telephone poles and cut the lines.

By 1930hrs, the official start-time for the assault, Murphy had not yet fired. No doubt the former Notre Dame football quarterback felt some uncertainty. He wanted to confirm that the huts to his rear were empty, even though reassured by guerrillas that they were. He also wanted to know for certain that each team was in position. He sent two men to check the huts and another back down the line to double-check the teams. His cautiousness is easy to understand – up to this point the mission had, against the odds, played out perfectly. Nonetheless, Mucci and Prince grew increasingly concerned with each passing minute.

At 1945hrs, Lieutenant Murphy concentrated on aligning three points: the peephole of his M1 rifle's rear sight, the front blade sight, and the head of a Japanese soldier. He took a deep breath, released a little air, and gently squeezed the trigger. The raid of was now under way.

Captain Robert W. Prince, Commanding Officer, Company C, 6th Ranger Infantry Battalion, after the Cabanatuan raid. He was also the assault commander. Pistols were commonly carried in shoulder holsters in the Ranger battalion. (US Army)

An explosion of fire erupted from around the three sides of the camp. The sentries at the gates, in the towers, and in the fighting positions were immediately cut down. A dead soldier tumbled from the southeast tower. Rangers shifted their fire from their primary targets to already obliterated adjacent positions just to make sure. They continued to fire into the guard quarters as they rushed forward. The bamboo huts were easily shredded with tracers and grenades showered into the Japanese positions even though the majority of the guards were already dead. Youngblood's team began cutting an opening through the fences as Prince fired a red flare from an M9 hand-projector.

Across from the front gate, 1st Platoon cut down the guards in less than half a minute and charged across the highway, firing and throwing grenades as they ran. Staff Sergeant Theodore Richardson was assigned to break open the gate. Rather than blasting the padlock with his Tommy gun he battered it with the gun's butt. Failing, he pulled his pistol to shoot the lock and a sentry rushing out of the guardhouse shot it out of his hand as a BAR man gunned down the sentry. Recovering the pistol undamaged, Richardson shot the lock off. As they threw the gate open a man ran toward them shouting "What's going on here?" The Rangers withheld fire thinking he was a prisoner, but he turned and shouted in Japanese.

They quickly brought him down and fired into the guards' quarters. First Lieuenant William O'Connell's 1st Platoon raced across the highway and through the gate within a minute of the start of the attack. The platoon rushed down the central street, firing into buildings and running shapes to the right, repeatedly emptying their weapons into the guards' quarters. The sheds containing the suspected tanks were 300yd (274m) inside the camp. A bazooka team closed to within 50yd (46m) and fired three rockets into them. Troops of the transiting Kinpeidan HQ who had been piling into two trucks were riddled with bullets and the trucks set aflame. As the headquarters troops rushed forward they were silhouetted by the burning sheds which made easy targets for the advancing Rangers.

The moment gunfire broke out at the camp, the guerrillas opened up with a rattling barrage into the Japanese bivouacs across the river from less than 300yd (274m). A cracking detonation burst from the bridge, too early for any Japanese to have started crossing. As the smoke and dust cleared it was seen that only a few feet of the bridge's east end was shattered. Pajota directed his automatic weapons to sight on the bridge's end and any Japanese trying to jump the gap. The tanks, at least, could not cross and pursue the raiders. Less than five minutes into the attack, the first Japanese emerged from the trees, rushing the bridge unaware of the newly formed gap. Streams of bullets tore into them as they attempted to leap across, and group after group charged only to be mowed down. The Japanese brought their machine-gun truck forward as additional support but this was quickly destroyed by some well-aimed bazooka fire, the survivors being picked off as they leapt clear.

At the camp, as the 2nd Platoon charged through the gate heading for the prisoner compound, there was complete pandemonium and confusion among the POWs. Some thought it was a guerrilla raid; others thought with horror that the Japanese were massacring them. Upon seeing Rangers in muddy green fatigues, field caps, strange boots, and carrying weapons they had never seen, they did not immediately know who they were. When they were captured, the army had worn khaki, but these men wore uniforms that looked frighteningly like the Japanese kit. Reportedly, the rescuers were shouting "We're Americans," "We're Yanks," and "We're Rangers," only to get responses like, "You don't look like Americans" and "What's a Ranger?" Some prisoners simply ran off and hid amidst the general confusion.

Rangers were forced to drag POWs out of their barracks, although more than 100 sick prisoners who had been housed in the hospital successfully made their own way to the main gate. But, generally, Rangers had to keep prisoners moving by pushing and yelling "Get the hell outa here!" As the situation sank home some prisoners began to shout in jubilation while others cried. Some had to be led out by hand as if they were children, many had to be carried. Tragically, Corporal James Herrick found a prisoner so weak he was unable to rise from his bunk. He picked up the man and carried him out, telling him that he was going home, despite the POW insisting: "Leave me, I'm going to die." Outside, the man went limp – he had died of a heart attack just yards from the gate.

Fifteen minutes into the raid, the Rangers had not suffered any casualties. Rangers were still mopping up across from the prisoner compound and the reserve waiting in the ditch opposite the gate spread out along the highway in case of Japanese counterattacks. As Rangers and the POWs began moving down the highway, three mortar rounds struck. These were fired from the far southeast corner of the camp and were probably 5cm grenade discharger (also known as "knee mortar") rounds. Company F Rangers in the rear opened fire on the trenches, silencing the discharger. Five men were wounded, but only one seriously. However, another Ranger – Captain

The Cabantuan raid begins with a burst of small arms firepower. Captain Prince's red flare falls to the ground as Staff Sergeant Theodore Richardson of 1st Platoon, Company C blasts the lock off the main gate with his .45, immediately after having it shot out of his hands and recovering it. (Howard Gerard © Osprey Publishing)

The internal layout of Cabanatuan
Prisoner of War Camp No. 1.
1) Guard Towers
2) Fighting positions ("pillboxes")
3) Main gate
4) Guardhouse
5) POW compound
6) POW hospital
7) Japanese officers' quarters
8) Japanese guards' quarters
9) Motor pool (tank sheds)
10) Signal center
11) Chapel
12) Water tower
13) Transient unit area
14) Rear guard quarters
15) Rear gate
16) Main attack
17) Escape hole cut.
(© Osprey Publishing)

Fisher, the medical officer – was soon discovered with a severe stomach wound. Two Rangers and two guerrillas carried him to the Pampanga River crossing, as soldiers and POWs, many of the latter wearing only underwear, streamed out of the camp. There was a fear that prisoners would become separated in the confusion and that the weak might be left behind as the moon rose to light their return.

Half an hour into the battle, the Japanese at the bridge had all but given up. In all probability most of the officers were dead, having wasted themselves in futile rushes. Small groups continued to fire at the guerrillas only to draw more fire in return. Occasional grenade discharger rounds landed behind the guerrilla positions but this ceased once the guerrillas used their bazooka to fire on the tanks and supporting troops.

Northeast of Cabanatuan City, on the Rizal Road, which the raiders and their freed prisoners would have to cross later, a roving P-61 detected the 2nd Shusei Battalion dispatched to Cabanatuan City from San Jose. The Black Widow's three devastating passes ensured the battalion never reached its destination, with a total of 12 trucks and one tank destroyed.

Most of the prisoners had vacated the camp by 2010hrs. Rangers and guerrillas had to carry most, piggy-backing them or making hasty litters from rifles and shirts. It was 2 miles (3.2km) to the Pampanga River, where carts waited to take them to Platero to be treated, fed, and organized. Many were still in shock and had not yet fully understood that they were free.

Captain Prince and others made a final search of the compound as Mucci sent the groups on their way. Prince fired the second red flare, signaling for everyone to head to the Pampanga. Joson's roadblock would remain in place for a time, but the Rangers with him and a few guerrillas linked up with the main body to assist prisoners. Six Rangers from the camp's south side had not reported in and Prince waited with 20 men outside the gate.

At the Cabu River, the Japanese made little effort to continue their attacks. A small group attempted to cross the river further north and was wiped out. Pajota would remain in place until the third red flare arched into the sky.

Seeing the second flare, the six Rangers remaining on the south fence skirted the camp on its east side when bullets cracked over them. Judging it to be random fire from the bridge battle, they moved on and began to take scattered fire from inside the camp. Tragically, two bullets fired by a fellow Ranger struck Corporal Roy Sweezy in the chest, dropping him into a ditch, where he died as a medic worked on him. These Rangers linked up with First Sergeant Bosard on the highway, who was distressed to learn the company had lost a man and had had to leave his body behind.

At 2040hrs, Captain Prince was at the Pampanga River supervising the loading of stumbling prisoners into 25 carts as Rangers and prisoners trickled in and Fisher and the wounded Scout were treated in the field hospital. The rest of the Scouts established an ambush at the crossing site. At 2045hrs, one hour after the raid was launched, Prince fired the third red flare and departed for Balangkare. Joson withdrew his roadblock and, while Pajota was under no pressure from the Japanese and free to withdraw, he stayed in place until 2200hrs just to make sure. His squadrons circled to the southeast and around behind the Japanese to arrive at the Pampanga three hours later. The Filipinos were ecstatic – they had utterly destroyed a superior-strength Japanese battalion in their first stand-up battle. They came out of it with only a few men slightly wounded and all would be heroes.

Over 270 Japanese lay dead or dying in the smoldering camp; most of the wounded dying by dawn as no aid was forthcoming. Japanese bodies were literally stacked at the Cabu bridge and scores more littered the riverside woods. Meanwhile, the loaded carabao carts were ordered on their way to Balangkare at 2145hrs. As the column of prisoners departed north, Prince called the Alamo Scouts in from their ambush to guard the medical team and the wounded Fisher. Some of Pajota's men set up an ambush on the Pampanga River to stall any Japanese attempt to pursue the raiders.

Some freed prisoners were in such bad shape that they had to be spoon-fed in the homes of Filipinos while passing through the small barrios. The grateful Filipinos gladly shared what little food they had. (US Army)

The column closed on Balangkare at 2230hrs where 15 more carts joined them. The radio team there had difficulty establishing contact, but the long-awaited message was finally received at Guimba, where Sixth Army staff officers waited in apprehension, at 2300hrs, "BAKER ZULU GEORGE BAKER LEAVING SOME WITH FRIENDS" (BZ meant Mission Accomplished, GB meant Starting Back). Tech. 4 James Irvine, who had remained awake for nearly 60 hours awaiting this crucial message, was able to announce jubilantly to the expectant officers, "They've done it!"

They left Balangkare before midnight. Mucci was at the column's head with a limping Prince bringing up the rear. After almost 4 miles (6.4km), they crossed the Morcon River and another mile brought them to Mataas Na Kahoy at 0200hrs on January 31. Here, 11 more carts waited as more prisoners weakened, and the convoy departed within half an hour of arriving. It was crucial that the column continued to move and some Rangers began taking Benzedrine to stay awake. The column stretched almost 2 miles (3.2km), making it extremely vulnerable to attack as it snaked back toward Allied lines. Reaching the Rizal Road, they encountered an obstacle. The column could not cross directly as a steep bank barred the north side. They had to travel 1 mile (1.6km) southeast down the road to Luna before they could turn off. Roadblocks were established up and down the road during the transit, which took the strung-out column an hour. In the meantime, Captain Fisher was carried by six men to Balangkare, arriving at 0205hrs. There, a work detail cleared a light aircraft runway.

Reaching the Casili River the column halted for a rest at 0530hrs to allow stragglers to catch up. They received word that Huks in a village ahead would not allow them to pass. Negotiations were made via runners, but the Huks remained adamant. Mucci finally had enough and told the Huks they were all coming through and that he would level the barrio if there were any difficulties. The column passed through enduring nothing worse than hateful glares. At Sibul they received a more cordial welcome at 0800hrs in the form of food, water, and 19 more carts.

With daylight and full bellies came the prisoners' realization that they were on their way home. This was evident in the smiling faces in the film footage taken that morning. At 0900hrs, Mucci learned via radio that Talavera, 12 miles (19km) closer than Guimba,

THE CABANATUAN RAID

1. Squadrons 213 and 2nd Platoon, Company F establish a roadblock southwest of the camp.
2. Guerrillas cut telephone lines 166yd (150m) east and west of the camp.
3. 2nd Platoon, Company F fire support teams neutralize guard towers and fighting positions.
4. 1st Platoon, Company C neutralizes gate sentry and tower then breaks into main gate.
5. Men from 2nd Section, 1st Platoon, Company A split into two parties to attack both the officer and guards quarters.
6. 1st and Special Weapons Sections, 1st Platoon, Company C attack tank sheds, signal area, and transient unit area.
7. 1st and 2nd Sections, 2nd Platoon, Company C break into POW compound and attack transient unit area.
8. Special Weapons Section, 1st Platoon, Company C destroys tank sheds and trucks.
9. 2nd Platoon, Company F team cuts escape hole through east fence.
10. POWs are ushered out of the compound and assemble outside of main gate.
11. Three grenade discharger rounds are fired onto highway.
12. Captain Fisher and several men are wounded by grenade discharger rounds.
13. As 2nd Platoon, Company F fire support teams are withdrawn to highway, Corporal Sweezy is shot by mistake.
14. All raid forces and freed POWs are withdrawn to Pampanga River crossing and await the arrival of the buffalo carts. (Howard Gerard © Osprey Publishing)

was in American hands. He requested trucks for 412 personnel and ambulances for 100 to meet them on Highway 20 in two hours. Nearing the highway, aircraft were heard approaching and panicking prisoners clambered from carts. Four P-51 Mustangs roared over and put on an air show for the cheering men. Soon they met a 1st Battalion, 1st Infantry patrol and the trucks and ambulances arrived. They were trucked to Guimba where a jubilant reception awaited, with cheering GIs lining the roadside, and the 92nd Evacuation Hospital then took charge of them. Here General MacArthur would visit the liberated POWs as they convalesced on February 1.

Back in Balangkare, Captain Fisher died at noon, the requested plane never having arrived. He was buried there and the small group, harassed by Huks, made its way to Talavera, arriving in the evening where they found sleeping Rangers. Corporal Roy Sweezy's body was subsequently recovered from the camp by guerrillas on January 31, and he was buried alongside Captain Fisher.

The Cabanatuan raid has gone down in the annals of US military history as one of the most perfectly planned and executed special operations raids. According to General MacArthur, the raid was "magnificent and reflects extraordinary credit on all concerned." The Sixth Army G2 weekly intelligence summary declared it "an almost perfect example of prior reconnaissance and planning." Few operations have since matched its success. Coincidentally, one of the few raids that did measure up to its standard was conducted just 24 days later, the Los Baños Internment Camp liberation by elements of the 11th Airborne Division under the control of the Eighth Army. Interestingly there was no mechanism or time for the Los Baños planners or Raiders to have learned anything from Cabanatuan.

The former Cabanatuan prisoners arrive at 6th Infantry Division lines, January 31, 1945. Many wore only underwear as they had to depart so fast. (US Army)

MARINE ELITES

The Raider battalions were the special-ops capable units that the Marine Corps never wanted. The Raider concept was born in the early days of World War II when America was perilously weak and needed forces that could harass and delay a stronger foe while maintaining national morale. President Franklin Roosevelt eagerly seized upon the commando model for guerrilla fighters and maritime raiders to pit against the Japanese Empire.

The Marine Corps' leadership wanted no part of the guerrilla role, and countered that amphibious raiding was one of the Corps' traditional roles. The commander-in-chief, of course, prevailed. The Marines therefore organized Raider battalions, but they lasted less than two years. In the final analysis they fought primarily as elite infantry rather than in their intended roles.

Individual Marines took different paths into the Raiders, and the process was dependent upon the beliefs of the commanders of the original Raider battalions. Though it has a reputation for being somewhat backward in attitude, the Corps actually encourages initiative, professional education, and creativity, and produces a disproportionate number of "characters" like the commanders of the first two Raider battalions, Merritt Austin Edson and Evans Carlson.

Lieutenant Colonel Merritt Austin Edson held the orthodox view that all Marine units should be capable of conducting maritime raids, the role of the "specialist" British Commandos. Nicknamed "Red Mike" for the flaming red beard that he had grown during long-range jungle patrols pursuing Nicaraguan guerrillas in the Banana Wars, Edson was a fighting intellectual. A small, ungainly man whose clothing and equipment always seemed too big, he led the national champion Marine Corps rifle and pistol teams, and authored the *Small Wars Manual*, a seminal document in counterinsurgency warfare. His cold, blue eyes never smiled. War correspondent Richard Tregaskis called him "… the bravest, the most effective killing machine I have met in fifteen years." Captain Henry Adams, who as an FBI Special Agent had hunted the most violent criminals, said he had "… never seen a guy as cool as that fellow. I don't think he was ever scared." Edson genuinely cared for his men, but was reserved and distant.

Red Mike seemed to possess a masochistic love of hiking. Marches with full field gear started at a few miles, and quickly grew in distance and severity. On one marathon the battalion marched from Quantico to the old Manassas battlefield 30 miles (48km) away, and returned the next day. Other training focused on increasing proficiency with weapons, and on improving cross-country navigation and map analysis. Much of the training was conducted at night, and Edson's emphasis on night combat would save many lives.

On December 7, with the Japanese attack on Pearl Harbor, the world changed for the Marine Corps. Edson increased the training to a numbing tempo. Holland Smith requested that the rubber-raft battalion be redesignated 1st Special Battalion, under direct command of the Amphibious Force Commander, and assigned to special missions. In January 1942 Edson's battalion was designated the 1st Separate Battalion, and the 2nd Separate Battalion was established under Major Evans Carlson in California.

The Corps was grappling with yet another problem. Evans Carlson's campaign to create a "guerrilla" force was gaining momentum with a request by Admiral Chester Nimitz, the newly appointed commander in the Pacific, for raiding forces to strike back at Japan. There was a very real threat that the President might insert Colonel William "Wild Bill" Donovan (a World War I Army hero and future leader of the OSS, predecessor to the Central Intelligence Agency – CIA) into the Corps to divert manpower and scarce resources to form guerrilla units, at the expense of the amphibious assault mission. Commandant Holcomb reluctantly dispatched two officers to observe British commando training, and resigned himself to the idea of special "trick" units.

A Douglas C-47A transport could carry up to 19 paratroopers. For the Los Baños jump Company B, 1st Battalion, 511th PIR loaded approximately 15 paratroopers in each of the nine transports. The jump door is off the left edge of the photograph.

Airborne forces provided the US Army with a large-scale special forces capability, and a new means of rapid battlefield deployment. Here a US paratrooper with a Thompson M1 submachine gun conducts combat training at an American base. (NARA)

On February 16, Edson's battalion became the 1st Raider Battalion but the ensuing changes almost wrecked his carefully crafted unit. Rather than taking the time-honored opportunity to dump his malcontents, Edson transferred his entire Company A, a machine-gun platoon, and a mortar section to form the core of Carlson's 2nd Raider Battalion. The rest of the 2nd Raider Battalion was a hand-picked unit shaped by Evans Carlson's unusual concept of a new kind of social order in the American military. The son of a Congregationalist minister, Evans Fordyce Carlson ran away from home at 14, lied about his age to join the Army at 16, and was a first sergeant at 19. After a brief stint as a civilian, he reenlisted in 1917, was promoted to lieutenant, chased Pancho Villa in Mexico, and served as a captain on General Pershing's staff after World War I. After another half-hearted and unsuccessful try at civilian life, he enlisted as a private in the Marines in 1922. Commissioned as an officer and assigned as a military aide at President Roosevelt's vacation home in Warm Springs, Georgia, he became a familiar of the President and his son James, a Reserve officer.

When assigned to his third tour as an intelligence officer and military observer of the communist forces in China, Carlson maintained private communications directly with the President, which did little to endear him to his superiors. In China he observed with admiration the apparent unity and political motivation of the Chinese communist forces fighting against the Japanese invaders. He marched over 2,500 miles (4,000km) through the mountains and deserts of northern China with the famous Eighth Route Army. Like many idealists, Carlson somehow missed noticing the brutality that underpinned Mao's system; the Chinese fighters marched so hard and fought so tenaciously not only out of political motivation, but also out of mortal fear of their own leaders.

"Red Mike" Edson (right), shown here with Commandant Holcomb on Guadalcanal, supported the orthodox Raider doctrine of "spearhead" assaults, and determined Raider unit organization. Both men are wearing summer dress clothing. Note the different designs of the shirt. Edson is wearing a non-standard pistol belt usually issued to Defense Battalions. As usual, his helmet seems too big. (USMCRC)

Though Carlson was not a communist (a devout Christianity-based socialism would probably be a better description of his beliefs), his public admiration for the communists aroused suspicion. He resigned from the Corps in April 1939 to write and speak publicly about Japanese atrocities in China. In May 1941 Carlson used his White House connections to re-enter the Corps as a Reserve captain, then was promoted to major.

Unlike the aloof Edson, Carlson was, according to Private Brian Quirk, "the nicest man you'd ever want to meet, and he was fearless. He was smart … flawlessly in control of himself. Never got excited, never raised his voice, and that's pretty hard to do when things are going bad."

Carlson's Raiders were hand picked, and he used his unique speeches to explain his philosophy to the new recruits. He introduced the term "Gung Ho" as a motto, speaking with a missionary's fervor of the need for postwar social equality and justice, and mutual self-sacrifice. Weekly Gung Ho sessions served as "town-hall" meetings to air complaints, conduct group singing, view movies, and listen to guest speakers on political and social issues. Higher-ranking officers found one of Carlson's practices – his egalitarian disregard for rank structure – profoundly disturbing. Officers fraternized openly with enlisted men, no rank badges were worn, and the Gung Ho sessions featured open criticism of officers without fear of retribution.

Carlson also placed great emphasis on physical fitness. Ervin Kaplan recalled, "We'd get up and run in a circle for twenty minutes … two or three miles. We'd go down in the Mission River valley, and somebody would carry us for a hundred feet, and we had to carry them back. I always seemed to pair up with some guy that ran about two-fifty [pounds]."

Route marching started slowly and worked up to two-day, 70-mile (112km) hikes. Others could not tolerate their colonel's vision of how dedicated warriors should live, with few comforts and no recreation. In addition to the usual weapons training and marches, Carlson placed more than usual emphasis on knives. His Raiders were issued two distinctive knives, the massive "Gung Ho" Bowie and a Raider stiletto patterned after those used by the Commandos. The young Marines took to the knife training with a vengeance.

Carlson's battalion received less training in the use of rubber boats – three weeks practicing off the California coast. After a transfer to the Hawaii Territory the battalion received additional training at Camp Catlin, Oahu. On May 22, Companies C and D were dispatched in great secrecy to reinforce Midway in anticipation of a Japanese invasion that never materialized. On June 28, Companies A, B, E, and F set sail north to the Aleutians as part of a plan to recapture Attu and Kiska from the Japanese. "About two days out," said McCullough, "we turned and went to Midway." It was not the most auspicious beginning for the elite units.

OPPOSITE: November–December 1943, Bougainville. US Marine Raiders and their dogs, which were used for scouting and running messages, start off for the jungle frontlines, warily watching out for Japanese ambush. (NARA)

In September 1942, Lieutenant Colonel Harry B. "Harry the Horse" Liversedge stood up the 3rd Raider Battalion. In October Lieutenant Colonel Jimmy Roosevelt raised the 4th Raider Battalion, and a Raider training battalion was established in California. (A victim of various diseases, Roosevelt relinquished command of the 4th Raider Battalion before the unit went overseas.) Liversedge was a by-the-book officer who represented the future of the Raiders as he rose to command the new 1st Raider Regiment (composed of the 1st and 4th Battalions) in March 1943. Sam Griffith, the new commanding officer (CO) of the 1st Battalion, was another fighting intellectual. The ten-man rifle squad was unwieldy in the jungle, and so Griffith reorganized the squad with a leader and three three-man fire teams. Each had a BAR, with a leader and assistant BAR man, both with the new M1 semi-automatic rifle.

Lieutenant Colonel Alan Shapley, the CO of the new 2nd Raider Regiment (raised on September 12, 1943 and composed of the 2nd and 3rd Raider Battalions) made it clear that he did not ascribe to the Raider mystique. "We had a lot of stuff like Raider boots. Everybody had to turn those in and they were burned up in a big fire," recalled Kaplan.

The Raiders were heavily committed to combat in the Pacific from August 1942, the first deployment being that of the 1st Raider Battalion to Tulagi and Guadalcanal during the bloody Guadalcanal campaign. Subsequent deployments included the Solomon Islands and New Georgia, but in many cases the Raiders were used more as conventional (albeit elite) Marine infantry rather than specialist raiders. An exception was the Makin Island raid of August 17–18, 1942. Admiral Nimitz was casting about for a diversionary operation in support of the landing on Guadalcanal, and his staff eventually settled on Butaritari Island, Makin Atoll. The small Japanese weather station and seaplane base made it a feasible target, close enough to the Solomons to be an effective diversion. The 2nd Raider Battalion was chosen for the mission. Reconnaissance was sketchy, consisting of a few photos taken on an aerial raid, and through a submarine's periscope. The battalion intelligence officer, Lieutenant Gerard Holtom, interviewed a fisherman from the island. All information seemed to suggest that there were few beach defenses.

The layout of the island was staked out near Barber's Point on Oahu for rehearsals, and the Raiders did a walk-through of each man's role. Each man had a specific mission on the island. Brian Quirk was one of six men hastily trained in demolitions, though "I didn't know Primacord, from a telephone [cord], from a piece of string." He was in Company B, but attached to the small headquarters unit. "My job was gonna be to go to that radio station [and destroy it], and assuming I had the landmarks to get there, I didn't care where you were going... We had rehearsed this thing lock, stock, and barrel."

Nimitz could make available only two of the Navy's three large submarines, *Nautilus* (APS-2) and *Argonaut* (APS-1), which limited the size of the raiding force. *Nautilus* could cram in 85 passengers, while the bigger *Argonaut* could take 134. Carlson pared his force by leaving behind 25 men from Company A and 30 from Company B, the two companies selected for the raid.

Carlson argued that only one senior officer was needed on the raid, and outlined the risks of having the President's eldest son fall captive. Roosevelt argued that his place was with his men. Eventually a phone call from Jimmy to his father secured his place on the raid.

Rubber-boat practice in some of Oahu's roughest surf revealed problems with the small outboard engines: improvised metal shields proved inadequate to protect the

Marine sniper Private First Class Mike Barrineau takes aim with an M1903A4 sniper rifle during the New Britain campaign, May 1944. Although snipers were found within regular Army and Marine units, they often performed the equivalent of special forces roles, including intelligence gathering and advance reconnaissance. (NARA)

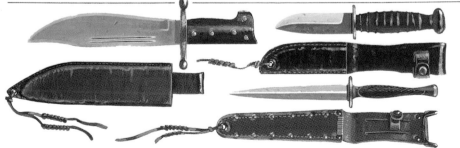

Raider weapons and uniforms, mid-1942. This 2nd Raider Battalion enlisted man (left figure) is wearing the black P1941 utilities and gym shoes unique to the Makin operation, and is armed with a Thompson gun. The Raider lieutenant next to him wears P1941 utilities that have been camouflaged with irregular splotches of brown, dark green, and even white paint. Surrounding weapons include the M1903A1 Springfield rifle, the M1941 Johnson light machine gun, the M1941 Johnson Automatic Rifle, the Reising submachine gun, the .55-cal Canadian-pattern Boys Anti-Tank Rifle, and various patterns of knife. (Michael Welply © Osprey Publishing)

ignition systems against salt water. Concerns about conditions aboard the submarines also led to the installation of crude air-conditioning systems.

On August 6, 1942 (August 7 in the Solomons), Pearl Harbor was abuzz with the news of the Guadalcanal landings. The next morning the Raiders boarded the submarines. To save space each man carried only his weapon and a cloth bag with field gear, including helmet and a change of clothing. The tightly packed rafts, outboards, and the fuel had already been loaded in great secrecy. At 0900hrs the submarines slipped out of the harbor. For the Raiders inside, there was nothing to do but lie in the bunk and think unwelcome thoughts. Crude bunks, stacked four high, were sheets of canvas stretched tightly over a wooden frame, and each bunk held four men. The temperature never dropped below 96 degrees F (36 degrees C). The closely packed bodies overwhelmed the air circulation, and pools of sweat accumulated in the bunks and on the decks. The air reeked of unwashed men, diesel fumes, and the smoke of cigarettes that were the only concession to morale. The grunting, snoring, and farting of men, and the rhythmic thumping of the diesel engines marked every minute of every day. The only punctuations were twice-daily meals, and the rare opportunity to go on deck and breathe clean air.

At 0300hrs on Sunday August 16, the faster *Nautilus* made landfall at Makin, and conducted a last-minute periscope reconnaissance. In the face of rain and an onshore wind the operational commander, Commodore John Haines, elected to proceed with the mission. At 0330hrs someone opened the forward hatch, drenching the men with seawater blown in by the storm. The 15ft (4.5m) waves broke over the deck, knocking men off their feet. Men struggled to mount outboard motors and fill fuel tanks. Loose gear was carried off by the wind and waves. Water filled the rafts as soon as they were lowered over the side, and men bailed frantically with helmets. Men fell into the water, saved from sinking only by the superhuman efforts of comrades. Two rafts filled with medical supplies and ammunition broke free and disappeared into the darkness. The men paddled madly toward the rendezvous point, only to be swept landward by the relentless wind. The rafts, and their landing sites, were hopelessly scrambled.

On the edge of the reef the raft plunged down the faces of the breakers, taking on water. Unable to steer, the man in charge of the motor cursed and unscrewed the wing nuts, letting it sink. When the raft grounded on the sand the exhausted Raiders leapt out and dragged it into the underbrush, then crouched in the darkness. The two companies had landed in a huge snarl along 200yd (183m) of beach. Lieutenant Oscar Peatross' platoon was nowhere to be found.

The Raiders decided to sit quietly until daylight, but just before dawn a private loading a BAR let the bolt slam home, releasing a long burst of fire into the silence. Officers and NCOs immediately scurried about organizing the units. Sergeant Ken McCullough recalls that it was about 20 minutes before the Japanese garrison responded.

A short while later one squad from Sergeant Herbert "Frenchie" LeClair's platoon sent to the far shore of the narrow island reported back that the units had landed exactly in position. The platoon spread out and started to move slowly through the scrub and tall palm trees, guiding on a narrow road. Suddenly the scout, Corporal Howard Young, dropped to the ground and warned the others. A truck slewed to a stop in the road. Japanese soldiers tumbled out and deployed in a skirmish line in the brush. Sergeant Clyde Thomason ran back and forth along the line, positioning men in an ambush with one flank pushed forward to form a cross fire. The inexperienced Marines opened fire with no thought for fire discipline or preserving ammunition. Thomason ignored shouts to get down, until a Japanese rifleman fatally wounded him.

The firing slackened after five full minutes in which the Japanese unit was wiped out, but as the 2nd Platoon arrived as reinforcement, more Japanese troops arrived and launched a screaming *banzai* attack. The two platoons drove the enemy back, but suffered heavy losses trying to move forward. Nothing in their training had taught them to expect snipers hidden in the treetops, and enemy marksmen concentrated on leaders like

The new Raider Training Battalion established in 1943 emphasized consistent, but still intense, training. These trainees are equipped with an odd mix of M1 rifles, BARs, and a Thompson gun. (USMC Museums)

Captain Holtom (promoted while on the raid) – who were identified by their hand signals – and the radiomen. Sergeant McCullough was in charge of communications. "We had these little SCR walky-talkies, and the damn things had chrome antennas. One or two of the guys were shot in the head." Five machine-gun rounds struck Frenchie. An enlisted man bandaged the ghastly wounds, tied his arm to his body with a belt, and he continued to stagger around the battlefield.

By 0700hrs most of the fighting was over. Major Roosevelt used one of the remaining radios to call in gunfire from *Nautilus*, which destroyed two Japanese vessels in the lagoon. The Japanese, alerted by a radio message from the doomed garrison, dispatched planes to see what was happening on Makin. One arrived at 0900hrs, two more at 1040hrs. Carlson pulled his skirmish line back to try and lure the enemy forward, and when a dozen enemy planes arrived at 1255hrs they bombed and strafed their own troops. The Raiders directed fire from machine guns, rifles, and two Boys Anti-Tank Rifles at the planes. One burst into flames and sank. The larger four-engine aircraft made a desperate attempt to take off again, but was riddled by fire as it rose from the water, staggered, and crashed.

Peatross' small group never linked up with the main body because other Raiders opened fire on them in the confusion. They looted and burned the enemy headquarters,

RIGHT: This Raider's utilities are not camouflaged, only filthy after days or weeks in the jungle. Note the captured Japanese equipment and the Marine identity discs. (USMC Museums)

OPPOSITE: This photo of the Carlsons, father and son, shows the boondocker boots, the most common pattern of Raider logging boots, and the hacked-off trouser legs. The younger Carlson won a Silver Star on the Long Patrol, became an aviator, and served in Korea. (USMCRC)

then withdrew to their isolated raft. By 2000hrs they were back aboard *Nautilus*, the only group to withdraw as planned.

Carlson planned to leave the beach at 1930hrs, but had not counted on the pitch-black night, the strength of the surf, or his burden of wounded, which included both his surgeons. Seven of the 18 boats, including Brian Quirk's, made it through the surf.

The other 11 boats made repeated attempts to breach the surf. The rafts filled with water, were spun about by the waves, and repeatedly pushed back. In some instances the rafts capsized and the men were flung back onto the beach before they gave up the struggle. Most would have lost shoes, clothing, and weapons. The survivors spent another miserable night in the rain.

Carlson fretted all night. The son of the President was trapped on the island, enemy planes would certainly return at daylight, and perhaps a powerful Japanese landing force. After all, their purpose was to draw a landing force. By some accounts a despondent Carlson penned a surrender note and dispatched it to the Japanese. Others, like McCullough, who was near him through the night, dispute the claim. McCullough wrote that for Carlson "… it could have been grocery shopping, or a day in training. He was about the most calm guy on the island." Carlson's major concern was relieved when around 0800hrs four more boats breached the surf line and met the submarines. One carried Major Roosevelt, though Carlson did not yet know that.

Ken McCullough wrote: "Peatross or somebody sent five men back in. One of them jumped out of the boat and swam in… He said that the ship's Captain said he would be there until we all got off. He swam back out, and he hadn't much more than got in the boat, 'til we seen the subs dive." Enemy planes machine-gunned the boat, and dropped bombs on the submerged submarines. Fortunately they had no depth charges.

Most of the men on the beach were despondent, but Carlson reorganized the men to sweep across the island killing any remaining Japanese and destroying facilities, the mission they had neglected in the confusion of the day before.

All the radios had been lost in the surf, and four of Carlson's communicators were killed by snipers. The sole survivor who knew Morse code was Ken McCullough. McCullough climbed a leaning coconut tree with the single surviving flashlight and signaled for the submarines. "I could feel them [Japanese] looking at me all over the place. I'd start and get two or three letters out, and they'd break me. Blink real fast – that means 'stop.'" The sailors kept signaling "Who?" Finally Haines blinked out a query about the odd nickname of a friend of Haines' father. Carlson recognized the name – "Squeegie" Long. After verifying his identity, McCullough blinked out instructions for the submarines to rendezvous at 2130hrs downwind of the island, where the huge raft would not have to fight the surf.

The trip turned into a two-hour ordeal. The last outboards died, and the paddlers struggled with the unwieldy raft. One group of men badgered Carlson until he gave them permission to break away and go ahead. The rubber boat and its occupants were never seen again. At the rendezvous McCullough signaled with his dying flashlight, and by 2308hrs the last of Carlson's men were on board the submarines. There was no time to account for the dead and missing, so the ships divided up the survivors and steered

a course for home. The wounded doctors provided "meatball surgery" in the fetid air of the crowded submarines.

The Raiders returned to a tumultuous welcome. They may not have been the first Americans to strike back at Japan, but they were ones the press and the brass could get their hands on. The raid provided a much-needed boost to national morale, rivaling the equally famous and equally token Doolittle Raid. The Raider exploits were shamelessly exaggerated, and they were the guests of honor at a no-holds-barred party at the Royal Hawaiian Hotel.

With exhaustion clearly etched on their faces, a group of US Marine Raiders gather in front of a captured Japanese dugout on Cap Totkina on Bougainville, Solomon Islands. (NARA)

The Raiders conducted several similar missions over the next two years, but by late 1943 it was clear that there was no role for the Raiders in the "new" Corps. There was no need for harassments or diversions, and ironically the Raiders were now becoming a morale problem. The "ordinary" officers and enlisted Marines who increasingly bore the brunt of the fighting resented the publicity lavished upon the Raiders, and "Gung Ho" became a derisive term. What was there to do with all these highly trained men?

In a stroke of organizational inspiration, the Raider units disbanded in February 1944 formed the core of the new 4th Marines, a regiment that in 1941 had been forced to surrender by the initial Japanese offensive in the Pacific. The Corps was determined that the only regiment ever to be surrendered would be reborn as a "special" unit. The 4th Marines went on to fight at Emirau, the recapture of Guam (the only major US territory to fall to the Japanese), and Okinawa. It was deliberately chosen to land in Japan to liberate the POW camps. For the emaciated and disease-ridden survivors of

Following the raid on Makin Island in the South Pacific in August 1942, Lieutenant Colonel Evans F. Carlson, USMCR (left), commanding officer of the Marine "Raider Battalion," and Major James Roosevelt, USMCR, the president's son and second-in-command display a war prize. (NARA)

1st Raider Regiment base camp, Dragon's Peninsula, New Georgia, July–August 1943. The accommodations at this rear-area base camp illustrate the hardships of the New Georgia campaign. The isolation of the Northern Landing Force in the coastal swamps on the northern coast required Colonel Harry Liversedge's Raiders to live and fight under exceedingly primitive conditions. (Michael Welply © Osprey Publishing)

Bataan and Corregidor, the Marines' code of honor was satisfied. Their regiment had at last come to take them home.

MARINE RECON

The Raiders were not the only elite combat forces developed within the Marine Corps during World War II in the Pacific. The Corps also formed specialized reconnaissance platoons, companies, and, eventually, an entire battalion dedicated to high-risk reconnaissance operations. When the first two Marine divisions were established, each

Raider training, like this practice off the coast of San Clemente Island, California, did not prepare Carlson's men for the high, breaking surf they would encounter off Makin Island. (Raider Museum)

included a scout company of seven officers and 132 men in a headquarters and three platoons. Organized in March 1941, these men were trained to scout on foot, from motorcycles, and from M3 armored cars. Subsequently these companies became part of the division's tank battalion with a motorized reconnaissance mission. On their arrival in the Pacific theater, rubber boats were issued and dismounted patrol techniques taught by old-timers with "Banana War" experience in jungle terrain. The scout cars remained through 1942, when they were replaced by jeeps. Eventually, "rubber boats and field shoes" became the most widely used methods of transport.

Wartime necessity accelerated developments and, in January 1942, a group of specialists was created in the Atlantic Fleet to develop amphibious reconnaissance techniques and equipment. They later went to the Pacific Fleet and formed the basis of the first amphibious reconnaissance company. In August 1942 the US Navy even formed the Amphibious Scout and Raider School at Fort Pierce, Florida, to train individual soldiers, sailors, and Marines in raiding and patrolling techniques. When the Marines began fighting in the South Pacific in 1942 they found that scouts, observers, and snipers were needed at regimental and battalion levels as well as with divisions and corps. Then in May 1944 the scout companies were renamed reconnaissance companies and assigned to the division headquarters battalion, with the strength of five officers and 122 men in three platoons.

Although scout and reconnaissance companies met the needs of the division, the various Marine senior commands did not have specialized recon forces when the war began. The corps-level commands solved patrolling needs in different ways. The I Marine Amphibious Corps (later III Amphibious Corps) operated in the south Pacific, with headquarters at Guadalcanal until it moved forward to Guam. In this corps the parachute and raider battalions were assigned patrols, and were well suited to behind-the-line actions. Other patrols were formed as needed from available American personnel, or with the help of Allied independent commandos and "coastwatchers." Active until 1943, these patrols varied in size from two to more than 40 men. Training was given in rubber boat handling, demolitions, and hydrography. Specialists were included, and were put ashore by submarine, seaplane, and ship. The results obtained were as varied as the patrols themselves; some had the benefit of experienced personnel and guides familiar with the objectives; others were too large, overcommitted, and inexperienced. The conclusion reached was that well planned, aggressive reconnaissance was worthwhile only if conducted by units organized, equipped, and trained for patrolling.

The V Amphibious Corps operated in the Central Pacific, with headquarters at Pearl Harbor. Its patrolling demands were met when a special unit – the Amphibious Reconnaissance Company led by James L. Jones – was formed in January 1943. Known as the "Recon Boys," the company consisted of a headquarters and four recon platoons. A platoon of 19 men was split into two recon squads of six men each and a platoon commander with a six-man headquarters. The six-man squad, the basic patrol size, was armed with an automatic rifle, two submachine guns, and three rifles. A platoon could embark in two ten-man rubber boats or three seven-man boats. After nine months of training, the company was sent to the Central Pacific for operations: the Gilberts in November 1943, the Marshalls in January and February 1944, and the Marianas from June–August 1944. The company's capture of Apama Atoll with a force of 68 men was described as a "brilliant sideshow" and a model amphibious operation by the V Amphibious Corps commander.

Frequently landing at night from submarines and other vessels prior to the main assaults, the Amphibious Reconnaissance Company rendered singular service on enemy-held islands. It entered areas where "friendly aircraft, naval gunfire, [and] other forms of support were not available," and under cover of darkness moved in hostile territory under the noses of Japanese troops. The company reconnoitered 31 atolls, and served as a rifle company during the assault on Eniwetok. After these operations it was decided to expand the company to battalion size. This expansion allowed for rotation of patrols on operations or in training and for simultaneous missions. A larger unit would also be more able to accommodate casualties.

THE AMPHIBIOUS RECONNAISSANCE BATTALION

In April 1944, a two-company Amphibious Reconnaissance Battalion, with 23 officers and 291 men under Major James Jones, was formed by the V Amphibious Corps. The battalion moved to the Western Pacific in June 1944 for landings on Saipan and Tinian. There it operated for the first time with the US Navy's UDTs (underwater demolition team) to conduct beach reconnaissance and hydrographic surveys before and after the

The Makin Raid landing, August 17, 1942. Despite intensive training, nothing prepared the Raiders for the unexpected storm and surf conditions they encountered at Butaritari. Men and equipment were soaked by breaking waves and cold rain, and entire boats filled with key equipment were swept away by the wind. (Michael Welply © Osprey Publishing)

UNDERWATER DEMOLITION TEAMS

In 1943 the US armed services recognized the need for special units to reconnoiter reefs, obstacles, and nearshore water conditions, as well as destroy manmade and natural obstacles in the path of the landing craft, and this was reinforced by the near failure of the November 1943 Tarawa assault. The Navy formed its first Underwater Demolition Teams (UDTs) in December 1943 using Navy, Army, and Marine personnel. First employed at Roi-Namur and Kwajalein in February 1944, the "frogmen," armed only with knives, conducted pre-invasion hydrographic reconnaissance from

the 3½ fathom (6.4m) curve to the high-water line. UDTs located and destroyed obstacles, blasted boat lanes through reefs, marked boat lanes, and reported on the natural conditions at the landing zone. Later, 92-man UDTs were formed solely from Navy personnel; many were raised by assembling six-man Navy combat demolition units, Seabees (the Navy's construction personnel), and others trained by the Joint Amphibious Scouts and Raiders School at Fort Pierce, Florida. All subsequent landings in the Pacific were preceded by UDT swimmers, who were instrumental in their success. The UDTs were subordinate to Underwater Demolition Flotilla, Amphibious Force, Pacific; and the Naval Combat Demolition Training and Experimental Base was established on Maui, Hawaii, in April 1944. By the war's end some 3,500 men were assigned to the UDTs, and it was planned to commit 30 teams to the invasion of Japan.

LEFT An explosive charge placed by a UDT detonates on the coast of Saipan in 1945. The UDTs laid the foundations for the establishment of the US Navy SEALs during the postwar period. (NARA)

landings. Using combat swimmers, these missions took place at night in unfamiliar waters.

In February 1945 one company was sent to operate with the UDT and 3rd, 4th, and 5th Marine Division reconnaissance companies for the Iwo Jima landings. This mission was accomplished by the novel use of amphibious tractors. The remainder of the battalion supported the Okinawa campaign. As the only reconnaissance unit available to the Tenth Army, it infiltrated and flanked enemy positions and landed on offshore islands within the Japanese defenses. Throughout the war various structures had been tried until a balance in personnel, equipment, and employment was found: a light infantry unit of company to battalion strength. An additional requirement was for reliable communications between patrols and transports, plus a vigilant attitude to security. One recon veteran recalled that any Marine infantry unit "with extensive training in scouting and patrolling" could carry out recon tasks; and that all Marine rifle companies should have training in rubber boat operations for coastal raiding and reconnaissance by the division. At the lowest levels, tasks merged with scouting routines for all infantry units, but infantry units were not always available, and were not trained in specialized amphibious techniques. Clearly there was a need for Marine commanders at all levels to have dedicated units equipped and trained to conduct amphibious or ground reconnaissance.

The Raiders and the Marine recon forces illustrate how the lines between elite and conventional forces were often blurred in World War II, at least practically if not theoretically. Other units in the US military fell into the same middle ground. One other famous example was the 5307th Composite Unit (Provisional), better known as "Merrill's Marauders" after its commander Frank Merrill. This 3,000-man formation was formed in 1943 specifically as a long-range deep-penetration force in the China–Burma–India (CBI) theater, each man being trained in specialist skills such as demolitions, jungle navigation, survival, camouflage, scouting, and close-quarters marksmanship. Travelling by foot, with support from mules and air drops, the Marauders entered Burma in 1944 and were a deep thorn in the side of the Japanese, attacking formations many times their own size. Eventually, however, combat losses and disease whittled down their numbers until they were no longer combat effective as a unit, and after a truly epic war in the jungle the Marauders were finally disbanded in August 1944.

The Marauders and similar sized elite units were the most visible end of special forces operations during World War II. In complete contrast, however, were far smaller, and more secretive, groups of men and women who would virtually define the notion of special forces, akin to today's SEAL Team 6 and Delta Force. These were the operatives of the Office of Strategic Services (OSS).

OFFICE OF STRATEGIC SERVICES

In July 1940, William J. Donovan was sent to Great Britain by the Roosevelt administration to determine if the island nation had the ability to fight on after the German victories in Western Europe during May and June. Donovan, a Medal of Honor holder from World War I and a successful Wall Street lawyer, met with Britain's leadership, toured her defenses, and was given access to her clandestine services – the Secret Intelligence Service (SIS) and the newly created Special Operations Executive (SOE). After delivering a report calling for increased American aid to Britain, Donovan advocated the creation of an American centralized intelligence service to combat enemy espionage and subversion, which was believed at that time to be a major factor in the fall of France. On July 11, 1941, by order of President Roosevelt, the

Five members of OG Team "Donald" beside the "Carpetbagger" B-24 that will drop them over Brittany in August 1944. They wear the British X-type parachute routinely used for clandestine night drops. OSS personnel who successfully completed British parachute training were entitled to wear British parachute wings; the man on the far left displays them below his SF wings. (NARA)

Coordinator of Information (COI) was established as a civilian agency with Donovan as its director. Its mission was to gather and analyze security information obtained from agents around the world and from government departments and agencies. COI was to report its findings to President Roosevelt and to government agencies as he deemed appropriate. The FBI and the military services mistrusted this new intelligence agency, which they believed could threaten their control over American intelligence-gathering.

Donovan first established the Foreign Information Service (FIS) branch under the direction of playwright Robert E. Sherwood, to prepare and distribute "white" or factual propaganda across Europe and the Pacific by radio, print, and film. The Research & Analysis (R&A) branch was created next, to evaluate information obtained by COI and distribute reports based on its findings. Other founding branches included the Foreign Nationalities branch, to interview arriving foreign immigrants; the Field

Photography Division; and a Special Activities section for spying, sabotage, and guerrilla warfare. After observing the damaging rivalry between Britain's separate SIS and SOE over the demarcation of responsibilities, Donovan decided to split Special Activities into a Secret Intelligence (SI) branch for intelligence-gathering, and a Special Operations (SO) branch for subversive operations, with the goal of better coordination with the respective British agencies while still operating under a single clandestine organization. Since COI was still getting itself established and directing its efforts towards Europe, it was not involved in the intelligence failure that preceded the attack on Pearl Harbor in December 1941.

With America now in the war, Donovan realized that unconventional warfare conducted by COI needed support from the newly established Joint Chiefs of Staff (JCS). Sherwood was concerned that putting COI under military control would hinder the ability of the civilian-staffed FIS to operate effectively. By contrast, Donovan believed that both "white" and "black" propaganda (designed to subvert the target audience by any devious means possible) were best employed under the direction of the military.

President Roosevelt settled the issue by signing Executive Order 9128 on June 13, 1942; this removed FIS from COI and placed it under the new Office of War Information. What was left of COI became the OSS, which would fight an entirely different type of war, and not just with guns and explosives.

ORGANIZATION

The OSS expanded from around 1,000 staff in 1941 to a peak of over 13,000 personnel by late 1944, and at least 24,000 people worked for the OSS at one time or another during its brief existence. Members from all the military branches served in the OSS, and it provided the USMC its few opportunities to engage in operations against the Germans. Civilian staff worked as clerks, analysts, scientists, engineers, and even behind enemy lines. About 4,000 women worked for the OSS either as civilians or in uniform, performing clerical roles and helping prepare missions in operational theaters, and some operated behind enemy lines.

The SI branch gathered and reported military intelligence from operational areas by unorthodox means, to include: the location, movement and patterns of activity of enemy units; the strength and capabilities of resistance movements; the location of infrastructure and industrial targets; and the gathering of economic, political, social, and psychological intelligence. This was accomplished by positioning agents in enemy territory, acting in direct liaison with resistance groups, and obtaining tactical intelligence for Allied troops near the frontlines. SI established its Technical Section to review and distribute agent reports pertaining to the German secret weapons program, and supplied over 2,000 reports on German atomic research to the Manhattan Project. As well as initiating their own operations, SI fulfilled specific requests from the military services, and also obtained reports from the clandestine services of Allied nations.

SI was divided into four Geographic Desks that coordinated operations in Europe, Africa, the Middle East, and the Far East, each being subdivided into sections devoted to specific countries. While most SI operations originated from the Geographic Desks in Washington, control was exercised by overseas field bases for better coordination and response to local situations. Washington did maintain direct control over SI operations in neutral nations, where the primary focus was on infiltrating agents into and obtaining intelligence from bordering enemy-occupied countries.

SI had difficulty finding enough experienced personnel not only to operate behind enemy lines, but also to staff the coordinating field bases. Consequently, many Americans who were recruited as agents in fact became operations officers (handlers) because of their language skills and knowledge of the local culture, while agents to actually operate in enemy territory were recruited from local populations. SI agents reported their findings to their SI handlers by portable radios, through couriers, or in person if they exfiltrated back through enemy lines.

Within SI, a Labor Section obtained industrial intelligence and recruited agents through the labor unions and organizations in different countries. The Ship Observer Unit (SOU), established in December 1942, gathered shipping intelligence from seamen's organizations and from sailors who had recently sailed from ports in neutral or enemy-held countries or in Germany itself. Informal interviews with – or actual agent recruitment among – seamen of neutral merchant fleets yielded information on harbor installations, naval bases, cargoes, and the current situation in occupied territories. Sailors recruited by SOU also obtained foreign publications, and helped infiltrate OSS agents into enemy territory.

The SO branch of the OSS was created to take the war directly to the enemy through unorthodox warfare – the direct sabotage of enemy targets and training local resistance forces in guerrilla warfare. Small SO teams or circuits sabotaged targets of strategic importance such as factories or railway tunnels, or targets of a tactical nature like bridges and supply dumps. SO teams organized, supplied, and trained local resistance groups with Allied weaponry to conduct a sustained insurgency campaign of sabotage and ambush. Since many of these activities were in direct support of Allied operations, SO units came under the authority of their respective Allied theater commanders. Several sections of SO – such as the Operational Groups, Maritime Unit, and Technical Development – later became separate OSS branches in their own right.

Established as a separate branch from SO in May 1943, Operational Groups (OGs) conducted irregular warfare directly against enemy forces – raiding installations, ambushing supply lines, occupying key infrastructure to prevent its destruction, as well as supplying, training, and operating alongside resistance groups. In contrast to other OSS operatives behind the lines, OGs always fought in military uniform. Uniquely, OGs were formed exclusively with first- or second-generation Americans of Norwegian, Greek, Italian, Yugoslavian, Polish, German, or French heritage. Recruited from US Army infantry and airborne units, each OG had at least several members who could speak the local language fluently. From August 1944, OGs in Europe were collectively identified as 2671st Special Reconnaissance Battalion (Provisional), which would be awarded the Presidential Unit Citation; Detachment 101 in Burma was the only other OSS unit to be so honored.

The Maritime Unit (MU) separated from SO in June 1943. Its purpose was to use the sea to place OSS operatives behind enemy lines, supply resistance movements, conduct shoreline reconnaissance, and sabotage maritime targets. Because of this unique mission, the MU developed its own special equipment independently of the Research & Development (R&D) branch.

MORALE OPERATIONS

This branch was established in January 1943, to cause disharmony and chaos among enemy troops and civilians by the use of "black" propaganda – lies and deception, spread by radio broadcasts and printed materials – to subvert enemy morale. A key distinction between Office of War Information (OWI) and Morale Operations (MO) propaganda was its perceived origins: OWI material was overtly advertised as coming directly from the Allies, but MO material was crafted to give the impression that it came from resistance movements or from the enemy itself. Although the direct impact of such methods is difficult to quantify precisely, countermeasures such as denials in official publications and the jamming of radio broadcasts proved that MO activities did not go unnoticed. Several instances were noted of rumors and lies that MO had spread behind enemy lines turning up later in Allied reports or the press.

MO transmitted its "black" radio programs into the Reich from stations around its periphery. The first originated from Tunisia in June 1943 and broadcast into Italy; it was called Italo Balbo after the late Italian air marshal. To create divisions between Italians and Germans it played on Italian suspicions that his death in 1940 was connected with his opposition to Italy's ties with Germany, and called for popular action against the Fascist regime. Italo Balbo ceased after the invasion of Sicily. Another MO station code-named Boston was established in Izmir, Turkey, to target German forces in the Balkans with news of military reverses and events on the German home front. It operated from August to October 1944, when several direct acts of sabotage forced its closure.

One of the most successful black radio programs was a joint effort with Britain's Political Warfare Executive (PWE) called Soldatensender-Calais, which began broadcasting to German forces in July 1944. Masquerading as a German radio station from that still-occupied French port (and renamed Soldatensender-West after Calais' liberation in September 1944), its programs actually originated from Milton Bryant in England. To maintain a captive audience for its subversive messages Soldatensender played popular American songs that were composed, sung, and recorded in German by artists such as Marlene Dietrich. After the July 1944 assassination attempt on Hitler, Soldatensender broadcast the names of alleged conspirators involved in the plot so that the Gestapo would disrupt the German leadership by pursuing these leads. The US 12th Army Group reported that 90 percent of German POWs taken in the summer of 1944 admitted to listening to this station.

As Allied armies reached the German border MO began to broadcast directly into Germany from stations on the continent. Programs such as Westdeutscher Volkssender and Volkssender Drei conjured up fictitious resistance groups within Germany, calling for a popular revolt against the Nazis. MO recruited German POWs to record broadcasts, including a major whose voice resembled that of General Ludwig Beck, the former Chief of General Staff who committed suicide after being implicated in the July 1944 attempt on Hitler's life. The convincingly impersonated "Beck" blamed Hitler for losing the war and called for an end to the Nazi regime if Germany was to survive. The Nazis' sensitivity was indicated by their very diligent jamming of further broadcasts from "General Beck."

One technological advantage that MO and PWE exploited in January–April 1945 was a 600,000-watt Aspidistra transmitter in Woburn, England; this overpowered and interrupted German radio broadcasts with false news bulletins, anti-Nazi rhetoric, and rebuttal of key points from the program that was being interrupted. The enemy could not jam these interruptions without blocking their own programs sharing the same frequency. When the Allies crossed into Germany, MO black radio announced false Allied movements and German defeats to confuse the Wehrmacht and reinforce the sentiment that further resistance was futile. MO also sent coded messages to fictitious resistance groups in Germany, with instructions to cross out letters of the Nazi party initials "NSDAP" on public display so only the N and the D remained; Allied troops found examples of this on posters and official party signs in the towns they passed through.

In the Far East, MO established a radio station near Chittagong, India, north of the Burmese border, to imitate the Thai-language Radio Tokyo broadcasts in Thailand. To increase plausibility the station broadcast near the same frequency and immediately before the regularly scheduled airtime of Radio Tokyo. Thai agents were used to announce news about Japanese battlefield setbacks, and this material was even printed

Major General William J. Donovan, director of the US Office of Strategic Services from 1942 to 1945. (LOC)

subsequently in Thai newspapers, since they were required to print what Radio Tokyo reported. Even after the Japanese compelled the Thai government to reveal that the MO broadcasts were phony they remained popular with Thai listeners. MO also established a radio station in Kunming, China, which was heard in the coastal areas occupied by the Japanese; these broadcasts encouraged nonviolent resistance and sent messages to fictitious Chinese guerrilla groups. One program based on a Chinese fortune-teller predicted that a major (albeit unspecified) disaster would directly hit Japan in early August 1945.

MO was also able to broadcast directly into the Japanese home islands, recruiting Nissei and Issei personnel to help produce the Voice of the People program in San Francisco; a Japanese POW was used to ensure that colloquial expressions in the broadcasts were contemporary for Japanese ears. These programs were recorded on disks and flown to Saipan, where, from April 1945 until the war's end, they were broadcast into Japan from an OWI transmitter. Ostensibly originating from Japan itself, these programs emphasized Japan's inevitable defeat, demanded an end to the war, and called on the populace to drive the militarists from power. Except for the first and last two transmissions, however, the Japanese successfully jammed all 124 broadcasts.

MO also produced printed materials to undermine enemy civilian and military morale, such as leaflets, false newspapers, documents, death notices, and poison pen letters. Leaflets were either air-dropped over a large area of territory or distributed by locally recruited agents; MO also provided resistance groups with materials so that they could produce leaflets on their own. In spring 1945 MO initiated Operation *Cornflakes*, where planes from the US Army Fifteenth Air Force attacked trains carrying German mail and simultaneously dropped mailbags full of MO material nearby; these were recovered during the clean-up, and their contents were mailed throughout the Reich.

The attempted assassination of Hitler in July 1944 provided a unique opportunity for a small MO team in Italy to conduct one of the most successful operations of the war. *Sauerkraut* put a small team of trusted German POWs across the frontlines in Italy

This plate shows different elements of secret intelligence. 1) SI agent; Harrington airfield, Northamptonshire, England, spring 1944. OSS agents who jumped into occupied territory wore British one-piece canvas "striptease suits" to protect their clothing from telltale dirt or damage during a parachute drop. 2) Special Force Detachment; HQ US Seventh Army, Southern France, summer 1944. OSS military personnel wore standard uniforms and insignia, depending on the service from which they were recruited. 3) SI agent; Italy, summer 1944. The Hi-Standard .22-cal silenced pistol was the most useful of the special weapons developed for the OSS. (Richard Hook © Osprey Publishing)

to distribute MO leaflets about the assassination attempt in Wehrmacht rear areas. Private Barbara Lauwers interviewed potential agents from a nearby POW camp and 14 reliable men were recruited; a few days later – supplied with German uniforms, rifles, false identities, and cover stories – these agents infiltrated enemy lines near Siena. Each carried 3,000 MO leaflets of a supposed proclamation by the German commander in Italy, Field Marshal Albert Kesselring, that he had resigned and that the war was lost. Each agent returned safely (with useful information about military positions) after posting the leaflets on walls, trees, trucks, and in other places where they would draw attention from German soldiers.

This success prompted MO to send a dozen more *Sauerkraut* missions across the lines in Italy before the war ended. On one of these, agents distributed material from the "League of Lonely German Women," a fictitious organization conceived by Lauwers to weaken the resolve of German soldiers at the front. The members of the League were supposedly German women on the home front who would freely copulate with any German soldier on leave who showed her a pin made with the leaflet's heart-shaped logo; the purpose of this offer was supposedly to increase the birthrate for the Fatherland. More conventionally, MO in Italy also distributed leaflets and safe-conduct passes to persuade Czech conscripts and Italian soldiers to desert their units, and it was estimated that they successfully instigated the desertion of at least 10,000 enemy soldiers.

Other printed materials that MO employed were fake newspapers from imaginary German underground political parties opposed to the regime. *Das Neue Deutschland*, a newspaper from a fictitious peace party, was circulated among German troops in Italy, and *Der Oesterreicher* was purportedly produced by an Austrian resistance group. An MO team in Stockholm produced "Handel und Wandel," a newsletter for businessmen who traveled between Sweden and Germany; printed from July 1944 to April 1945, it combined reliable business news with propaganda about the inevitable defeat of Germany. MO also successfully used the Germans' own propaganda leaflets against them. *Skorpion West* was a Wehrmacht operation in the fall of 1944 to drop leaflets promising final victory to encourage its soldiers to fight on; MO duplicated these leaflets with plenty of black propaganda designed to subvert this message, thus forcing the Germans to terminate this program.

In the Far East, MO was able to mail black messages directly to Japan in the summer of 1944 when a team based in New Delhi, India, came across a pouch of 475 postcards home, already passed by the Japanese Army censors, from soldiers of a Japanese unit that had since been wiped out. With the assistance of Nissei interpreters MO gently erased the original last messages home and replaced them with news of starvation and a sense of abandonment in the jungle. The altered cards were then placed in a pouch and left south of Mogaung in Burma for the Japanese to find and mail back home.

The same MO unit was able to persuade Japanese soldiers in Burma to surrender by the use of forged Japanese Army documents; Elizabeth MacDonald came up with the idea of forging an order from the Japanese high command allowing troops in hopeless battle situations to surrender instead of fighting to the death. A perfect forgery was produced with the help of a Japanese POW; copies were slipped into Japanese-occupied Burma by Detachment 101, and air-dropped by the OWI. In China, MO was able to establish secret bases behind enemy lines to produce leaflets printed on local presses, which were distributed by Chinese agents and air-dropped by the US Army Fourteenth Air Force.

X-2 COUNTERESPIONAGE

Before X-2 was created in June 1943, SI handled all counterespionage matters. In response to a request by the OSS for access to Ultra decrypts, the British agreed on the condition that the OSS established its own self-contained counterespionage branch, which would be given exclusive access to Ultra and their counterespionage files. X-2

R&A branch amassed a large library of German language materials as references for the reports that it produced for the OSS. Here a civilian employee at OSS headquarters in London browses a shelf of German books on law, administration, and politics. (NARA)

As Allied armies advanced up Italy in 1944, OGs were parachuted into the northern half of the country to work with partisan groups against the Germans. Note on the right the "Special Recon Bn" sleeve title above the Fifth Army patch on this man's tank jacket. (NARA)

used its special status to check the backgrounds of potential OSS agents, reject proposed OSS operations on security grounds, protect OSS activities overseas from enemy penetration, operate directly against enemy operatives in neutral nations, and capture and turn enemy "stay-behind" agents in France and Italy. The operational headquarters of X-2 was established in London, due to its close proximity to Bletchley Park and the other Allied counterespionage services. While X-2 in London directed operations in Europe and the Mediterranean, X-2 in Washington directed counterespionage operations in the Far East.

X-2 in London was divided into geographic sections for Western Europe, the Iberian Peninsula, Scandinavia, and the Middle East, each subdivided into desks dealing with specific countries. In March 1945 these desks shifted their focus to branches of the German Abwehr and Sicherheitsdienst intelligence services. Each of these desks collected and collated all available information into a central card registry that kept track of all persons of interest, and by 1945 the registry had over 400,000 entries. They were color-coded by category: pink for Abwehr or Sicherheitsdienst personnel, buff for political traitors and suspected collaborators, white for friendly persons, and blue for those still unclassified. X-2 focused on the operational procedures and working relationships of the German intelligence services, and on uncovering their plans for intelligence-gathering and sabotage; it was thus able to disrupt these operations directly through the employment of its Special Counterintelligence (SCI) teams (see below). In late 1944, X-2 created the Art Looting Investigating Unit to help in the retrieval of items of value plundered by the Nazis, but its primary purpose was to obtain information on people who might use these ill-gotten treasures to fund Nazi activities after the war.

In the Far East, X-2 was only able to establish itself at Kunming, China, in September 1944. It soon discovered that the Nationalist Chinese counterespionage effort against the Japanese by General Tai Li's Bureau of Investigation and Statistics (BIS) was unreliable or nonexistent. To overcome the obstacles of the BIS having sole authority to arrest enemy agents and the obvious limitations of American personnel operating in the field, X-2 recruited local Chinese agents; several networks were established in both occupied and unoccupied China, and successfully uncovered several Japanese spy rings. X-2 then turned this information over to the BIS, who neutralized these threats. The X-2 card file eventually contained 15,000 entries on people, organizations, and places of interest. Despite this success, OSS bases and operations were effectively infiltrated by Communist Chinese agents.

To take rapid advantage of any intelligence-related opportunities during the Allied advance across France, X-2 established SCI teams that were attached to the G-2 of each US army and army group, working in cooperation with Counterintelligence Corps (CIC) personnel. Traveling just behind (or sometimes just ahead of) US units, their mission was to apply counterespionage information to protect Allied assets, neutralize enemy stay-behind agents, garner intelligence from captured enemy agents and documents, and debrief SI agents whom the advance caught up with. One SCI team captured the Gestapo HQ in Rennes complete with its personnel and files; another captured an Abwehr NCO who led them to several hidden caches of sabotage equipment for use against Allied installations.

As the Germans retreated from France they left stay-behind agents equipped with hidden radios to report on Allied movements; SCI units had to race to find these agents, not only to thwart this activity but also to obtain any valuable intelligence they might provide before they were caught and summarily executed by the resistance. X-2 in London provided the intercepts from enemy agents to the nearest SCI teams, who could then apprehend them and convince them that it was in their best interests to cooperate with X-2. A case officer was then assigned to control the turned agent, providing false information to be reported back to Berlin. This ruse was so effective that the Iron Cross was awarded in absentia to three turned agents.

RESEARCH & ANALYSIS

Donovan believed that academia could play an important intelligence role by using data and analysis to pinpoint enemy weak points. The R&A branch was thus created and divided into primary geographic divisions for Europe-Africa, Far East, USSR, and Latin America, each subdivided into economic, political, and specific geographic sections. R&A employed prominent historians, economists, sociologists, diplomats, and other experts for their intellectual, analytical, and research abilities. Materials from the Library of Congress, university libraries, research institutions, government agencies, and from OSS agents in the field were used by R&A to produce reports either on demand or on its own initiative. These reports were provided to other OSS branches, the military and government agencies; they dealt with the military and economic potential of enemy and Allied countries, diplomatic issues, and supplementary information for the planning of military operations. In the summer of 1942 R&A was informed of Allied plans to invade North Africa; the entire staff worked day and night for several weeks to produce several detailed reports on Morocco, Algeria, and Tunisia, much to the astonished satisfaction of the military. R&A also produced the *Soldier's Guides* for American troops stationed overseas.

R&A established a Map Division (MD) that produced unique maps incorporating the economic, political, and military situation of a specific country or area; information on these specially prepared maps included transportation routes, communications, industry, natural resources, terrain, and weather. MD also amassed a large collection of foreign maps to assist with OSS operations overseas. The Central Information Division (CID) was created to collate R&A reports and other information for effective access; CID created a vast card catalog system that allowed it to provide extensive information at short notice. By 1945 over three million 3x5 cards, 300,000 captioned photographs, 300,000 classified intelligence documents, one million maps, 350,000 foreign serial publications, 50,000 books, thousands of biographical files, and 3,000 research studies had been compiled.

R&A sent personnel overseas to directly distribute needed information, forward the latest intelligence to R&A headquarters in Washington, and help analyze data obtained in theater. Operating behind the Allied advance, R&A sought out important publications and reported on the economic and political issues in liberated areas. (Valuable industrial, technical, and military information regarding Japan was also uncovered in France and Italy.) R&A also traveled to former battlefields to examine German vehicles and equipment, recording factory markings and serial numbers; analysis of this information allowed R&A economists to estimate with a certain degree of accuracy the current production levels of equipment throughout occupied Europe. (The new location of an aircraft factory was found when R&A noticed that the inscription on a compass from a plane wreck had changed from "Focke-Wulf Bremen"

to "Focke-Wulf Marienburg.") Such intelligence was passed on to the Enemy Objectives Unit (EOU) based at the American Embassy in London, whose primary purpose was to identify critical targets for the strategic bombing campaign. Other intelligence used by EOU came from air reconnaissance, POW interrogations, and agents operating on the Continent.

RESEARCH & DEVELOPMENT

Originally the Technical Development Section of SO, R&D became a separate branch in October 1942 in order to facilitate the development and production of special weapons and equipment used by OSS agents. Very few of these items were produced by R&D directly; it arranged for their development through contracts to government, academic, and corporate laboratories. R&D established a working relationship with the National Defense Research Committee (which later became an advisory board to its successor, the Office of Scientific Research and Development), whose Division 19 enlisted the assistance of such laboratories. R&D's Technical Division observed the

The OSS Air Crew Rescue Unit was formed in summer 1944 to evacuate Allied airmen forced down in either Partisan or Chetnik territory in Yugoslavia. Lieutenant Nick Lalich (left), team leader of the "Halyard" Mission with Lieutenant Mike Rajacich (right), is interviewing a P-51 pilot who was shot down south of Belgrade in September 1944. Their names are a reminder that the OSS sought out Americans of suitable national heritage to operate in particular countries. (NARA) development of items to ensure they stayed within the bounds of reality, and then tested them to determine if they warranted full production. R&D also obtained special devices from the British that were manufactured and supplied to the OSS. The Documentation Division of R&D was responsible for counterfeiting enemy documents for use by OSS agents in occupied territory. The Camouflage Division ensured that agents and their equipment remained inconspicuous; this included supplying European-style suitcases to carry clandestine radios, clothing suitable to the operational area, and the correct accessories to be carried in pockets.

FIELD PHOTOGRAPHIC

The Field Photographic branch was the brainchild of Hollywood director John Ford, who believed that a specialized unit of skilled cameramen would be a valuable asset in the support of military operations. Unofficially organized as a US Naval Reserve unit in 1939 (Ford had been a US Navy Reserve officer since 1934), it was funded and equipped by Ford himself to document military activities and conduct photographic reconnaissance. Rebuffed by the US Navy, Field Photo did not become operational until it was recruited by Donovan for the COI in September 1941. Field Photo was part of SI when the OSS was established in June 1942, and did not become a separate branch until January 1943. Despite its predominantly naval character, personnel from all the military services were recruited into its ranks.

Field Photo made three types of films: special projects, strategic, and documentary. The first were films specifically requested by the military or government agencies. Strategic photography involved filming and photographing geographical areas that had intelligence value. For instance, the Intelligence Photographic Documentation Project, a joint effort with R&A in 1944, created by means of air photography a large file of high-value military and industrial installations and important geographical areas in Europe and the Far East. The documentaries were training films for OSS recruits that demonstrated weapons, equipment, and techniques, or general instructional films on

RIGHT: REPORTING FROM THE FIELD
1) "Line-crosser"; southeast France, summer 1944. Local civilians and resistance fighters recruited by the OSS provided tactical intelligence such as the location of German positions, units, and supply dumps. 2) Liaison with the partisans; central Yugoslavia, fall 1943. Intelligence from deep within enemy territory was obtained by OSS liaisons with resistance groups such as Tito's Partisans (though the quality of the intelligence was at the mercy of the Partisans who provided it, and who saw it as a form of leverage). This agent has started to prepare a coded message for his SSTR-1 suitcase radio. 3) SI agent; Germany, spring 1945. One advantage enjoyed by OSS agents in Germany during the chaotic final months of the war was the Joan-Eleanor system; Joan was a hand-held transceiver that could communicate with an Eleanor-equipped Mosquito aircraft orbiting up to 30 miles (48km) away. This agent had to hold Joan no more than 3in (7cm) from his mouth, and in the same exact spot to maintain the frequency and direction of the signal. Joan was best used in clear, flat fields or on high rooftops, as nearby metal and concrete structures degraded its performance. (Richard Hook © Osprey Publishing)

It takes a special kind of bravery to operate in enemy-occupied territory, and especially while wearing full USMC uniform. Captain Peter Ortiz is seen here consulting with the local Maquis as part of the inter-Allied "Union" Mission in early 1944. (NARA)

subjects as varied as the identification of enemy uniforms and life on the Japanese home islands. Field Photo also documented OSS and some other military operations worldwide.

COMMUNICATIONS

The small Code & Cable Section left over from COI had insufficient staff and resources to support clandestine operations overseas, and in September 1942 the Communications branch was established to provide training and communication channels for OSS operations. Military personnel and civilian amateur radio operators with the necessary skills were actively recruited. The Communications branch established a Research & Development Division (not to be confused with the separate R&D Branch) to devise special equipment for agents in the field, and developed and maintained the security of the codes and ciphers used by the OSS. The branch managed the radio traffic between field agents, overseas bases, and OSS headquarters in Washington, which by 1944 was receiving 60,000 messages a month.

SPECIAL FUNDS

After its establishment, Special Funds operated under various branches before becoming independent in May 1944. Its role was to finance secret OSS operations with funds that were not officially accounted for, in order to maintain security. Special Funds obtained intelligence on exchange rates, which currencies could or could not be used in particular places, foreign restrictions on the transfer of currency, and the financial situation of areas where agents operated (errors over the type and amount of currency they were provided could jeopardize a mission). Special Funds also paid sub-agents to conduct missions and covered their equipment costs and operational expenses, handled the salaries of civilian employees working in neutral countries, and provided currency to French and Italian resistance groups to finance their operations.

Special Funds obtained foreign currency through banks, brokers, and black market operations in neutral countries and North Africa. It also had to ensure that the money used in clandestine operations was not traceable. The Gestapo would record serial numbers or leave special markings on French francs before sending them into the black market to trap undercover agents; to avoid this, Special Funds examined all foreign currency against a list of all known marked notes. Fresh banknotes brought immediate suspicion upon an agent, so they were dumped on the floor and walked on until they became dirty and worn enough to be convincing. Gold was also obtained to purchase

Special Force Detachments were established in early 1944 to coordinate OSS activities with the operations of each of the American armies in northwest Europe. Here a convoy from SF Detachment 11 is leaving Third Army's headquarters at Chalons sur Marne as the advance continues eastward. Nothing in their uniforms or equipment sets them apart as OSS personnel. (NARA)

One important source of intelligence was German newspapers obtained in neutral countries and sent to R&A branch for analysis. One key benefit of R&A obtaining foreign publications was its ability to produce accurate statistics on German battle casualties, since German families were required to publish in their local newspapers the death notices of relatives killed in action. (NARA)

foreign currency, or as another medium of payment or bribery by agents, and in the Far East silver rupees and opium were also supplied. One of the greatest challenges Special Funds faced was from other OSS branches who believed that it had stockpiles of foreign money ready at a moment's notice; not realizing that considerable time and planning were involved, many OSS officers made requests to Special Funds only hours before their agents were to be dropped behind enemy lines.

MEDICAL SERVICES

Established as an independent branch in January 1944, Medical Services initially focused on ensuring proper medical care for OSS personnel at training areas and overseas bases. It also assessed the health situation of resistance groups and provided them with medical supplies. Through these channels it was able to obtain intelligence about medical conditions in occupied territory, to forewarn Allied forces and relief agencies of any potential epidemics or other health-related concerns in areas soon to be liberated. Medical Services personnel also provided medical supplies to line-crossers as barter for information, and one side-benefit of its efforts was the ability to obtain political and other non-medical intelligence unavailable to other OSS branches. Medical Services examined abandoned German medical facilities and equipment to determine the health status of the Wehrmacht, and also gathered information on the Germans' potential to conduct chemical and biological warfare.

OPERATIONS

Given the passages above on Secret Intelligence, Special Operations, and Operational Groups, in this chapter repetitive explanations of the exact functions of OSS missions are avoided. The information the OSS gathered behind the lines included the identification and location of enemy units, targets for Allied air power, and the local political and economic situation. Operations against the enemy in conjunction with resistance, partisan, and guerrilla groups were either indirect – through the sabotage of roads, railroad tracks, bridges, and communication lines – or direct, through the ambush of convoys and the harassment of enemy units and outposts. The OSS also organized, trained, supplied, and advised these irregular formations to support Allied operations directly by attacking enemy positions, capturing towns, rescuing downed Allied airmen, and seizing bridges, power stations, and dams before they could be destroyed by the retreating enemy.

The geographical range of OSS operations was exceptional, from the deserts of North Africa to the jungles of Burma, and from the internecine complexities of Yugoslavia to the underground war against the Nazis in occupied France. It also operated in neutral countries such as Switzerland and Spain. Given the breadth of missions, a complete study here is impossible. Instead we will gain insight into the OSS through three of its primary theaters: France and the Low Countries, Southeast Asia (Burma, Thailand, and the Pacific), and China.

SPECIAL FORCE DETACHMENTS

SF Detachments were established in January 1944 to coordinate the operations of each US army and army group with OSS teams and resistance forces operating in their areas. The detachments contained personnel from SI and SO who worked under the G-2 and G-3 of each army or army group respectively; they passed on pertinent intelligence received from either agents in the field or the resistance, or forwarded from London. In August 1944, as the US Army approached Paris, SI in London provided the latest locations of German military depots in the French capital 36 hours after the request was received from an SF Detachment. Agents locally recruited by SF Detachments were sent behind the lines either on foot or by parachute to obtain information specifically requested by US Army units, and sabotage and ambushes by the resistance were also arranged to support offensive operations. SF Detachments also debriefed OSS agents and teams and resistance fighters after advancing American forces overran them.

The inter-Allied Jedburgh teams in France used a mixture of US and British equipment. While the American "Jed" in left foreground wears the M42 US paratrooper jump uniform the others are wearing British battledress and 1937-pattern webbing. Team "Ronald," seen here, operated in Brittany in August–September 1944. (NARA)

FRANCE AND THE LOW COUNTRIES

February 1943 saw the first OSS agent (independent of any particular branch) infiltrate France from the French submarine *Casabianca* to set up a clandestine radio station in the southern port of Toulon. Other radio stations followed, and while they eventually fell under the jurisdiction of SI, the first official penetration into France by that branch came in August 1943 when the "Penny-Farthing" team parachuted in and set up a base in Lyon. As more SI teams landed in southern France, chains of sub-agents were formed, their information being either radioed to OSS headquarters in Algiers or sent by courier across the Pyrenees to OSS stations in Spain. Intelligence gathered by these networks played a key role in the successful Allied landings on the Riviera coast in August 1944.

In the more challenging environment of occupied northern France, SI participated in a joint operation with the British SIS called *Sussex*, whereby two-man teams of an observer and a radio operator were placed near rail yards, road intersections, airfields, and river crossings to report on German movements. The first Sussex teams were parachuted in April 1944 and, by the use of sub-agents, began reporting on the location of German units, supply dumps, and V-1 launching sites; some of these targets were bombed not long afterwards. After the Normandy landings SI initiated Operation *Proust*, by which agents gathered tactical intelligence at the direct request of US armies. They would rendezvous with the French Maquis to locate the enemy, and the Proust agent would then report to the Special Force Detachment (see feature box) attached to the specific army for which the agent was gathering information.

As the US First Army advanced into Belgium, its SF Detachment recruited resistance fighters from the Belgian Secret Army to scout, gather intelligence, and mop up bypassed German pockets. Despite this accomplishment, the G-2 at US First Army did not hold the SF Detachment in high regard, and obtained its withdrawal in September 1944 – a decision that contributed to the First Army being caught off guard by the German offensive in the Ardennes the following December.

In September 1944 the SI "Melanie" Mission deployed to Eindhoven in Holland to report the intelligence gathered by the various Dutch resistance groups and by line-crossers.

The first SO agents to land in France in June 1943 were instructors and radio operators to provide assistance to British SOE "F-Circuits" already in place. Each F-Circuit normally had an organizer, his lieutenant, and a radio operator, and recruited, trained, and equipped resistance fighters in its region. SO personnel operated in many SOE F-Circuits, and also established several of their own beginning with "Sacristan" in June 1943. Virginia Hall, who had previously worked undercover in Vichy France for the SOE, organized the only SO circuit to be led by a woman. Hall armed over 400 Maquis who conducted ambushes, derailed several trains in their tunnels, and demolished several railroad bridges in the summer of 1944.

Operation *Jedburgh* was a joint effort between SO, SOE, and the Free French to establish three-man teams that could quickly organize, supply, train, and accompany resistance groups in direct support of advancing Allied armies. In contrast to the regionally rooted F-Circuits, Jedburghs could be parachuted anywhere into France depending on the battlefield situation. To avoid alerting the Germans, General Eisenhower forbade the first Jedburgh team from deploying to France until the night

Major Peter Ortiz (second from left) returned to France as head of the "Union II" Mission that landed in the French Alps on August 1, 1944. Weeks later, Ortiz and three teammates were surrounded while fighting in the village of Centron; they surrendered after the Germans agreed to spare the village. (NARA)

of the Normandy invasion, but soon afterwards teams began parachuting across France. (The Jedburghs were also successful in keeping resistance groups of different political loyalties focused on fighting the Germans instead of each other.)

In August 1944 additional Jedburgh teams were parachuted in to protect General Patton's flanks as his troops simultaneously advanced on the port city of Brest and towards the German border, organizing local resistance groups to block and harass German units. However, many Jedburgh teams were unable to fulfill their mission because they were overrun by the faster-than-expected American advance.

In September 1944 Jedburgh teams were attached to the airborne divisions in Operation *Market Garden* in Holland, to recruit the local Dutch resistance to provide assistance and intelligence and to establish a communications link between the airborne forces and SFHQ in London. The Jedburghs landed along with the paratroopers, which did not allow them sufficient time; many of their radios were lost or damaged, and most teams were unable to fulfill their missions due to the incessant German attacks along the airborne perimeters, though Jedburghs near Nijmegen were more successful. The tri-national Jedburgh team "Dudley" was deployed separately in eastern Holland; it conducted intelligence and sabotage operations, but by the end of 1944 its effectiveness had suffered from disunity among Dutch resistance groups and from German countermeasures.

From June to September 1944, OG teams openly engaged the Germans in infrastructure sabotage and ambushes; paradoxically, they also seized hydroelectric plants and dams to prevent their destruction. On some of these missions OG teams operated alongside the British Special Air Service (SAS), inter-Allied Jedburgh teams, and the French resistance, which they also supplied and trained. With help from the Maquis, OG teams were able to exaggerate their size and bluff entire German garrisons into surrendering; this tactic successfully convinced more than 10,000 Germans to surrender out of the belief that the Americans would treat them better than the French.

BURMA

Detachment 101 was the first SO unit deployed overseas, and recruited indigenous tribesmen in Burma for espionage, sabotage, and guerrilla warfare. This irregular campaign helped the Allies reopen the Burma Road to China and liberate the country from Japanese occupation. Detachment 101 established its base at a tea plantation near Nazira in eastern India in October 1942, and trained British, Burmese, Anglo-Burmese, and Anglo-Indian agents in intelligence-gathering and sabotage. The Air Transport Command agreed to drop supplies and personnel behind the lines in return for Detachment 101 helping to rescue downed airmen. The first agents infiltrated Burma in January 1943 to report intelligence, carry out sabotage, and guide Allied bombers to

This plate shows two Detachment 101 soldiers operating in Burma between 1943 and 1945, supported by a Kachin guerrilla (far right). Before the Kachin guerrillas were issued with US military clothing they fought in their native garb, always with their shortswords strapped across their chests. (Richard Hook © Osprey Publishing)

Detachment 404 based in Ceylon sent teams from the Arakan Field Unit on missions to reconnoiter beaches and rivers on the Burmese coast. This OG team prepares to carry its rubber boats down to waiting British landing craft for an amphibious operation. (NARA)

Japanese targets. Some of the bases established behind the lines had rough airstrips used by light planes to bring in visitors and evacuate the wounded. From these bases Detachment 101 recruited the Kachins of northern Burma, who were very familiar with the jungle terrain; once trained, they became effective guerrillas and radio operators. (Kachin loyalty stemmed from their prewar relationship with Christian missionaries, from the medical care provided for them.) Nissei personnel in Detachment 101 interrogated Japanese captured in these operations, and also led Kachins into action, but only after their faces were carefully studied to avoid them being mistaken for the enemy.

In the spring of 1944, Detachment 101 supported Allied offensives into Burma with Kachin battalions scouting ahead of Allied units, providing flank protection, and attacking Japanese lines of communication. The Arakan Field Unit (AFU) – composed of SI, OG, and MU personnel from Detachment 404 – surveyed beaches and rivers along the Burmese coast, dropped off agents and supported several British landings in the spring of 1945. Based in Ceylon, the AFU was absorbed by Detachment 101 in March 1945. The following month Detachment 101, with close air support, began to single-handedly clear eastern Burma to make the Burma Road secure. It also harassed the Japanese retreat along the Taunggyi–Kentung road into Thailand, and the seizure of several key towns finally severed the road completely in June 1945. With the Japanese forced out of Burma, Detachment 101 was disbanded in July 1945.

THAILAND

As one of the few independent countries in Asia, Thailand formed an alliance with Japan to maintain its autonomy, declaring war on the United States in January 1942. This declaration was not reciprocated, and the OSS recruited agents from the pro-Allied Free Thai movement. Chinese obstruction delayed plans to infiltrate Free Thai agents overland, and those who were finally inserted in June 1944 were either killed or captured by Thai police. Shortly afterwards the pro-Japanese government was replaced by one headed by Pridi Phanomyong, a secret supporter of the Allies. In September 1944 a Free Thai agent was parachuted in to make OSS contact with Pridi, who had one of the captured agents radio his favorable reply. In January 1945 OSS officers Richard Greenlee and John Wester landed in the Gulf of Thailand from an RAF Catalina and reached Pridi's residence undetected, and Pridi agreed to pass on intelligence to be radioed back by SI agents in Bangkok to Detachment 404 in Ceylon. Unfortunately the information supplied was of little value before SI officers shared intelligence-gathering techniques. Free Thai agents also set up a network across Thailand to radio intelligence back to Ceylon. To show support for the Thai underground and to maintain the flow of intelligence, secret bases staffed by SO and MU instructors were established throughout the country, supplied either by parachute or by C-47s landing at hidden airfields. Japan knew of these activities, but could not counter them effectively before the end of the war in August 1945.

OSS plans to penetrate French Indochina directly had little success. The independent Gordon-Bernard-Tan intelligence network provided the only source of information before it was crippled by the Japanese takeover from the Vichy French authorities in March 1945. The following month the SO "Gorilla" Team that had parachuted near a withdrawing French column was itself forced to retreat to the Chinese border after fighting its way out of a Japanese ambush. Attempts by the OSS to recruit French agents to infiltrate Indochina were frustrated by the lack of French cooperation. A viable alternative was found after the OSS received reports of skirmishes between the Japanese and the Viet Minh, the Communist underground movement led by Ho Chi Minh astride Vietnam's far northern border with China. In July 1945 the SO "Deer" Team parachuted in to train and supply the Viet Minh for sabotage operations. Christened the "Bo Doi Viet-My" (Vietnamese–American Unit), it was still training when news of the Japanese surrender arrived on August 15, 1945. Meanwhile the "Quail" Team, a POW Mercy Mission with OSS personnel, landed at Hanoi's Gia Lam airport and evacuated Allied POWs without incident.

THE PACIFIC

Although the OSS was not allowed to operate in the Pacific Theater, Admiral Nimitz did accept the transfer of an MU (Maritime Unit) Operational Swimmer Group to help form UDT-10 in Hawaii in June 1944. The US Navy created UDTs after the heavy casualties suffered at Tarawa, where reefs and shallow water forced Marines to wade ashore under fire. UDTs were trained to scout the approaches to landing beaches, demolish any natural or man-made obstacles, and help guide landing craft to the beach. UDT-10's first assignment became the only UDT mission launched from a submarine during the war, when a five-man team was assigned to the USS *Burrfish* to scout the Yap and Palau Islands in August 1944; three men did not return from a nighttime reconnaissance of Gagil Tomil, and their fate remains uncertain. The rest of UDT-10 operated from the transport USS *Ratheburne* when they surveyed beaches and demolished coral for the landings at Anguar and Ulithi Atoll in September 1944. UDT-10's last wartime missions were scouting landing beaches at Leyte in October 1944 and Luzon in January 1945.

CHINA

The exclusion of the OSS from the Pacific Theater made Donovan look to China as the best opportunity for operations against Japan. Tai Li, who headed the Chinese intelligence service BIS, did not want an American service functioning in China outside his control. He was amicable with Captain Milton Miles, leader of the US Naval Group China that reported on Japanese coastal shipping and the weather in support of US Navy operations in the Pacific. Miles believed that absolute cooperation with Tai Li was the only way to operate successfully in China, so, anxious to establish itself in-country, the OSS joined with Tai Li and Miles to form the Sino-American Cooperative Organization (SACO) in April 1943, with Tai Li as its director and Miles as his deputy. Miles also doubled as the head of both the US Naval Group and the OSS in China. The OSS provided supplies and instructors to SACO, but its plans to gather intelligence independently were thwarted by Tai Li, who wished to conceal China's actual internal situation from the Americans. Miles, who did not want the mission of the Naval Group jeopardized by another organization that he directed, was unhelpful, and Donovan personally fired him from the OSS in Chungking in December 1943. Although OSS personnel served in SACO for the rest of the war, Donovan believed the OSS would have more freedom of action by joining forces with another American unit in China, the US Army Fourteenth Air Force.

The OSS teams operated in a diverse range of tactical scenarios. Here we see 1) "Camel" Team, southeast China, spring 1945; 2) Jedburgh team, central France, summer 1944; 3) "Union II" Mission, southern France, summer 1944. Note how many OSS personnel in China wore Nationalist Chinese uniforms. (Richard Hook © Osprey Publishing)

General Claire Chennault's legendary status in China as the founder of the "Flying Tigers" was beyond reproach, even by Tai Li. In April 1944 the Air and Ground Forces Resources and Technical Staff (AGFRTS) was formed with staff from both the OSS and Chennault's Fourteenth Air Force. AGFRTS allowed the OSS to gather intelligence independently, and to help Chennault employ his limited air assets effectively. In April 1944 the Japanese launched a series of offensives in central and southern China to seize USAAF bases and a secure land route between Beijing and French Indochina. With nationalist Chinese forces routed, AGFRTS teams conducted a sabotage and ambush campaign in an attempt to slow the Japanese advance, and were forced to demolish several USAAF bases before they could be captured. AGFRTS was fully absorbed into the OSS in April 1945.

In July 1944 OSS personnel participated in a mission to Yenan to liaise with the communist Chinese and assess their potential as part of the "Dixie Mission." They provided the mission with a communication link with Chungking, supplied the communists with radio equipment, demonstrated demolition techniques, and joined the communists as observers on operations behind Japanese lines. The communists provided information on Japanese units and allowed the OSS to microfilm their collection of

OG instructors use a derelict C-47 fuselage to demonstrate the proper jump procedure to future Chinese Commandos. (NARA)

Japanese documents and newspapers. Not all these interactions went smoothly. The OSS wanted to use Yenan as a base to infiltrate SI teams into northern China, Manchuria, and Korea, and also to arm and train the communists for sabotage operations against the Japanese. These plans were shelved after the communists demanded a $20 million loan (which was the total amount of unvouchered funds budgeted to the OSS in 1944). However, the Dixie Mission in one form or another remained in Yenan until March 1947.

In May 1945 the SO "Spaniel" Team parachuted into northern China to enlist the Chinese for intelligence and sabotage operations, but were detained by the communists, who had not been informed in advance. The communists wanted to maintain their monopoly of providing intelligence, and to prevent any independent contacts that might reveal – contrary to their propaganda – their fairly tranquil coexistence with the Japanese. The Spaniel Team was held incommunicado until the end of the war.

In February 1945 the new CBI theater commander, General Wedemeyer, ordered the OSS to be made an independent command as Detachment 202, in charge of all American clandestine operations in China. This allowed SI to set up independent networks in southern China. The Japanese did not occupy large rural areas but kept their garrisons in the towns, and SO teams exploited this when leading Chinese guerrillas on a sustained campaign of sabotage and ambush. In April 1945 OG personnel started training the Chinese Commando units that became their country's first paratroopers, and in July, accompanied by their OG advisors, the Commandos supported a Nationalist Chinese offensive in southern China. Deployed by parachute or sampan, they disrupted river and road traffic and helped seize an airfield. Two other Commando units served as the honor guard for the surrender talks at Nanking in August 1945.

WEAPONS AND EQUIPMENT

R&D helped develop special weapons and equipment for the OSS, but most of them either never left the drawingboard, never progressed beyond prototypes, or never found a use in the field. For reasons of space, only those that saw use with the OSS will be mentioned here, and the full range of standard-issue military weapons that formed the bulk of OSS technology will not be considered.

SPECIAL WEAPONS

The OSS issued its own variant of the Sykes-Fairbairn knife, with a thinner blade than that issued to the British Commandos. While this made it very effective for slashing and stabbing, the tip of the brittle blade often broke. One OSS veteran only saw them being

Elements of OSS Research & Development. 1) An engineer is preparing to test-fire the "Big Joe 5" crossbow, designed to silently take out sentries and guard dogs. 2) A member of the Field Photographic Unit. 3) A US-based analyst using a Recordak Model C microfilm reader, which accepted both 16mm and 35mm film and was specifically designed to view microfilmed copies of newspapers, mechanical drawings, and diagrams. (Richard Hook © Osprey Publishing)

used to open ration cans; others believed that the standard issue M3 trench knife was more practical for the field.

The United Defense Model 42 (UD-42) 9mm submachine gun, known as the Marlin after the company subcontracted to manufacture it, was initially produced for the Dutch East Indies forces, but the OSS took over the contract when those colonies fell to the Japanese in 1942. They used it worldwide, and supplied significant quantities to resistance forces. Able to fire at 750rpm, it was noted by OG teams as being handy at close range; two 20-round magazines were clipped together in staggered fashion for fast reloading.

With its suppressed discharge and lack of muzzle flash, the ten-shot HiStandard .22-cal silenced pistol was ideal for eliminating enemy personnel at close range virtually undetected. Its built-in "silencer" reduced the sound of discharge by 90 percent, and out

In the radio hut at Detachment 404 HQ in Ceylon, radio operators wait to receive transmissions from agents in the field. The OSS employed a wide variety of radios, including the civilian RCA receivers seen here. Note the paperback novel beyond the typewriter (center); agents had to memorize a particular line from a specific book to use as the base code when encrypting messages for transmission back to base. (NARA)

of doors the remaining report (similar to snapping fingers) could easily be smothered by everyday background noise. HiStandard also produced a special barrel for the M3 "grease gun" submachine gun that also reduced the sound of discharge by 90 percent; this saw action with Detachment 101 in Burma and SO teams in China.

The Liberator pistol did not originate with the OSS but from the Military Intelligence Service at the War Department. Cheaply made out of seamless tubing and stamped sheet metal, the Liberator was an extremely crude single-shot .45-cal smooth-bore pistol with an effective range of only 10ft (3m). It was shipped in great numbers to Europe and the Southwest Pacific, where it did see action in the Philippines. Plans to drop Liberators to resistance groups in Europe were shelved because of fears that spreading thousands of these un-numbered weapons across the countryside would pose a serious postwar criminal problem. The OSS received a large number of Liberators, but neither OSS personnel nor guerrilla groups were interested in them since vastly more reliable weapons, either Allied-supplied or Axis captures, were readily available. Most of the Liberators that found their way to OSS personnel were kept simply as souvenirs.

SABOTAGE

Many of the sabotage devices employed were improved versions of originally British inventions. Composition C was the primary explosive used by the OSS against infrastructure targets, in designations C-1 through C-3 indicating different combinations of explosive and plasticizing ingredients. The Limpet was designed for maritime sabotage; a waterproof plastic case holding 2½lb (1.1kg) of Torpex could be attached to a steel hull with six Alnico magnets. A variant called the Pin-Up Girl used a pin-firing device instead of magnets to secure itself to a wooden hull. Used on land, the Clam was a plastic case holding a ½lb (0.2kg) plastic charge that could be attached to any metal surface with four magnets.

The firing devices used by the OSS to initiate explosions were (with three exceptions) of British origin, and relied upon a timing device, the pulling out of a pin, pressure, or pressure-release. The US-designed Mole was intended to derail entire trains inside tunnels; its photo-cell eye, normally exposed to daylight, would trigger an explosion when blacked out by the train entering the tunnel. Another sophisticated US device was the Anerometer, a 6in (15cm) cylinder attached to a short fabric tube of plastic explosive. Designed to destroy aircraft in flight, it was initiated by a drop in external atmospheric pressure, normally at 1,500ft (457m) after takeoff.

The Pocket Incendiary was designed to spontaneously combust after a time delay; containing napalm powder and several acids, it would burn by itself for 8–12 minutes after ignition of a celluloid capsule of potassium chlorate by two Signal Relay Incendiary Pencils using regular match-heads. The Firefly was an incendiary device

OPPOSITE: Lieutenant Ray Kellogg of the US Naval Reserve at work photographing wreckage of a German aircraft shot down near Bizerte, North Africa. Kellogg was in charge of OSS operations in this theater. (NARA)

small enough to slip into a vehicle's gas tank or a fuel drum; small holes admitted gasoline, causing two rubber washers to swell, which triggered a small amount of TNT and magnesium.

COMMUNICATIONS TECHNOLOGIES

To allow OSS agents to transmit intelligence while operating undercover, in late 1942 the Communications branch developed the Special Services Transmitter Receiver Model No.1 (SSTR-1). This had three components – a transmitter, a receiver, and a power supply – that were all compact enough to fit together in a small suitcase. Various power supply units gave a total weight range of between 20lb (9kg) and 44lb (20kg). The SSTR-1 had a transmission range of 300–1,000 miles (480–1,600km), and messages were tapped out with a telegraph key on a continuous wave; it used interchangeable crystals that allowed it to operate on different frequencies. Unfortunately the SSTR-1 was fragile, and many were damaged during parachute drops. Its power pack proved troublesome due to poor connections, shorts, insufficient insulation, and overheating. The 6-volt battery that powered it had a short life, but could be recharged in the field with portable thermocouple chargers that burned wood or gasoline. The SSTR-1 itself could be powered by a hand-cranked generator, car batteries, or from the electrical current of a building. OSS agents also used SOE communication equipment including the Type 3 Mk II and Type A Mk III suitcase radios; these weighed 32lb (14.5kg) and 39lb (17.7kg) respectively and had a transmission range of at least 500 miles (800km).

OSS agents who transmitted while undercover always risked being located by German radio detection equipment, often operated in mobile vans, and the Joan-Eleanor (J-E) system was invented in response. J-E came in two components: Joan was an SSTC-502 transceiver powered by two 1.5-volt and two 67.5-volt batteries; its signals could be received by an orbiting plane from 30 miles (48km) away and, weighing only 3½lb (1.6kg), its small size made it ideal for undercover work. Joan worked best in clear, open surroundings. Its counterpart was Eleanor, a 40lb (18.2kg) unit consisting of an SSTR-6 transceiver, wire recorder, antenna extension support, manual directional control, dynamotor, and a power supply containing four 6-volt wet cell batteries. Mounted aboard an aircraft, Eleanor could record 60 minutes of transmissions verbatim on a spool of wire. Eleanor was located in the bomb bay of several British-supplied USAAF Mosquito PR XVIs; at 30,000ft (9,144m), Eleanor had to be turned on every half-hour to keep it from freezing. J-E's narrow UHF beam made detection impossible and codes unnecessary. J-E proved successful when it was first used in occupied Holland in November 1944, and was supplied to several teams that parachuted into Germany in 1945. The Eleanor operator and the agent were able

In contrast to other OSS branches, the role of OGs was to engage with the enemy directly; they thus wore conventional uniforms, although they were unlikely to receive the treatment guaranteed by the Geneva Convention if they fell into German hands. Here we see 1) OGs in France, 1944; 2) Greece, summer 1944; 3) Norway, spring 1945. (Richard Hook © Osprey Publishing)

to talk with each other from 10–30 miles away (16–48km), and clarify any details being reported. Special broadcasts by the BBC were used to schedule these rendezvous between the agent and the circling Mosquito.

The OSS also used standard US Army Signal Corps radios for field operations. The 35lb (16kg) SCR-300 was a backpack radio that transmitted voice messages over ranges of 3–5 miles (5–8km). The SCR-694 could transmit voice and coded messages with a transmission range of 15–30 miles (24–48km); it weighed nearly 200lb (91kg), but could be broken down and carried in several components, and SO teams in China powered it with the GN-58 hand-cranked generator. For small unit actions, SO and OG teams used the SCR-536 "handi-talkie" with its 1-mile (0.6km) transmission range. Each SF Detachment was equipped with three jeep-mounted SCR-193 radios and a truck-mounted SCR-399. The SCR-193, with a range of 15–60 miles (24–96.5km), would maintain contact between liaison officers in the field and the SCR-399 at army headquarters; the SCR-399, with a range of 100–250 miles (161–402km), would pass and receive messages to and from SFHQ in London.

CIPHERS

Although "code" is the term generically used, "code" and "cipher" are distinct. Codes have entire words replaced by other words, letters, numbers, or symbols. Ciphers have individual letters in messages replaced by other letters.

OSS agents initially coded their messages with a double transposition system. The agent would select a specific line from a poem, song, or book; this would identify a transmission's origin and become the agent's base cipher when preparing messages. For security reasons, only the agent and the headquarters that received the messages knew what the line was. This system proved to be too time-consuming and vulnerable to garbled radio traffic and human error. It was soon replaced by one of the most unbreakable ciphers ever devised: the one-time pad (OTP).

Invented after World War I, this was first supplied by the SOE before the OSS provided its own version. The OTP is a polyalphabetic cipher where any letter in the alphabet can be substituted for any letter in a message without a set key or pattern. The letters on the OTP to code the message were completely random, so two identical letters in one plain text message would have a different cipher letter. The OTP was a tablet of 100 sheets of nitrate rice paper that could easily be burned, dissolved or eaten. Each sheet was glued on top of the next so that only one could be used at a time. Rows of random letters in sets of five were printed on each sheet. The letters of the plain text message would be written under the letters on the OTP. Next, a table of letters printed on a silk handkerchief was used to obtain the needed cipher letters; the cipher letters used in the transmission were where the plain text and the OTP letters intersected on the table. This process was reversed when an OTP message was deciphered. The agent and headquarters required the exact OTP for this ciphering system to work. Each sheet could only be used once, and each following sheet would provide a coded message dissimilar from the previous one. This meant that if an OTP and its conversion table fell into enemy hands it still could not be used to break other OTP messages because of the randomness of its letters.

UNDERCOVER: CLOTHING, DOCUMENTS, ACCESSORIES

The OSS bought, scrounged, or made civilian clothing for its agents sent into occupied territory. Continental styles were noticeably different from American or British fashions. The OSS at first obtained suits, overcoats, hats, shoes, and other items from European refugees and second-hand shops, but since these only offered a limited supply authentic copies were tailor-made, perfect down to the parallel threading of the buttons. Towards the end of the war the OSS faced a shortage of German-style clothing, so one OSS supply officer followed American troops into Cologne and collected clothing and personal items from abandoned shops before anyone else could loot them. The OSS also obtained German uniforms from POW camps or captured stocks; these were mostly worn by German and Austrian agents who went behind the lines to gather intelligence or spread MO material – one female agent parachuted behind the lines dressed as a German Army nurse. Before going on these missions, some agents actually infiltrated POW camps in German uniforms to gather intelligence and to learn the current colloquial style and mannerisms of German soldiers.

The most important things an agent carried were identity papers and any occupation permits necessary to operate freely. For instance, in France an OSS agent needed an identity card, ration cards (for food, clothing, and tobacco), census card, occupation card, certificate of residence, medical certificate (to excuse the agent from labor or military service), work permit, and birth certificate. Agents operating in Germany required additional papers such as travel permits and police registrations for employment and housing. Depending on an agent's cover, a foreign worker passport or a Wehrmacht pay book would also be issued. R&D forged most of these documents from genuine examples collected by undercover agents; German papers were gathered in captured towns, POW camps, and from dead enemy soldiers. German typewriters, stamps, watermarks, ink, and blank cards and permits were highly sought-after by R&D personnel, since genuine documents that were simply filled out withstood greater scrutiny than those fabricated from scratch. Some documents were difficult to forge, such as German ration cards that were valid for only four weeks at a time. Recently bombed cities or areas were listed as the agent's place of birth or current residence to make background checks of his cover story difficult. Any mistake could doom an agent;

OSS TRANSPORTATION

Royal Air Force Special Duty squadrons based in Britain and the Mediterranean to support SIS and SOE operations also dropped OSS agents into Europe. A Halifax parachuted the first OSS agents into France in June 1943 and Germany in September 1944. SD squadrons of Halifaxes and Stirlings also dropped Jedburgh and OG teams, while Lysanders landed OSS agents individually in France. In the Far East, RAF Liberators, Dakotas, and Catalinas supported OSS operations in Burma and Thailand.

In November 1943 the USAAF established the 801st Bombardment Group (redesignated 492nd BG in August 1944) with B-24 Liberator squadrons that had previously flown patrols against U-boats; their long-distance night flying experience made these aircrews ideal for supporting clandestine operations in Europe. Nicknamed the "Carpetbaggers," they flew their first missions in January 1944 from Tempsford, and later from Harrington. Each glossy black B-24 was specially modified to drop up to eight agents and 12 supply containers. After September 1944, with most of Northwest Europe liberated, a few Carpetbagger squadrons were transferred to Italy, while other Carpetbagger B-24s had their armament removed to fly supplies into Sweden for the Sepals. Supply missions were also flown for the resistance in Norway and Denmark. Due to the strong antiaircraft defenses over Germany the slow B-24s only flew over the southwest corner of the Reich, while faster A-26 Invaders were used to drop OSS agents over the rest of Germany. The agent in the A-26 would sit on a hinged plywood floor in the bomb bay; once over the drop zone the agent would fall out when the floor folded from beneath him. The last Carpetbagger mission was flown in April 1945.

Along with Royal Navy MTBs and Italian MAS boats, US Navy Patrol Torpedo boats of RON 15 landed OSS agents throughout the western Mediterranean from 1943 to 1944. RON 2 (2), based at Dartmouth on the English Channel, had three PT boats under the command of Commander John D. Bulkeley; these landed and picked up OSS and other Allied agents along the French coast in the spring of 1944. The PT boats were painted a shade called "Mountbatten pink" that made them almost invisible in the dawn and dusk. All the operations of RON 2 (2) were accomplished successfully without ever coming into contact with the Germans.

one was caught when his work permit was found to have been signed supposedly in two different cities with the same handwriting.

The simplest things carried in agents' pockets could support or jeopardize their cover stories. Before they left for the field they were searched for such obvious items as London theater-ticket stubs. One agent maintained his cover in France by carrying Lotterie Nationale tickets and a letter sent to his Paris address that he had someone write for him. Another agent infiltrating Rome even lined his pockets with Italian tobacco shavings.

Cameras were issued to OSS agents, the Minox miniature camera being the ideal. Manufactured in Latvia, the Minox remained scarce despite a nationwide search by the OSS. To make up for the shortage the OSS developed its own miniature Matchbox camera (this came with German, Swedish and Japanese labels to make it look like a simple box of matches, hence its name). It could take 34 pictures on 16mm film, but could only be reloaded in the dark. Agents knew that a camera would be incriminating if discovered during a search, so many either did quick sketches of important targets or just committed them to memory.

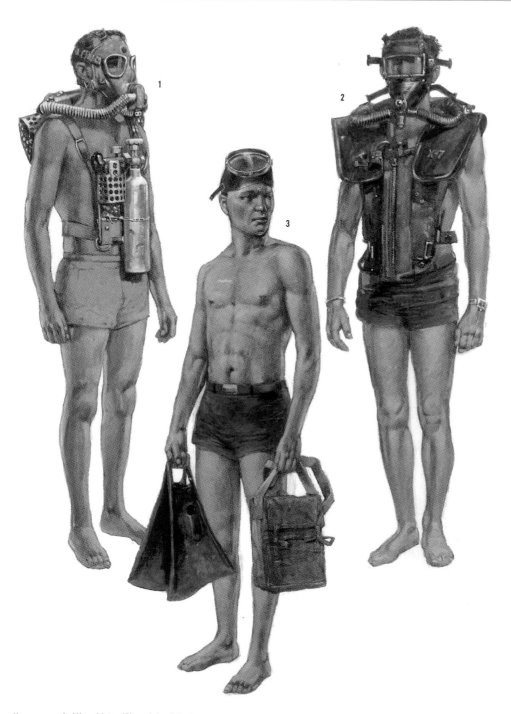

Here are early (1) and later (2) models of the LARU, a self-contained underwater "rebreather" device designed to allow OSS Maritime Unit swimmers to conduct maritime sabotage undetected. We also see UDT-10 (3), operating in the Central Pacific, summer 1944. Although no longer part of the OSS, most of the personnel of UDT-10 were swimmers from the Maritime Unit. (Richard Hook © Osprey Publishing)

Detachment 404 also dropped off agents on coastlines throughout the Indian Ocean, although P564 – an 85ft (26m) Air Sea Rescue launch – was limited by its short 500-mile (805km) range to infiltrating agents along the Burmese coast. (NARA)

In the event of capture, OSS agents were supplied with the rubber-coated potassium cyanide "L" (for lethal) pill for a quick suicide. One female agent used one in 1945 after being shot by a German patrol while attempting to cross into Switzerland from Germany.

MARITIME EQUIPMENT

Invented by Dr Christian Lambertsen, the Lambertsen Amphibious Respiratory Unit (LARU) was adopted by the OSS after it was demonstrated to them in a swimming pool in November 1942; the LARU came in four different models, weighing 28–35lb (10.5–16kg). This self-contained apparatus allowed a diver to stay undetected for several hours underwater at depths of 50–100ft (15–30m) by preventing any telltale bubbles escaping. Pure oxygen at a pressure of 2,000lb (909kg) per square inch flowed from a cylinder attached to the diver's chest into his face piece and a rubber "lung" on his back. The exhaled air went through a canister of lime above the lung that absorbed the carbon dioxide before being breathed again by the diver. Divers had to discipline themselves to breathe slowly and evenly for the CO_2 to be completely absorbed; breathing too quickly overloaded the LARU and caused discomfort. The diver was also supplied with oxygen from the lung, which was replenished from the cylinder when necessary. The LARU proved its worth in July 1944, when Operational Swimmer Group 2 used them to swim undetected through the antisubmarine nets at Guantanamo Bay, Cuba. Despite this success, the LARU was never employed on missions against the enemy.

The surfboard was a pneumatic rubber floatation device that could be inflated in minutes with a compressed air cylinder. It was 10ft 6in (3.2m) long, 3ft (0.9m) wide and weighed 310lb (141kg), and could carry two men and their equipment to a total of 900lb (409kg). It was propelled by a silent electric motor at 5 knots (9km/h) with a range of 15 miles (24km). It was successfully used by the MU on the Adriatic coast of Italy in the summer of 1944. The MU also employed a two-man kayak for coastal operations; this had a plywood frame fitted together with metal pipe and covered in rubberized canvas, and was propelled by two collapsible double-bladed paddles. Carried in two backpacks weighing 50lb (22.7kg) each, the 16ft 6in (5m) kayak could be assembled in five to ten minutes, weighed 104lb (47.3kg) and had a carrying capacity of 800lb (364kg). It was widely used by MU teams for reconnaissance along the Burmese coast in early 1945.

The OSS were a breed apart during World War II, true "cloak and dagger" operatives that would, in the Cold War, evolve into the Central Intelligence Agency (CIA) as well as inform the tactical development of several other secretive special forces units. For when the war ended in September 1945, the wartime elites, whatever their nature, faced the inevitable cutbacks and restructuring. Yet the idea of elite troops, dedicated to special-purpose operations, was now well established at the heart of the US military. It would take the Cold War to cement that idea in more permanent units and formations.

VIETNAM AND COLD WAR SPECIAL FORCES

LEFT: A Special Forces team searches for the enemy during a practical training exercise in North Carolina's Pisgah National Forest. The mountain stream offers convenient track coverage. (NARA)

WHILE THE FOUNDATIONS OF SOF were undoubtedly laid during World War II, it was in the Cold War era that special forces truly took shape as a defined concept within the US military. The former World War II Allies descended into an ideological staring contest between the capitalist West and communist Soviet Union, and proxy conflicts flared up around the world at various locations, from the Balkans to Southeast Asia. Sometimes these conflicts were outright wars of invasion and attempted conquest, such as the Korean War (1950–53), yet many were struggles of insurgency and subversion that required counterinsurgency (COIN) tactics in response. In this environment, the need arose for men to fight clandestine battles in distant parts of the globe, often conducting missions that were of necessity hidden from public view. The Vietnam War (1963–75) in particular, a war as highly politicized as it was hard fought, spawned or expanded SOF units in significant numbers as the US military attempted to gain the advantage over an elusive enemy in an unforgiving wilderness. What this effort produced was an extraordinary body of elite soldiery.

KOREAN WAR

The end of World War II brought the inevitably massive reduction in US forces. Former elite troops were no exception, and thousands of men of the airborne force, the UDTs, Jedburgh Teams, Rangers, and so forth found themselves having to adjust to lives of comparative mundanity back in the United States.

Yet it was not long before the first of the major Cold War conflicts, the Korean War, forced a revisiting of the SOF concept. When North Korean forces poured across the 38th Parallel on June 25, 1950, they employed some of their many infantry regiments not as conventional assault formations, but as infiltrators through South Korean lines to seize objectives in the rear. Several US commanders saw the value of a similar capability, and Korea's mountainous terrain was thought to be ideal for infiltrating small raider units. General J. Lawton Collins, Army Chief of Staff, after visiting Korea, issued a directive on August 29, 1950, recommending the formation of "Marauder Companies." One company was to be attached to each division to conduct through-the-lines infiltration to attack headquarters, communications, and combat support units. Revisiting the Ranger concept, Army G3 recommended they be designated "Airborne Ranger Companies," and action was immediately taken to implement their formation. Each was to consist of five officers and 107 enlisted men organized into a small HQ and three rifle platoons of three squads each. A call for volunteers went out in mid-September to the 11th and 82nd Airborne Divisions, as volunteers were required to be airborne qualified. Colonel John G. Van Houton was chosen to organize the Ranger Training Center (Airborne) at Fort Benning, Georgia, activated on September 29, 1950.

The first six-week course began on October 2, concentrating on raid and sabotage tactics, forced marches, demolitions, US and enemy weapons, land navigation, and directing artillery and air support. The 1st–4th Ranger Infantry Companies (Airborne) graduated on November 13. The 1st, 2nd, and 4th immediately prepared for movement to Korea, while the 3rd remained to assist with the second cycle. The 2nd Company (initially designated the 4th) was an all-black unit. The 5th–8th Companies completed the second cycle (now eight weeks long) in January 1951, followed by four weeks of cold weather and mountain warfare training at Camp Carson, Colorado. Some units conducted additional training at Eglin Field, Florida.

Then came deployments for the new Ranger units. The 3rd, 5th, and 8th Companies were shipped to Korea; the 6th went to West Germany, where it was assigned to Seventh Army and acted primarily as "aggressors." The 7th Company remained at Fort Benning as a replacement training unit and to assist the Ranger Training Command.

The six Ranger companies operating in Korea were assigned to Eighth Army, but attached primarily to divisions, and sometimes to corps HQs and other units. They executed raids, ambushes, and reconnaissance patrols, led assaults, and were employed as regimental reserves to conduct counterattacks. Often misapplied and lacking sufficient logistical support, they were sometimes not too highly thought of by their higher headquarters. Misuse cost some companies up to 90 percent losses. Replacements, however, were usually available, both from the USA and from volunteers from their parent divisions.

The 2nd and 4th Ranger Companies were attached to the 187th Airborne Regimental Combat Team (ARCT) on March 3, 1951. They and the 187th executed a combat jump on March 23 near Munsan-ni in an effort to cut off retreating North Korean forces. The Ranger companies' specific mission was to strike southeast from the drop zone and take the town of Munsan-ni. They were re-attached to their parent divisions on April 4.

The seven later Ranger companies were sent to various locations. The 9th and 15th remained at Fort Benning and were assigned to Third Army. The 10th and 11th were made up of National Guardsmen from the 45th (Oklahoma) and 40th (California) Infantry Divisions respectively: both were inactivated in Japan while the divisions were en route to Korea. The 12th was assigned to Fifth Army and the 13th to Second Army, both in the USA; the 14th was attached to the 4th Infantry Division, also in the USA.

There was, however, an even earlier Korean War Ranger unit. The 8213th Army Unit, Eighth Army Ranger Company was activated in August 1950 at Camp Drake, Japan. This 77-man unit was formed of mainly airborne volunteers from combat units stationed in Japan. It was sent to Korea on October 12 and attached to IX Corps, and then to the 25th Infantry Division, with which it took part in a number of actions including the drive to the Yalu River, before being inactivated in March 1951.

Another Ranger-type unit which operated in Korea was the 8245th Army Unit, Eighth Army Raider Company, active from November 1950 to April 1951. It was attached to the 3rd Infantry Division until December 26 and then placed under the 8227th Army Unit, Special Activities Group. Three provisional Ranger companies were also formed. The 2nd Armored Division Provo Ranger Company was formed in 1951, and the 1st Armored Division Provo Ranger Company in 1952, both at Fort Hood, Texas (these may in fact have been the same unit). The third was the 28th Infantry Division Ranger Company (Provisional) at Camp Atterbury, Indiana, in 1951–52.

Lack of logistical support (the companies relied on their parent divisions for everything from cooks to trucks), and the problems faced by a mere captain commanding officer working with the divisional staff, caused some staff officers to feel that a return to the battalion organization might prove more effective. This was proposed, but was not to take place. Two short-lived Ranger companies (A and B) were formed at Fort Benning before the end of the war, and these may have been the intended beginnings of a battalion (or may have been only training units).

Due to many perceived and some real problems, it was directed in July 1951 that all Ranger companies be inactivated. Other reasons given for their disbanding were the fact that non-Oriental troops faced difficulties when operating behind enemy lines; and that the static nature which the war increasingly took on limited their utility. Additionally, the "manning slots" were to be used for the formation of SF. The companies in Korea were all inactivated on August 1, 1951; their airborne-qualified personnel were transferred to the 187th ARCT, and non-airborne personnel were transferred to infantry regiments of the companies' parent divisions. The other companies were inactivated in September–December 1951. The Rangers were not to die out, however, as they had after World War II. The Ranger Training Command was inactivated on October 17, 1951, but its place was taken by the Ranger Department, formed on October 10, with the task of turning out Ranger-qualified junior officers and NCOs, who returned to their units to pass on Ranger skills.

US ARMY SPECIAL FORCES

As noted above, while the Rangers in Korea were being disbanded, another force was coming into being. The seed had been planted by Brigadier General Robert A. McClure, Chief of the Army Psychological Warfare Staff Section; and the unlikely garden plot was in the forest of the Pentagon. General McClure's goal was to form a guerrilla or unconventional warfare (UW) organization within the US Army: a difficult task, as the army was conventional in thought, convinced that "push button" warfare was well within sight, felt it could rely on nuclear weapons, and tended to regard so-called "elite" units

OPPOSITE: A UDT shoves off in a Landing Craft, Vehicle, Personnel (LCVP) from USS *Dichenko* for Wonsan Harbor, where they will transfer to rubber boats for completion of their mission of exploding some 1,500 to 2,000 mines placed in the harbor by North Koreans. (NARA)

with some disdain. To accomplish his goal General McClure formed a Special Operations Section under his staff in 1951. Heading it was Colonel Wendell Fertig, while the Plans Officer was Colonel Russell W. Volckman. Both had commanded guerrillas in the Philippines. The Operations Officer was Colonel Aaron Bank, a former Jedburgh Team member with three missions in France and one in Indochina under his belt. The section also included other former members of OSS, Merrill's Marauders, and other World War II

Here Green Beret Cecil Williams is making a final inspection of his parachute prior to boarding an aircraft for a field maneuver. Sixty officers and men, elements of the 20th Special Forces Group, participated in an early morning surprise attack on an "enemy" outpost. (NARA)

special operations organizations. These pioneers in modern UW doctrine developed operational concepts, individual and unit training programs, proposals for wartime contingency plans, tables of organization and equipment (TO&E) for proposed units, and countless staff briefings to sell their theories to the US Army hierarchy. Besides bringing to this task their vast personal experiences, they based many of their concepts on the OSS' Special Operations Branch (the Jedburghs) and Operational Group Command.

Training, organization, and techniques of operations were derived from those programs. The tradition-bound Army produced many opponents of the concept of a formally organized unit with the mission of guerrilla warfare. Outside the OSS — considered an unusual organization at best — there had been nothing like it before. It meant providing manpower slots at the cost of "real" combat units, and it might mean that another "elite" formation would appear. Guerrilla warfare and other special operations were looked upon by many as a minor effort that could not have a major impact on the overall outcome of a war. Special operations units were also condemned for drawing off valuable and skilled manpower needed elsewhere. (This argument has force; but opponents fail to see the value of the possible rewards from the results achieved by special operations units if supported and properly employed.) The stumbling blocks were many; and not all were produced by the Army.

The new CIA (backed quietly by the State Department) and the US Air Force were also major opponents. They had jointly developed their own plans for the conduct of UW in any future war. The Air Force envisioned the use of massive airpower to bring an enemy to its knees. CIA agents were to be dropped into enemy territory to organize guerrillas. They were to be supplied by airdrop provided by the Air Force, and were to receive tactical close air support. The guerrillas, under CIA control and supported by the Air Force, were to further disrupt the enemy forces disorganized by Air Force bombs in their rear areas, while the Army merely mopped up after the devastation caused by the Air Force in the frontlines.

The Army and Air Force/CIA proposals were brought before the Joint Chiefs of Staff (JCS) in early 1952. The Air Force contended that guerrilla operations would be conducted in strategic areas, which were their turf. Likewise the CIA maintained that it was responsible for behind-the-lines covert activities. The CIA lost out when it was decided that the Department of Defense (DOD) would be responsible for handling guerrilla forces within war zones. As the Army was responsible for ground combat, it was charged with organizing these forces, while the Air Force was tasked to support them.

The Army in the meantime reluctantly accepted the proposals for a UW unit. General J. Lawton Collins, Army Chief of Staff, backed the idea, and was able to sell it to President Eisenhower; 2,300 manning slots were made available, primarily by the decision to inactivate the 14 Ranger companies. (The theory seemed to be that special operations units all have the same function and could perform each other's roles with little difficulty – a consensus of misunderstanding that still persists today, although to a lesser degree.) The title for this new group was Special Forces (SF), originally a 1944 term used to identify collectively all OSS and British SOE operating units. The group

A Special Forces Training Group, Phase I Field Training Exercise, Camp Mackall, North Carolina, 1960s. While M16 rifles and M60 machine guns were available, the students carried 7.62mm M14 rifles and .30-cal M1919A6 machine guns, for the simple reason that they were heavier. (Kevin Lyles © Osprey Publishing)

organization was borrowed from that of the OSS Operational Group Command, but expanded to make it more self-sufficient.

In April 1952, Colonel Aaron Bank was reassigned to the Psychological Operations Division (then at Fort Riley, Kansas, and a component of the General Staff School) and sent to Fort Bragg, North Carolina with instructions to select a site for the future Psychological Warfare School and the planned SF unit. On June 20, 1952, the 10th Special Forces Group (Airborne) – 10th SFGA – was activated at Fort Bragg under the command of Colonel Bank. It was activated without fanfare or publicity. The group was quartered in World War II barracks in a section of the post known as "Smoke Bomb Hill," a name that became part of the SF vocabulary.

Recruiting had begun in April, when a pamphlet was distributed outlining the requirements to be met in order to volunteer for the new organization. It was worded to appeal to the kind of men that Bank was looking for: skilled professionals, mature individuals willing to accept responsibilities beyond their rank, those experienced in travel overseas and skilled in a foreign language, and willing to take risks not expected of conventional units. The volunteers began to appear in May, and were just what Bank was looking for – paratroopers and Rangers; former OSS personnel; former members of Merrill's Marauders, 1st Special Service Force, Ranger battalions, and every other

January 1968, California. AUS Navy SEAL Team 1 trainees prepare to fire a 57mm recoilless rifle during a drill in the desert area near the Chocolate Mountains. (NARA)

World War II special operations unit that had existed, including Lodge Act personnel (displaced persons from communist-dominated countries who would receive US citizenship in exchange for a hitch in the Army). There were also some younger, less-experienced soldiers, but all professionals regardless.

Former OSS and other experienced officers were quickly formed into a training staff to develop the unit's training program. Training began at the individual level, and all troops were trained in their respective specialty: operations and intelligence, weapons, demolitions, communications, and medical. Specialty cross-training was also begun.

Emphasis was placed on the many aspects of UW to include security, sabotage, formation and operation of intelligence, escape and evasion systems (called "nets" by the Army), and so on. Training progressed to team level and cross-training was continued, conducted within and by the teams. Team members had to show initiative, be able to instruct others, and possess leadership and organizational skills. The Psychological Warfare Center and School was established at Fort Bragg in October 1952, with the SF School as a component element.

In October the 10th SFGA began a group-level maneuver in Georgia's Chatahoochie National Forest. The planning staff modeled the exercise on those conducted by the Jedburgh Teams; and it was to begin a tradition of SF's use of civilian involvement in its training exercises. Civilians living in the area acted as a guerrilla support organization, providing live and dead letter drops, safe houses, information on aggressor forces, and operating an escape and evasion net. Local law enforcement agencies and a Georgia Army National Guard military police unit acted as the aggressor counterguerrilla force. SF teams were rotated in the role of guerrillas. Advanced training in amphibious operations was followed by mountain and cold weather training in Colorado. The next phase was the conduct of the Army Training Test, a battalion of the 82nd Airborne Division providing the aggressors, which was to become another tradition. The tests were totally successful. Sixty-four members of the 10th SFGA were sent to Korea in early 1953 to act as UW advisors to Far East Command, but no actual detachments were deployed.

It was in June 1953 that the workers' revolt broke out in communist-dominated East Berlin. It was quickly and harshly crushed, but it had the effect of making the Army realize that 10th SFGA needed to be in Europe in order to respond rapidly to critical situations. About half of the group's assigned strength, 782 troops, sailed to Germany in November. The other half – primarily the new arrivals who were not fully trained, plus a cadre of trained officers and NCOs – remained to form the 77th SFGA, which had been activated on September 23. The 10th was quartered in the luxurious Flint Kaserne in the Bavarian town of Bad Tölz.

The 10th SFGA continued to train in its new surroundings, making use of the local population in its exercises; German border police, US troops, and Allied units made excellent guerrilla and counterguerrilla forces. The 10th also acted as aggressors for exercises by conventional units when the employment of guerrillas was desired. Training exercises, exchange programs, and mobile training teams were soon being mounted in other countries. The new 77th SFGA trained up to group level and was prepared for worldwide deployment. The Psychological Warfare Center was redesignated the Special Warfare Center and School on May 1, 1957.

It was in the mid-1950s that SF began to look to the Far East. It was obvious that trouble was brewing in the area. The 77th formed and sent two special training teams to Japan in 1956. They conducted training missions in various Southeast Asian countries – including in South Vietnam. In 1957 these two teams were moved to Okinawa, and formed the cadre for the 1st SFGA activated on June 24 at Fort Buckner. The 1st began deploying teams to Vietnam, Thailand, and Nationalist China as well as to other Allied countries throughout Asia and the Pacific.

In July 1959 the 77th SFGA deployed Operation *White Star* to Laos for the purpose of training the Royal Laotian Army. The teams (later augmented by the 1st SFGA) were redesignated White Star Mobile Training Teams in April 1961, and remained there until October 1962. The 77th was redesignated 7th SFGA on May 20, 1960 to place its designation in line with projected groups. An old enemy in a new form began to rear its ugly head in the late 1950s. Instead of massed tank armies swarming across Western Europe, guerrilla warfare was being used to achieve political/military goals in other parts of the world. SF now became concerned about this aspect of UW counterinsurgency. They were to be the guerrillas themselves in a sense, but now they were increasingly involved in training small countries' armed forces to combat guerrillas.

EXPANSION AND GROWTH

President John F. Kennedy's concern over the increase in the number of communist-inspired "wars of liberation" had a great influence on the expansion of special forces. The logic was simple: what better force to combat guerrillas than one trained as guerrillas themselves? UW was still to remain SF's primary mission, but assisting small nations in their counterinsurgency efforts became a major part of their role. In October 1961 President Kennedy visited Fort Bragg to see for himself the capabilities of this little-known organization. A massive effort had been made by the Special Warfare Center and the 7th SFGA to impress the President. Their demonstrations of techniques and equipment made a favorable impression. Fully realizing the turn that world events were taking, the President ordered the expansion of SF.

Expansion of a force that requires high-quality personnel and lengthy specialist training brings its own inherent problems, and SF was no exception. The three existing groups were brought up to strength and funds were made available for much-needed equipment and training. The 5th SFGA was activated on December 5, 1961 to support missions in Southeast Asia. The 3rd, 6th, and 8th SFGAs were formed in 1963. To support this massive expansion, the SF Training Group was formed to provide a continuous flow of personnel. Small SF units had first been formed in the Army Reserve and Army National Guard in 1959. In 1961 these units were expanded into the 2nd, 9th, 11th,

John F. Kennedy was a president fascinated by the possibilities of special forces, and did more than most US leaders to embed the concept of an elite within the US military. (NARA)

12th, 13th, 17th, and 24th Reserve and the 16th, 19th, 20th, and 21st National Guard SFGAs. In 1966 these small groups were consolidated into the Reserve's 11th and 12th and the National Guard's 19th and 20th SFGAs.

It must be admitted that this expansion did lower the overall quality of SF personnel. Selection and training standards were relaxed somewhat, although the personnel were still triple volunteers, and of much higher quality than the bulk of the Army. In 1965 first enlistment soldiers and second lieutenants were allowed to volunteer for the first time. To gain public support and sufficient volunteers, publicity campaigns were instituted, which caused some displeasure among the old hands and amusement among SF's detractors. Though there were problems involved in SF's expansion, there were also benefits. The increased recruiting efforts and publicity attracted many fine troops who might not have had an opportunity to volunteer in the past. The development of new items of equipment and techniques of operation would not have been possible without the expansion program. Training funds for both individuals and units, so critical in the development of an effective organization, would otherwise have been out of reach. Regardless of its growing pains, SF accomplished the multitude of missions assigned to it. From entire groups down to a single individual, detachments were deployed on countless missions to just about every Allied and friendly country.

The US SF soldiers found themselves deployed across extremely diverse parts of the world during the 1960s, as the Cold War became increasingly hotter. The 1st SFGA continued to deploy teams throughout Asia and the Pacific area. They conducted innumerable civic action projects, trained military and police in counterinsurgency, conducted special operations in Southeast Asia (often in support of other SF units already deployed there), and were instrumental in training and developing many nations' own SF units. Laos, Thailand, the Philippines, South Vietnam, South Korea, and Taiwan were the countries in which most of the operations took place. The 3rd SFGA was activated on December 5, 1963 at Fort Bragg. It was made responsible for Africa, where a number of small and mostly unpublicized missions were conducted in the Cameroons, Congo, Ethiopia, Guinea, Kenya, Mali, Senegal, and other countries. The 10th SFGA had been involved in some of these prior to the formation of the 3rd. Most of these were small-scale advisory and assistance operations, although a team from the 10th accomplished a risky rescue of over 200 Belgian refugees during the 1960 Congo revolution.

For a brief period prior to the activation of the 6th SFGA on May 1, 1963, at Fort Bragg, Company C of the 10th was responsible for North Africa, the Middle East, and part of Southwest Asia. The 6th took over responsibility for the Middle East in 1964: training missions were conducted by SF in Iran, Jordan, Pakistan, Saudi Arabia, Turkey, and elsewhere, and SF was instrumental in developing these nations' own special operations units.

Concern over the situation in Latin America, due to the proliferation of insurgency movements in a region so close to home, led to what would become one of the larger operations outside Southeast Asia. The 7th SFGA, as part of its worldwide deployment mission, began conducting advisory operations in various Latin American countries in 1961. Company D of the 7th was moved to the Panama Canal Zone the following year. The next year it was to form the nucleus for the 8th SFGA, activated on April 1 at Fort Gurlick. The 8th sent training teams to almost every country in Central and South America where civic action operations, counterinsurgency training, and development of various special operations units were successfully accomplished.

With all of these missions being conducted throughout the world, the major concern of SF was a remote little corner of Asia that few Americans had even heard of. The first SF unit to operate in Southeast Asia was a detachment from the 77th SFGA that trained the Thai Rangers in 1954. The first SF unit in Vietnam was the 14th Special Forces Operational Detachment (SFOD), formed from personnel of the 77th, which spent a brief period there in 1957 instructing Vietnamese Commandos. Thus began what was to become the largest, longest, and most controversial of SF's many missions.

VIETNAM

The first teams of the 1st SFGA arrived in Vietnam in late 1957. There had already been a US presence there since 1950 in the form of the US Military Assistance Advisory Group Indochina. Vietnam was a country divided. With the defeat of the French Union forces by the Viet Minh (Communist Vietnam Independence League), the countries of the former French colony of Indochina (Vietnam, Laos, and Cambodia) were given their independence by agreement to Geneva Accords in 1954. Vietnam was divided into a communist-controlled North Vietnam and a Western-oriented South Vietnam. A brief peace ensued, but it was not long before the Communist National Liberation Front and its military arm, the Viet Cong (VC), made their presence in South Vietnam known. They received support from North Vietnam in the form of limited amounts of supplies, weapons, and infiltrated cadre personnel.

Since 1957 SF had been training Vietnamese personnel at the Commando Training Center in Nha Trang. These men would eventually become the nucleus for the Vietnamese SF. Members of the 77th SFGA began training the first Vietnamese Ranger units shortly afterwards. The mission continued with the primary task of providing the Army of the Republic of Vietnam (ARVN) with its own special operations and offensive UW units. Teams from both the 1st and 77th (later 7th) SFGAs were deployed to Vietnam for this purpose. Until 1961 the US advisory effort was oriented towards developing the ARVN into a conventional force capable of

defending the new nation from a Korean-style invasion by North Vietnam: a role that was to change.

In the early 1960s the Vietnamese government had virtually no military or administrative control over the Central Highlands and large areas of the Mekong Delta. Control of these areas by the government was critical. Just as neglected were the various minority groups that populated them. The development of indigenous minority groups into a military force has always been a recognized SF concept. Living in remote rural areas, often in poverty, they are used to physical hardship, and they know the area and how to survive in it. Due to their minority status, however, they tend to be somewhat neglected, ignored, or even persecuted by the national government. Their situation varies from complacency with their lot to discontent verging on rebellion. Either way, they are generally ripe for exploitation by whichever side reaches them first. This may mean anything from forced service in an insurgent unit to total inclusion in the legal government's national goals. One hazard for the legal government is that even though a minority group may side with it, their ultimate goals may not necessarily be the same. In Vietnam's case the problems were further aggravated by the centuries-old racial and religious prejudices of the ethnic Vietnamese.

Sergeant First Class Johnny F. Cooper instructs a group of Montagnard tribesmen in the use of a 60mm mortar. Language was one of the main problems in such training operations. Kneeling at Cooper's left is an interpreter who translates from English to Vietnamese; standing behind Cooper is another interpreter who translates the Vietnamese into a Montagnard dialect. (NARA)

VIETNAMESE SF

The Vietnamese SF were formed in 1957 from a group of 58 men trained by the 14th SFOD; these men became the cadre for the Vietnamese 77th Observation Group, an SF-type unit. After several reorganizations it evolved in 1963 into the Lac Luong Dac Biet (LLDB) Command, similar to a USSF group. An LLDB team (slightly smaller than its USSF counterpart) was assigned to each strike force camp. Sad to say, the relationship between the USSF team and its LLDB counterpart was not always as it should have been. Attitudes ranged from totally ignoring each other to outright hostility in a few instances. In most cases, though, a workable relationship evolved, and things ran more or less smoothly. Quite often the LLDB handled the day-to-day administration and operation of the camp, while the USSF ran the combat operations of the strike force. There were a number of reasons for this conflict, and a simple clash of cultures was a primary one. The LLDB were not necessarily as well trained as their US counterparts; but they had been at it for a long time, and would remain at it long after the "hard charging" Americans had completed their six-month tour and had been replaced by more Americans, with more new ideas on how to change things. There were cases of corruption, laziness, and reluctance to fight on the part of some members of the LLDB, but there were also many good ones. It was not unusual for an LLDB team and its USSF counterpart to develop a good working relationship.

Vietnam has a number of ethnic and religious minorities, which were ignored or actually ill-treated by the government in Saigon. The VC was beginning to exploit these groups. In order to secure the critical areas, expand government presence, limit the exploitation of the minorities, and bring them into the national struggle, it was decided to employ SF elements to organize them into local self-defense forces.

The heart of most SF efforts in Vietnam was the Civilian Irregular Defense Group program (CIDG-pronounced "cidge"); it was begun in 1961 as the Area Development Program, and was not officially designated CIDG until the following year. The CIDG were civilian employees of the US Army, and not part of the ARVN. They were recruited, trained, clothed, equipped, fed, housed, and paid by the USSF. The CIDG program was initially composed exclusively of Montagnards (French for "highlanders"), who were of a completely different racial stock than the Vietnamese, had long been despised by them; referred to as *moi* (savages), they were not recognized as citizens. They are simple people who do not have a common language, and in the more remote areas it is difficult for them to understand the dialect of the village on a neighboring mountain. Only the Jarai and Rhade, the most advanced tribes, had a crude written language. The SF troops

LEFT: STAFF SERGEANT, US ARMY SPECIAL FORCES, VIETNAM, 1963.
He wears mostly standard M1956 LBE with an indigenous rucksack. World War II and Korean War era web gear was also widely used. The early tropical combat boots ("jungle boots") varied in pattern as they were test items. (Kevin Lyles © Osprey Publishing)

quickly developed a close relationship with these people, and in many cases were even made members of the tribe in elaborate ceremonies. A dangerous situation did develop in 1964 when some Rhade Montagnard strike forces revolted and killed some Vietnamese SF troops; the USSF managed to negotiate a peaceful settlement.

The first experimental SF camp was established at Buon Enao, near Ban Me Thuot, by half of 1st SFGA's Detachment A-35 in late 1961. The purpose of the program was to establish and train both village defense and local security forces for some 40 villages in the area. It was so successful that by the next year over 200 villages were involved in the program with 12,000 armed Rhade Montagnards.

During 1962 a number of separate COIN and paramilitary programs were instituted by the US Military Assistance Advisory Command-Vietnam and the CIA's US Operations Mission. These were all to be incorporated into the CIDG program under the auspices of SF on July 1, 1963. Besides village security and defense, the CIDG were progressively tasked with more aggressive missions. A Mountain Commando (later Mountain Scouts) Training Center was established, and reconnaissance missions were conducted into remote areas. Another program was the Trailwatchers (later Border Surveillance), which conducted surveillance missions on infiltration trails in the border areas. The village defense program was expanded into other areas of Vietnam as well. By the end of 1963 there were 18,000 CIDG strike force and 43,000 hamlet militia (the redesignated village self-defense) troops advised by two B Teams and 22 A Teams.

US Army Special Forces Vietnam (Provisional) or USASFV – in effect, a small SF group – was formed in September 1962 for the control of all SF elements in the country. Teams from the 1st, 5th, and 7th SFGAs were rotated to Vietnam for six-month temporary duty hours. This system had the advantage of retaining team integrity, but it sacrificed continuity of the advisory effort, and forced the relieving team to learn the area, the troops, and the effective methods of operation anew with each rotation. The in-country team provided the relieving team with information on the area and their operations, and upon their arrival conducted briefings and orientation patrols before departing. By 1964 the CIDG were actively conducting strike operations, and had expanded to include other minority groups. These included the Khmers (ethnic Cambodians born and raised in Vietnam), Nungs (ethnic Chinese mountain tribesmen), Chams and other ethnic Chinese from the coastal regions, and the Cao Dai and Hoa Hao militant religious sects (ethnic Vietnamese). These minority groups and their SF advisors rapidly developed a mutual respect and loyalty; many of the kind of men that SF attracts have a natural leaning towards the "underdog" to begin with.

Although highly conducive to the war effort and the accomplishment of assigned unit missions, this close relationship between the CIDG strikers and the SF troopers led to the almost total exclusion of the Vietnamese SF (Lac Luong Dac Biet – LLDB) from the chain of command in many strike forces. The predominantly Vietnamese (and usually prejudiced) LLDB were officially in command of the strike forces, while the USSF were supposedly to act only as advisors to them; this was often not the case in practice.

A lesser problem also developed in that conventional US units and higher commanders often looked upon the CIDG as SF's "private army." The problem was compounded by the fact that strike companies and combat reconnaissance platoons were in practice commanded by SF NCOs, often junior ones, in positions held by captains and lieutenants in conventional units. More than one battalion commander was surprised to find that the company commander with whom he had been conducting a joint operation was only a buck sergeant.

In September 1964 USASFV was disbanded, and the 5th SFGA was relocated to Vietnam by phasing in its teams. There were now some 40 camps. The six-month tour became a thing of the past, and one-year tours were required, as by other US personnel. This meant that a team was assigned to a specific camp where it remained. The personnel rotated in and out of the teams on their one-year tours, thus ensuring a continuity of the advisory effort, as there were always 'old hands' in the teams who were familiar with the strike force and the area. The arrival of the 5th SFGA also signaled another expansion of the CIDG program.

The war was escalating at a rapid pace. North Vietnamese Army (NVA) units, and massive amounts of supplies and equipment, were flowing into the south by way of the Ho Chi Minh Trail network through Laos and Cambodia. By 1967 it could no

A CIDG Camp Strike Force company departs for a patrol. In the background is a typical camp wood-frame administrative building. Such buildings were not provided with protection. An outdoor movie screen is mounted on the building's side. (DOD)

longer be termed a guerrilla war: massive, prolonged multi-division battles were being fought by both sides.

The primary missions of the strike force camps were border security, infiltration trail network interdiction, local village security, civic action and medical coverage for the local populace, and general intelligence collection. In addition SF also had an advisory role for the Regional and Popular Forces (RF/PF or "Ruff-Puffs" – territorial and local militia) in some areas. By 1969 the CIDG had grown into a well-armed and trained professional force, with its own traditions and lineages, of almost 40,000 strikers in the Camp Strike Forces alone. Several thousands more were employed by the Mobile Strike Forces and reconnaissance projects. All were trained, advised, and supported by a mere 2,300 USSF.

The Mobile Strike Force ("Mike Force") concept grew out of a need for SF to have a reaction force under its own control to reinforce camps that were under attack or siege. US and ARVN units could not always be relied upon to provide this support when, where, and in the manner needed. The concept was derived from a II Corps reaction force known as "Eagle Flight," formed in late 1964. Since the early 1960s the term "mobile strike force" had been used to designate locally raised reaction forces as well. In July 1965 a battalion-size Mobile Strike Force was authorized for each C Team for employment in their corps area. A fifth force was formed for employment by the 5th SFGA on a countrywide basis to provide an additional backup element. Each had an A Team in command of it, and did not receive an LLDB team until late 1966. That same year their strength was increased to between two and five battalions each, plus a reconnaissance company.

In late 1967 a B Team was assigned to each Mike Force, providing a Mobile Strike Force Command for each corps area (1st to 4th) and the 5th directly under group control. The 1st, 2nd, and 5th were predominantly Montagnards, while the 3rd and 4th were mostly Nungs and Cambodians. They were airborne qualified at the SF-run jump school at the LLDB Training Center, trained in more offensive-type operations, and more heavily armed than their Camp Strike Force comrades. The Mike Forces took part in a large number of operations which saved or took the pressure off hard-pressed camps. Additionally they conducted their own offensive operations, along with three successful battalion-size airborne assaults in 1967 and one in 1968.

An off-shoot of the Mike Force concept was the Mobile Guerrilla Force (MGF) created in mid-1966. These consisted of a specially trained CIDG Strike Force Company and a Reconnaissance Platoon under the command of a USSF A Team with no LLDB. One was assigned to each corps area, with the mission to infiltrate remote enemy-controlled areas and conduct ambushes and raids; these "Blackjack" operations were very effective. At the end of 1967 the MGFs were absorbed into the expanding Mike Forces, which continued similar missions. The height of SF deployment in Vietnam was 1969.

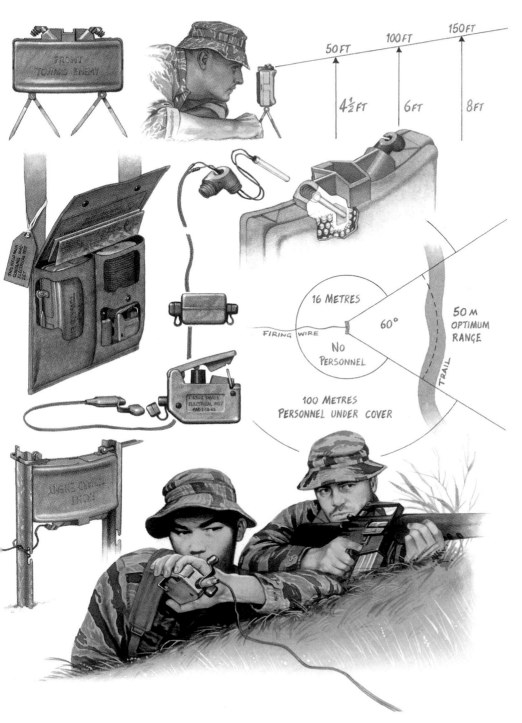

The Claymore M18A1 antipersonnel mine seen here proved to be most devastating ambush weapon in the US Special Forces arsenal in Vietnam. A curved, rectangular fiberglass box contained 704 steel ball bearings embedded in a plastic matrix and backed by 1½lb (680g) of C4 plastic explosive. (Kevin Lyles © Osprey Publishing)

The 5th SFGA was organized and deployed as follows: The Special Forces Operations Base (SFOB) was at Nha Trang. It contained the Group Headquarters, Signal Company, Logistical Support Center, 5th Mobile Strike Force Command (SFOB B-55), and numerous special detachments (military intelligence, signal, engineer, etc.). The Military Assistance Command Vietnam (MACV) Recondo School (operated by 5th SFGA since 1966) was also here. Companies C, B, A, and D were responsible for the I, II, III, and IV Corps Tactical Zones (CTZs) respectively. Each had one C Team, two to four B Teams, and from eight to 14 A Teams. Company E was responsible for special missions, and had eight B Teams. The C Teams were co-located (except for that of Company E) with an LLDB C Team, and provided command and control and logistical support for its A and B Teams. One B Team in each company was the Mobile Strike Force Command while the others, usually located in province capitals, controlled a varied number of A Teams. There was a counterpart LLDB A and B Team co-located with each USSF one.

A Camp Strike Force consisted of three or four 130-man companies, a Combat Reconnaissance Platoon, and a Political Warfare (civic action) Team. Many camps had an

A special forces camp in Vietnam could look extremely rundown and battered. They were never finished, being constantly rebuilt, repaired, and upgraded. (DOD)

D, 1st SFGA. It was responsible for training and advising the Royal Thai Army SF, Rangers, and Border Police. It also conducted various special operations into Laos and Cambodia; and acted as advisers to the Thai "Queen's Cobras" Regiment and "Black Panther" Division, which were sent to Vietnam. On March 3, 1972 the assets of the 46th Company were used to form 3rd Battalion, 1st SFGA, at the time a classified designation; it actually had the cover designation of US Army SF, Thailand. After leaving Thailand the unit was inactivated at Fort Bragg on March 27, 1974 – it was never physically part of the 1st SFGA.

THE SF EXPERIENCE

The popular image of SF during the Vietnam War is far from reality. It has unfortunately been influenced by the inane vision of John Rambo and other equally far-fetched motion picture characters. Other distortions come from Robin Moore's fictionalization of some more "glamorous" SF exploits, *The Green Berets* (1964); John Wayne's motion picture of the same title (1968); and Staff Sergeant Berry Saddler's popular song, "The Ballad of the Green Berets" (1966). Rumors, assumptions, war stories, and the efforts of the John F. Kennedy Center for Special Warfare to promote its capabilities in countering communist-sponsored "people's wars" were just as much responsible for the popular image of SF.

Soldiers invariably reflect the society that spawned them, and SF soldiers often demonstrated the highest values of American society. Most SF troopers were conservative by nature, but virtually apolitical. A typical SF trooper, although most would resent such a generalization, was of higher than average intelligence (determined by extensive testing), no more physically fit than other paratroopers, generally moderate in temperament, and able to maintain a sense of humor (a critical requirement in Vietnam), which often leaned toward the dark side. There were heavy drinkers and teetotallers, hardcore lifers, rednecks, cowboys, intellectuals, surfers, and motorcycle-gangers, to name a few. None were fanatical or ultra-right wing as often envisioned by a paranoid Hollywood.

There was a tendency to cut-up during training, and pranks were commonly inflicted on non-SF units and themselves without prejudice. However, SF was not a group of wild, rebellious misfits as portrayed in many motion pictures, although some senior commanders might argue otherwise. Regardless of personal attitudes, they were professional in appearance and actions. They were distinct individualists from a broad range of backgrounds with several things in common. Most were looking for something different and challenging, they wanted to prove themselves, and they were idealistic in a mildly patriotic, and at that time, unpopular way. Admittedly, most troopers distrusted overbearing, power-hungry, overly career-oriented officers.

Though it was not the goal of the selection process, troopers tended to have common attributes. Most were somewhat rebellious and independent, but still capable of working as members of a team; plus they tended to support the underdog, an invaluable attribute when it came to working with indigenous troops. They were all strongly anti-communist, though not because of indoctrination or political nurturing. All were triple volunteers, for the Army, Airborne, and Special Forces. They had to be at least 20 years old, have the same General Technical score (a form of IQ score) as required of officers, and have no police record. However, a surprising number had been in minor trouble with the law. A comparatively clean record was needed to obtain the required security clearance.

They represented all sectors of society, but most had middle-class backgrounds. No figures exist, but minorities were poorly represented. Blacks, Hispanics, Indians, and other minorities were found in numbers far below the Army-wide average. However, among the minorities accepted into SF, race discrimination was a rare complaint; one

The Stoner 63 Weapon System was a forward-looking attempt to create a modular assault rifle/light machine gun for infantry use. Although not adopted by the US military generally, it was put to good use by special forces in Vietnam, particularly the US Navy SEALs. (NARA)

had only to prove oneself as an SF soldier and acceptance was complete. Religion was not a subject of discussion. One practiced or did not practice as one saw fit. A typical A Team's age spanned over 20 years, ranging from young SF soldiers on their first enlistment to a team sergeant who might be looking toward retirement. Military experiences were many and varied.

SF soldiers worked hard and played with the same vigor. SF had its heavy drinkers, but a lower than average number of smokers at a time when smoking remained common (cigarettes were still included in C-rations). There were some genuine troublemakers, but they remained in SF because they could contribute. There were ongoing feuds between individuals, some resulting from real or perceived mistakes made in combat or even on training exercises, competition for promotion, women troubles (SF was said to have the highest divorce rate in the Army), and simple personality conflicts between strong-willed individuals.

SF was not a branch. No one was permanently assigned, although most NCOs served their entire careers in SF, with only occasional stints elsewhere. Officers were detached from combat arms branches to which they would return after an SF tour. Some returned to serve with SF, others did not. A small number of officers served much of their career with SF (limiting their future progression and assignments) and many of them were key in charting SF's course and development. But, it was the senior SF career NCOs who defined the organization's character.

SF resisted institutionalization and the formalities common elsewhere in the military. Such traditions as organization day, prop-blast ceremonies, dinings-in, and NCO academies were shunned. The key social event for an SF unit was a family barbecue in the unit area or someone's home (a practice observed even in Vietnam, *sans* families). SF was basically comprised of men loyal to an operational concept: special warfare.

SF as an organization was not a model of military theory and practice. Many in SF only reluctantly admitted association to the US Army, insisting that their organization was US Special Forces (USSF) and not US Army Special Forces (USASF). When a 1,200-man SF group was required to attend, for example, a retirement ceremony at Fort Bragg, its five companies might make their way individually to the parade ground where the group would assemble as a body and depart in the same manner. Realistically, no attempt would be made to march the group on to the parade ground or conduct a pass in review; it had been tried and it seldom went smoothly. The "other Army" was too rigid, too regimented, and far too noisy. SF troopers were appalled at how conventional soldiers were treated by their officers, although their treatment was still high by any other army's standards. However, after the more relaxed attitudes of SF, it seemed almost draconian. Within SF, even specialist 4s and buck sergeants were permitted a remarkable degree of latitude and responsibility.

Specialist 4 Jim Messengill, Team 22, Company H (Ranger), 75th Infantry Regiment, reports contact with enemy forces during a patrol northeast of Kuan Loc, along the Dong Nai River, in 1970. (US Army)

The most significant attitude in SF was that everyone did whatever it took to accomplish the mission, regardless of their rank. Paratroopers of the 82nd Airborne Division at Fort Bragg were stunned to see long-serving master sergeants and sergeants first class policing up pine cones in SF unit areas or shaking out parachutes alongside specialist 4s, because their A Team had been assigned the duty. That is one of the primary factors of SF effectiveness, and that is why SF buck sergeants with less than two years' service were able to lead indigenous companies in Vietnam without supervision.

All of this resulted in a group of well-trained individuals welded into functional teams with the flexibility, ingenuity, imagination, experience, maturity, and desire to accomplish whatever mission they had been given.

Special Forces soldiers engage the enemy in a firefight in the jungles of Vietnam. They use the three classic small arms of the era: the M16A1 assault rifle, the M60 machine gun, and the M79 "Blooper" grenade launcher. (Kevin Lyles © Osprey Publishing)

The lack of a rigid doctrine allowed them the leeway to accomplish their tasks in unusual environments and circumstances, with austere support, low visibility, and limited political repercussions. A common attitude found among SF soldiers when given a task, be it a menial work detail or a mission to raise and train a village defense force, was, "Tell me what you want done and I'll do it, but don't tell me how to do it."

Most future SF troopers had enlisted in the regular Army at a time when it was more popular for young Americans to join the National Guard or gain an educational or

An SF student vigorously exits the 34ft (10.4m) tower. He will fall only a few feet before sliding down the cables to the mound. The sensation is not unlike, in some aspects, jumping from an aircraft in flight. (US Army)

Members of the 5th Special Forces Group Command Readiness Team inspect the condition of a fighting/living bunker. The CRT visited every camp about twice a year to ensure standards were being met and to recommend improvements from lessons learned visiting other camps. (DOD)

conscientious objector deferment. Many were airborne qualified prior to volunteering for SF. The three-week Airborne Course (Jump School), at Fort Benning, Georgia, demanded high physical and performance standards. Men had to complete five qualifying jumps, but it was neither as tough nor as dangerous as often portrayed.

There were several ways that servicemen came to volunteer for SF. Some men, based on records screening, were approached by SF recruiting NCOs while attending Basic Combat Training (BCT) or the Airborne Course. SF recruiters had no quota and they actually attempted to discourage prospective volunteers. Others volunteered after two or more years' service; many men from the 82nd or 101st Airborne Divisions chose this route. Servicemen who had been exposed to SF in-country during a Vietnam tour, were another source of recruits. While most enlisted volunteers were infantrymen, they could possess any military occupation specialty (MOS). Unusual non-combatant MOSs were considered to provide SF troopers with a broader background when mixed with the predominating infantrymen.

The stipulation that enlisted men be triple volunteers – Army, Airborne, SF – like everything else in the Army, could be waived to accommodate qualified draftees. A soldier volunteering for the Army enlisted for three years and was designated Regular Army, his serial number prefixed by "RA." An inducted soldier, a draftee, was called to the colors for two years, his serial number was preceded by "US." In order to volunteer for SF, a draftee was required to extend his enlistment to three years or more and was redesignated "RA." A soldier was required to have at least 18 months remaining on his enlistment once he completed SF training. RA volunteers enlisting in the Army to attend specific training courses would not attend that training if they joined SF. Junior officers often faced an uphill battle to enter SF. All units during the Vietnam War were critically short of officers. Commanders were reluctant to lose good officers to the "Snake Eaters" and sternly warned hopefuls that an SF tour could adversely affect their careers.

SF officers could be of any combat arms branch: Infantry, Armor, Field and Air Defense Artillery, Engineer, and Military Police. Military Intelligence, Signal, Medical, Quartermaster officers, and others could be assigned to SF to fill certain support functions, and not all attended the SF Officer Course. However, all were required to have completed their basic branch course before acceptance.

Both officers and enlisted men took the Army Physical Readiness Test (APRT), meeting airborne standards, and successfully completed the Combat Water Survival Test (CWST), a simple swimming test. Enlisted men had to additionally pass the mentally grueling Special Forces Selection Battery, which included personality, critical decision making, self-location (using a series of photos), and Morse code aptitude tests, which many men purposely failed in order to avoid a somewhat unpopular duty.

A common eight-week BCT course was attended by all men entering the Army. It was conducted at one of 12 training centers (the number varied slightly over the war

Newly assigned 5th SFGA troopers, who are attending the Combat Orientation Course, prepare to practice a break contract drill on Hon Tra Island off the coast from Na Trang. They have already purchased their tiger-stripe "boonie" hats, but will not be issued tiger-striped uniforms until assigned to their camps. (US Army)

years) and provided a good foundation in basic military skills: physical fitness; dismounted drill; military customs and courtesies; bayonet and hand-to-hand combat; individual combat skills; first aid; and, most importantly, two weeks of rifle marksmanship. The use of grenades was the only other weapons training provided. "Basic" was followed by Advanced Individual Training (AIT) in one of scores of MOSs offered at the training centers or one of over 20 branch or specialty schools. AIT could last from eight weeks to many months depending on the MOS. Light Weapons Infantry AIT (MOS 11B) was eight weeks at one of seven infantry training centers. All except Fort Dix, New Jersey, were rated as "Vietnam oriented." Fort Dix was reserved for infantrymen slated for Germany, Korea, Alaska, and Panama.

Infantry AIT covered squad tactics, combat and reconnaissance patrolling, land navigation, radio-telephone procedures, mine warfare, more physical fitness instruction, and three weeks of machine gun, automatic rifle, 40mm grenade launcher, and antitank weapons training. BCT and 11B AIT called for 10–14 hours a day, five days a week, with Saturdays dedicated to inspections and administration.

Once accepted, the future SF trooper was sent to the US Army John F. Kennedy Center for Special Warfare (Airborne), which was identified by the awkward abbreviation of USAJFKCSW (ABN). The fact that it was the only organization within the Army that bore an individual's name was an indicator that it was different to anything experienced elsewhere in the Army. The SF student was expected to be on time for daily classes, but he was not marched there in formation. Once released from his training company's morning formation, he was on his own. After a week's processing, the student was assigned to one of the four training companies in Special Forces Training Group (SFTG). Often he would have to wait several weeks before being assigned a class date. In the meantime he pulled KP (Kitchen Police), guard duty, and other work details to include roadside trash pick-up; it was a humbling experience. This was to take place between all phases of SF training. But one of the details was sought after, and proved to be of benefit to his training. Groups of SF students awaiting their next phase were employed as "guerrillas" (Gs) to be trained by other students or "counterguerrillas" (CGs) to act as an aggressor force in field exercises during the different training phases. It was considered a lot of fun to chase someone or even be chased through the woods for a week or two, especially when it spared one from KP, formations, and inspections.

Phase I of the Special Forces Tactics and Techniques Course was of only four weeks' duration. Students came from throughout the Army. Some had volunteered to flee boring Stateside assignments, others had completed an overseas tour and sported specialist 4 or sergeant stripes, a small handful had even been to Vietnam, but most were privates and privates first class with only Basic, AIT, and Jump School under their belts. All were eager to meet the challenges of this new adventure.

Personnel from SFGA. 1) Corporal, Weapons Specialist, 77th SFGA; Uwharrie National Forest, North Carolina, 1955. 2) Sergeant, Demolitions Specialist, 6th SFGA; Fort Greely, Alaska, 1970. 3) First Lieutenant, A Detachment Executive Officer, 11th SFGA; Camp Drum, New York, 1972. (Ron Volstad © Osprey Publishing)

The first class in Phase I was a math refresher, much to our student's surprise. But, the rest of the course concentrated on patrolling techniques, land navigation, basic survival, and methods of instruction. The teaching role assumed paramount importance. He found out that the SF soldier was a teacher first and commando second. All of the hands-on instruction was given by NCOs, many with two or three tours in Vietnam behind them, and their years of practical experience were passed on to the student. The student himself taught progressively longer classes on a broad range of military subjects to his own group and was required to make his own training aids. The summation of the course was the Phase I Field Training Exercise (FTX), a week-long ordeal at Camp Mackall, southwest of Fort Bragg. After making a night jump into the dense pine forests, classes of 50 or more students conducted demanding, around the clock land navigation exercises, ambushes, reconnaissance patrols, and raids, all with virtually no food and while enthusiastically hounded by the "CGs" – other students. Severely deprived of food and sleep the entire week, a grueling 12-mile (20km)+ evasion and escape course followed. Upon completion of this phase he was awarded the green beret in a simple ceremony, but he was still a long way from being SF qualified. The 1st Special Forces crest adorned his beret, but no unit flash was authorized.

Another break in training followed, bringing with it work details and speculation as to what SF MOS course he might draw during Phase II. An interview by an officer determined the soldier's MOS, but it was preceded by the warning, "Tell me which MOS you want and I'll tell you why you can't have it." All enlisted men were trained in one of five skills. Officers were trained separately in the 12-week Special Forces Officer Course (SFOC). Each of the MOS courses, except the medical, ended with a week-long FTX to practice new found skills. The officers undertook a two-week unconventional warfare FTX known as Exercise *Gobbler Woods*.

The ten-week Engineer Course (MOS 12B) covered conventional and unconventional (home-made) explosives (a week of each); demolition techniques; obstacles; light building and bridge construction; and engineer reconnaissance. The course's highlight was to build a bridge one week and blow it up the next. Most went on to heavy equipment operator training at Fort Belvior, Virginia, the Engineer School.

The eight-week Weapons Course was divided into light and heavy weapons phases. The five-week light weapons portion (MOS 11B) trained the student to operate and disassemble some 55 small arms. Timed disassembly and assembly tests were frequent. Current and obsolete US, Allied, and Communist Bloc weapons were studied along with basic small unit tactics. The two-week heavy weapons (MOS 11C) portion dealt with 57mm and 106mm recoilless rifles, the LAW and 3.5in rocket launcher, and mortars, predominantly on the 60mm, 81mm, and 4.2in mortars, as well as fire direction center operations. After a one-week tactical exercise and live firing of all weapons, graduates were awarded both MOSs.

In the 12-week Operations & Intelligence (O&I) Course (MOS 11F) for NCOs, students were required to be at least sergeants. They were taught the many aspects of mission planning, and unconventional warfare and special operations intelligence techniques. The skills learned ranged from photography, fingerprinting, and briefing procedures, to establishing agent nets.

The 16-week Communications Course (MOS 05B) covered operation of specialized radios and burst-transmission message devices, on- and off-line crypto-graphic systems, clandestine comms techniques, and special emphasis on manual Morse code. The SF standard was to send and receive 18 words per minute (wpm), the highest standard in the US armed forces, with the exception of nuclear submarine communicators, who operated at 20wpm.

The extremely challenging 32-week Medical Course (MOS 91C) was conducted in four sub-phases. The first was an eight-week Special Forces Basic Aidman's Course (MOS 91A), which was modified from the regular course with more emphasis on tropical diseases and less on ward care. This was followed by attendance on the 12-week Clinical Specialist Course (MOS 91C) at Fort Sam, Houston, Texas, the Army's Medical Training Center. From there, students spent six-weeks "internship" at an Army hospital working in emergency rooms and wards. They returned to Bragg for the most challenging portion of the course: the Medical Aid Procedures Course, which was unique to Special Forces medics and taught students skills normally reserved for physicians. The six weeks began with three weeks' clinical training followed by "Dog Lab," where each student received a dog that was treated the same as a human patient. After being cured of existing ailments, the "patient" was anesthetized and shot in a hind leg with a .22-cal rifle, which was treated and another leg later amputated. The graduates of this most demanding of Special Forces MOSs were highly respected by the other troops and Army surgeons. The civilian position of physician's assistant (PA) was originally created to utilize the skills of former SF medics.

An interesting aspect of the Training Group was that the students were intermixed within companies regardless of MOS and training phase. All the various MOSs might

A typically uniformed SF trooper about to depart on a patrol. Note the can of serum albumin behind his neck, the M18 colored smoke grenade, and the olive drab tape applied to the handguard of his M16A1 rifle to break up its solid black appearance, which otherwise tended to stand out. (US Army)

be represented within a single eight-man room. It was a situation that, when coupled with a variety of previous military training, led to a great deal of unofficial cross-fertilization of skills. The practice was, however, eliminated in late 1968 when students were concentrated into companies by phase and MOS. The change undoubtedly eased administration, but informal professional development suffered.

Now with a new MOS, the student was assigned to a group of students that possessed all SF MOSs to undertake Phase III. It was here that the student was taught the basics of unconventional warfare operations: concepts, techniques, organization, mission planning, air support, low-level tradecraft, and more. He learned the nature of guerrillas, how to deal with them, how to organize them, and to motivate them to undertake missions that were beneficial to the military and political goals of the US and its allies, rather than the guerrilla's own, frequently short-sighted, aims. He was also taught how to demobilize a guerrilla force once a conflict was over.

The final two weeks of the six-week phase were spent in an unconventional warfare exercise. Students planned and prepared for the mission, then parachuted into Uwharrie National Forest northwest of Fort Bragg. Each student A Team linked up with its "guerrilla" force (made up of instructor-led SF students). The student A Teams organized and trained the "Gs," and then assisted them in the execution of raids, ambushes, and other missions while pursued by the "CGs," often provided by the 82d Airborne Division during this phase. The trust of the guerrilla leaders had to be gained but they often proved uncooperative and had to be persuaded to undertake some missions. Upon graduation from Phase III the student was now considered "flash-qualified" (authorized to sew his assigned group's flash on his beret) and had an "S" special skill identifier tacked on to the end of his MOS. Officers were designated by a "3" skill identifier. From 1969, the SF Qualification Course was rated as an NCO course, and graduating enlisted men were automatically promoted to sergeant (E5). Previously they had had to work their way through the ranks.

The words of Berry Saddler's "Ballad of the Green Berets," which says: "One hundred men we'll test today, but only one will win the green beret," are not entirely accurate, but it was a demanding program with an extremely high attrition rate. Counting the pre-screening and selection battery tests, one out of 100 may well have been the end success rate.

The new SF trooper was now assigned to an SF group, the 3rd, 6th, or 7th at Fort Bragg, 1st on Okinawa, 8th in Panama, or the 10th in Germany. Small numbers were selected for assignment to the 46th SF Company in Thailand. Most of the graduating E4s and E5s were placed directly in E6 and E7 A Team positions. Many of those remaining at Bragg were eventually destined for Vietnam. The training actually never ended; it was continued in the groups by unit-level training, exercises, and attendance at specialized courses. Even when our trooper arrived in Vietnam, he undertook the two-week Combat Orientation Course at the Special Forces-run MACV Recondo School. Contrary to popular perception, few of the new troopers were taught a foreign language or cross-trained in a second MOS. This was usually reserved for those who re-enlisted.

The new SF troopers were by no means supermen, but they were trained to a high degree of proficiency, were extremely motivated, mentally and physically fit for the rigors ahead, and possessed an innate desire to accomplish the SF motto, *De Oppresso Liber* (Free the Oppressed).

There were few A Teams that did not possess several pets, which, in Vietnam, ranged from scarce cats to pythons. Dogs were universally the favorite and were considered part of the team. In the background is Camp Thuong Duc's, A-109, concrete-capped commo bunker. (US Army)

DEPLOYMENT TO VIETNAM

The SF soldier selected for Vietnam duty was notified by the Department of the Army 120 days in advance by receipt of his alert orders. Those volunteering for Vietnam, a feat accomplished by a phone call to the Department of the Army's Special Assignments Section, often had a longer delay as they had to await vacancies in the next available allotment. In the meantime, the trooper undertook a pre-deployment physical, received numerous inoculations, took care of any dental work (none was available in Vietnam except for severe emergencies), completed a will, granted power of attorney to next of kin, and took a 30-day leave. His deployment orders directed that he report to either Fort Lewis, Washington, or Port of Embarkation, San Francisco, California. He spent a week there completing paperwork and received an issue of tropical uniforms. Regular troops were required to possess at least one field cap (baseball cap), and if not in possession of one, they had to purchase one at Quartermaster Clothing Sales. SF soldiers were not required to have one; and they became a clothing item that no self-respecting trooper would be caught with. They did, however, rush to on-post dry cleaners to have name and "U.S. ARMY" tapes sewn on their new jungle fatigues at their own expense. Only the SF knew what unit they were going to, and they had their "Lighting Bolt" patch and jump wings sewn on. Between processing, the days were spent on post work details and the evenings at enlisted or NCO clubs. The flight to Vietnam was on a chartered commercial Boeing 707 with all the usual airline amenities, and it took the better part of a day.

Most SF troops processed through Fort Lewis arrived at Cam Ranh Bay in II CTZ and the 22nd Replacement Battalion. Those from California arrived at Tan Son Nut Air Base in Saigon and went on to the 90th Replacement. More paperwork awaited them on arrival, including filling out next-of-kin notification cards. A soldier could specify that his next of kin not be notified if he was lightly wounded (most did this); regulations required that they be notified if he was seriously wounded, killed, or reported missing. Soldiers were also issued a Geneva Convention Card and MACV Ration Card (to control the purchase of electrical appliances, cameras, liquor, and cigarettes as a black market control measure). American dollars were exchanged for Military Payment Certificates (MPCs), which were the standard medium of exchange in Vietnam. Our trooper brushed his teeth with a special one-time use fluoridated toothpaste, was cautioned on the danger of venereal diseases, and sternly briefed on the necessity of taking all of his daily and weekly antimalaria pills. The conventional soldiers were assigned to units and after a few days were shipped out. The SF soldiers were even sooner flown to the SFOB at Nha Trang and began another round of paperwork.

Troops in Vietnam were paid in MPCs. It was a violation of regulations to even possess US dollars or spend MPCs on the local economy. MPCs could be spent in post exchanges (PX), military clubs, Army post offices, and authorized Vietnamese concessionaires on bases (barbers, tailors, etc.). American car dealers also had salesmen on major rear bases. A soldier could select his car (the next year's model), arrange for payroll deductions, and pick up his new car when he returned to the States (if he were killed the payments made would be reimbursed to his next of kin). MPCs were to be exchanged for Vietnamese piasters at military pay offices and banks at a rate of US $1.00 = 115$VN (115 piasters or "Pees") in 1969. Troops were cautioned not to exchange dollars or MPCs for piasters on the black market, where they received a substantially better exchange rate, up to 200 percent. Most soldiers had a percentage of their pay deducted and banked in checking or savings accounts. The First National City and Chase Manhattan Banks had branch offices in Saigon offering 10 percent interest on savings accounts, higher than the Stateside standard. Money could also be sent home by postal money order obtained from Army post officers.

A US Special Forces officer inspects the Danish Madsen 9mm M/50 submachine guns of a platoon of Rhade Montagnard Mountain Scouts. Some in the left-rear are armed with .30-cal M1903 rifles. Note the officer's World War II-era jungle boots. (US Army)

In 1969, an SF sergeant (E5) on his first tour had a monthly base pay of about $350 to which were added $65 hostile fire (combat) pay, $55 hazardous duty (jump) pay, $77.10 subsistence allowance (rations not available) pay, and $13 overseas allowance (no one could figure out what it was really for); all tax exempt in Vietnam. Letters home were free, but packages had to be paid for.

After processing through the 5th SFGA, the newly arrived SF trooper was attached to the Combat Orientation Course (COC or "Cock Course") under the tutelage of the MACV Recondo School, which was operated by the 5th SFGA. While waiting for the next course to begin, he was free to explore Nha Trang, to become familiar with Vietnamese culture, and to exchange the US dollars he had "forgotten" to declare for black market piasters. Restaurants, bars, steam baths, and tailor shops served as cultural classrooms. Wherever he looked he saw the three most common features in Vietnam: sandbags, barbed wire, and motorbikes.

Upon completing the COC our trooper received his assignment and within 48 hours he was on his way to some far corner of Vietnam. His first stop would be the C Team, where a small group would spend a few days awaiting transport to their B Team. The trooper would meet the company commander and sergeant-major, receive a briefing from the S-2, S-3, and S-5 sections, and draw an M16A1 rifle. When he arrived at the B Team by helicopter or air transport, much the same process would be repeated and, if such was his posting, he would find out at which camp he would be spending the next year.

LIFE IN THE FIELD

When SF soldiers reflect upon their service with the US Army's complex and controversial involvement in Vietnam, they rarely relate similar experiences. Such men were asked to fulfill a wide variety of operations and missions – camp strike forces, mobile strike forces, mobile guerrilla forces, special reconnaissance projects, training missions, and headquarters duty – and each provided vastly different circumstances for SF soldiers.

The span of time was an equally important factor that affected the experiences of SF soldiers. SF involvement in Vietnam began in 1957 and ended in 1973. Even a difference of one year would result in contrasting perspectives, as the war was fought in a constantly changing environment. Terrain and weather conditions were similarly important. Vietnam offered varied geographic environments, ranging from chilly, forested mountains in the north, vast open plains in the central highlands, triple-canopy inland jungles, dense coastal swamps, and the inundated flood plains of the Mekong Delta. It was often said that Vietnam has three seasons; wet, dry, and dusty, which recur at approximately hourly intervals.

OPPOSITE: Fort McClellan, Alabama, 1963. Sergeant Cecil Williams demonstrates the method of disposing of a guard on post during unconventional warfare and guerrilla tactics training. Both men seen here were members of the 20th Special Forces Group – "Green Berets." (NARA)

The effectiveness of an SF detachment was often determined by the personality of its members. While a certain degree of guidance was provided in the operation of A-camps and other SF activities, there was no official doctrine guiding day-to-day operations. In Vietnam, there was only "lore," and what was found to work best in a given situation. Expedients, substitutes, ingenious makeshift efforts, and resourcefulness were a matter of course. There were inevitably similarities between camps, but differences in routine were often vast.

Before moving on to look at other US SOF of the Vietnam era, we will briefly focus on the general experiences of SF troops involved with camp strike forces. The more glamorous SF missions, reconnaissance projects, and MIKE Forces for example, are more publicized in popular literature, but it was the A-camps that epitomized the heart and soul of Special Forces in Vietnam.

The camps, which were usually staffed by fewer than a dozen Americans in some of

The senior SF medic and team commander enter into a friendly competition with their favorite handguns, an M1911A1 pistol and an M1917 revolver, both .45-cal, at Camp Tong Le Chon. (US Army)

the most remote and inhospitable regions of Vietnam, were bases for indigenous, irregular COIN forces. They struggled to stifle the flow of enemy forces and supplies from across the borders, and they secured isolated ethnic minority villages to prevent their exploitation by ruthless enemy forces. The A-camps experienced COIN at grassroots level and were involved in all aspects of counterguerrilla warfare, training, advising, and fighting with indigenous troops. To this end, they were also involved in the interrelated field of psychological operations (influencing the opinions, attitudes, and behavior of enemy forces, indigenous populations, friendly and military), civic action (improving local economic and social conditions), and intelligence collection (through reconnaissance, informers, and low-level agent nets in the camp's area). Away from the battlefield, SF gave medical, educational, agricultural, and housing construction assistance to the troops' families and local villagers. MEDCAP (Medical/Civic Action Program) visits to local villages were routinely made.

Combat operations conducted in the camp's TAOR were of limited duration and scale. They focused on area denial and interdiction of enemy forces. The lightly armed strikers were not intended for long-duration, high-tempo operations against major enemy units; their operations tended to be simple in both plan and goals. Most engagements were small, chance encounter firefights and ambushes fought against small Local Force VC elements. The strikers and VC were fairly evenly matched, except that the strikers were normally in company strength and they could call for artillery, attack helicopters, and air strikes, which suddenly made an action rather one-sided and the result inevitable.

Many of the tactics and techniques used by both sides were similar. SF soldiers tend to read history, especially at the tactical level, more than their conventional counterparts, borrowing techniques from past guerrilla wars. They seldom closely imitated tactics outlined by the "Fort Benning School for Boys" – Officer Candidate School.

Vicious battles with Main Force VC and NVA units increasingly took place as the war escalated. By 1968, Vietnam was not a guerrilla war, but a mid-intensity conflict with large, conventional maneuver forces being employed by both sides.

For the most part, however, strike force operations were at the low end of the tactical spectrum. Operations were generally around five days in duration, with one company kept in the field at all times. The combat reconnaissance platoon would run similar length operations every couple of weeks or might work in conjunction with a company. The companies usually walked into and out of their AOs (the area of operations was a temporarily assigned area in which units conducted combat operations) but helicopters were sometimes provided. In such cases, a company going into the field could be inserted by helicopter in the morning and the same choppers would pick up the in-coming company from a different area within the TAOR.

Two Americans and one or two LLDB would accompany each operation. A single interpreter and two radio-telephone operators (RTOs) would be detailed to them while the LLDB would have his own RTO. The operation itself consisted of simply conducting sweeps through areas suspected of containing VC. In dense forests and steep terrain, the company would move in a column, with appropriate outer security, a "long green line." In areas with light underbrush an "open box" would be formed, with one platoon on line across the front and the others in columns on the flanks (sides) of the box. Local villages would be checked along with known trails and possible water points. In many instances the strikers were native to the area they operated in and visits to villages became homecoming affairs. Information on local VC activities was freely provided by the villagers. Day and night ambushes would be established on likely enemy routes.

Each of the companies' three platoons had two or three 40mm M79 grenade launchers with 30 rounds apiece. Though a weapons platoon was authorized to have two 60mm mortars and M60 machine guns, the authorization existed only on paper. The two M60s, with each gun's 800 rounds distributed between riflemen, were simply attached to the lead platoons, while the mortars remained in camp as they were too heavy to take to the field. In any case, artillery could be called as needed along with air strikes. While few fragmentation (frag) grenades were carried, they were dangerous in the dense forest; lots of colored smoke grenades were hung on rucksacks for air-to-ground marking so that helicopter gunships and strike fighters could identify friendly positions. Claymores were liberally distributed for ambushes and night defense.

The company would begin moving at daybreak, usually with little if anything in the way of breakfast. It would move until about 1100hrs, then halt for a couple of hours for rest and lunch. It would continue moving until an hour or so before sunset, break for dinner, and then move until last light, at which time it would occupy its night position, called the RON (remain overnight). Security and ambushes would be put out, guards mounted, and usually the night was spent in relative peace. The VC, contrary to popular belief, did not stealthily sneak through the jungles endlessly. Indeed, they feared the night and moved off of trails only out of necessity, often using flashlights. Nevertheless, the VC were excellent fighters and a challenging foe due to motivation, practical training, and local knowledge. The Americans reported into the camp by radio in the morning, during pok time, at 1500hrs, and after occupying the RON. All in all it was fairly routine and even boring work. The occasional contacts were, of course, memorable and were usually nasty, for one side or the other. The VC and NVA simply did not take CIDG prisoners, but USSF prisoners were sought, though few were captured.

The gear carried by an SF trooper in the field varied by preference, but a typical rucksack load follows. A poncho liner was placed in the indigenous ("indig") rucksack where it would act as a pad between the gear and the bearer's back. On either side were pockets for 1qt canteens. A third pocket was centered on the back. In this was placed a plastic bag containing extra field dressings, gauze rolls, adhesive tape, antiseptic, morphine, Compazine and ephedrine syrettes, sterile packets of pre-threaded sutures, and a bottle of assorted pills. A can containing serum albumin, a blood expander, and an intravenous injection set was also carried. While the team medics had trained a couple of strikers in each company in basic medic skills, it was the Americans who provided real emergency treatment in the field. All SF troopers received additional training from their team medics.

The usual rations were Packet, Indigenous Ration (PIR), one meal per day for the operation's planned five days, plus one spare, just in case. An equal number of cans of mackerel and cereal bars were packed. Included too was a plastic bag of coffee, sugar, cream, cocoa, chewing gum, toilet paper, and a couple of plastic spoons, all hoarded from the LRP and C-rations that occasionally came the team's way. Bottles of antimalaria pills and halazone (water purification) tablets were included.

Another plastic bag contained an empty C-ration can with slits cut in the side, a tube of matches, and half an M112 demolition charge – ¾lb (0.3kg) of C4 plastic explosive. A jawbreaker-sized ball of C4 would be placed in the silted can and lit. It burned like a small blowtorch and would bring a canteen cup of water to boil in a few minutes. It was safe enough, as long as one did not inhale the pungent fumes (causing brain damage) or attempt to stamp out the burning glob of C4, which would detonate. The boiling water was then added to the PIR instant rice. While the rice was heating up and expanding in its tube-like plastic bag, a can of mackerel would be heated. The canteen cup, now filled with more water, would have a packet of pre-sweetened Koolaid poured in. After only a cereal bar and a cup of lukewarm coffee for breakfast and no lunch, the rice and mackerel never seemed to heat fast enough for the much-anticipated single meal of the day.

Still another plastic bag held a pair of socks and OG undershirt and boxer undershorts. The latter item was not intended as underwear, but as an outer garment. Tiger-stripes were of comparatively flimsy construction and it was common for the crotch to rip out when crawling up stream banks or over fallen trees. The boxer shorts were simply pulled over the trousers as a quick fix.

A tightly rolled nylon indig hammock, with an 18in (45cm) extension sewn to one end to accommodate an American, was shoved in. An indig poncho, also with an 18in (45cm) extension, with the hood removed and its opening covered with a patch, was placed on top. This was used as a fly pitched over the hammock rather than as a rain garment. Two white-star parachute pop-up flares, for self-illumination, were shoved into the sides along with a penlight and Air Force survival knife. Most troopers did not look at this excellent knife as a weapon, but as a tool, and carried it where it would not be lost. M18 smoke grenades, one each in red, yellow, and violet, were attached to web loops on the rucksack's back.

Two Special Forces engineer NCOs cut a length of detonating cord to prepare demolition materials in order to clear trees hampering the approach to Camp Duc Hue's A-325 airfield. One man carries an M1 rifle with an M2 flash hider. (US Army)

The small rucksack weighed less than 30lb (14kg). However, unlike many US infantrymen, who often fastened all their gear to their rucksack or carried only limited items on their web gear, SF tended to load their harnesses down.

A field bivouac simply entailed selecting two suitable trees and stringing the hammock between them. If it looked like rain the poncho was erected as a simple fly. The web gear and rucksack were stowed under the hammock. The RTO turned over the radio, also placed under the hammock, and the trooper slept (fully clothed) with the handset tucked beside his ear. The poncho was needed only during the dry season with its comparatively cool nights and an issue sweater was comfortable in the northern mountains. Insect repellent was used rather than a bulky mosquito net regardless of the density and aggressiveness of these insects.

The camps themselves were natural targets for attacks by the VC and NVA, resulting in numerous battles of extraordinary brutality. The Camp Nam Dong attack is an example of a vicious close-quarters battle to prevent a camp from being completely overrun. The camp, in the northern portion of I CTZ in a remote area, was located at the intersection of two valleys used by the VC as infiltration routes, some 15 miles (24km) from Laos. It was also responsible for protecting nine Montagnard villages and their 5,000 inhabitants, but it had been decided to turn the camp over to the Vietnamese and convert it to Civil Guard use (predecessor of the Regional Forces) because of the area's poor recruiting potential. The three CIDG companies each numbered 80-plus men rather than 154. Two companies were Montagnard and one Vietnamese.

The situation at Nam Dong was perilous. The camp was situated on less-than-desirable defensive terrain, the Vietnamese district chief was uncooperative, relations with the LLDB were strained, and there were fights between the Vietnamese company and the USSF team's Chinese Nung bodyguards. This degenerated into a shootout between the Nungs and Vietnamese the day before the attack, but the Americans put a halt to it before there were casualties. Some 100 miles (160km) to the south, undermanned Camp Polei Krong in II CTZ had been overrun on July

A Special Forces NCO instructs a Montagnard striker in close-reconnaissance techniques. Although SF provided training to the often-experienced strikers, it was a two-way exchange. The SF learned much from the strikers, particularly the Montagnards, who were totally attuned to their natural environment. (US Army)

4, 1964. Seven USSF were wounded in the attack, but all SF personnel escaped. Unfortunately the USSF at Nam Dong had not been informed of Polei Krong's fall, which occurred two days before the attack on their camp.

Detachment A-726, detached from the 7th SFGA in the United States, arrived for a six-month tour at the end of May to relieve the in-place team. A-726 would continue making improvements to the camp, turn it over to the Civil Guard, then establish a new camp closer to the border at Ta Co. As soon as the new team arrived the VC increased its propaganda effort and harassment of local villages. In the days before the attack, patrols reported the villagers to be nervous and refusing to provide information. About 20 VC sympathizers were suspected in the Vietnamese company. These unstable conditions were exacerbated by the fact that almost 300 surplus weapons were in the camp awaiting shipment out, making an attack on the camp all the more desirable to the VC.

The 12-man USSF team with an attached Australian advisor, 60 Nungs, seven LLDB, and 381 strikers defended the camp. CIDG dependents lived in Nam Dong Village a few hundred yards to the northeast. A Seabee-built north–south gravel airstrip was situated a couple of hundred yards to the east, and a small river flowed parallel with the airfield about 550yd (500m) further east. A small outpost was located 165yd (151m) to the south-southeast on a ridge. Forested low ridges several hundred yards away surrounded the camp. Further off, mountains rose over the camp.

The camp was a freeform, roughly oval shape, as was common for early camps, and measured about 820ft x 1,150ft (250 x 350m). The perimeter trench relied on firing steps with a few open machine gun positions. There were machine gun bunkers at the main gate and in the southeast and southwest corners. The only barrier was a 4ft (1.2m) high five-strand barbed wire fence with punji stakes. Because of the camp's scheduled conversion, grass had been allowed to grow high in the wire. Striker barracks were positioned around the perimeter. The entry road ran north from the northeast corner, with a gate in both the outer and inner wire barriers. The gates, wood-frame with interwoven barbed wire, were kept locked at night and were not opened under any circumstances. A man-sized gate beside the main gate allowed access to the inner perimeter. It could only be opened at night with an American present and covered by a Nung. A helicopter pad was located on the west side of the road just outside the outer perimeter.

The inner perimeter was larger than usual: 260ft x 395ft (79 x 20m), oval, and surrounded by a similar wire fence only 100–130ft (30–39m) inside the outer perimeter. There was no perimeter berm or trench. The inner buildings were partly protected by 3ft (1m) thick, 4ft (1.2m) high log crib anti-sniper walls. The buildings themselves were built in the local Montagnard-style with thatch roofs and rattan walls. Besides several small buildings, there were 24ft x 60ft and 24ft x 40ft (7 x 16 and 7 x 12m) longhouses containing the USSF team house and other facilities. Some references suggest that the

A 3rd MSF striker carries a load of 7.62mm SKS carbines found in a large cache near Rang Rang, 50 miles (80km) north of Saigon, one of the largest caches found with over 3,000 small arms and numerous crew-served weapons, in December 1969. (US Government)

inner perimeter was built around a former French outpost, but this was not the case. On the inner perimeter's east side was a large pit, known as the "swimming pool," the future TOC, and a 7ft (2.1m) high mound of earth and rocks plus three stacks of concrete blocks.

On the east side, but outside the inner perimeter's wire, were three sandbag ammunition bunkers enclosed in their own wire. Inside the inner perimeter were three 81mm and two 60mm mortar pits manned by USSF and Nungs. The mortar pits were semi-sunk with the below-ground sides revetted with smooth rounded rocks and low sandbag parapets. Each mortar pit had 350 rounds with more in the main ammunition bunkers. Some of the pits had recently had concrete ammunition bunkers added. The mortar pits were to become individual strong points that held out through the assault. A single 57mm recoilless rifle was to be carried by the team sergeant to where it was needed. The strike companies each had only one 60mm handheld mortar with 12 rounds, and two machine guns.

The USSF and Nungs were on full alert on the morning of the attack, July 6. The strikers were lackadaisical, with most turning in. Years later it was found that some 100 strikers were VC with orders to slit the throats of those sleeping nearby, remove their own uniforms, and join the assault wearing loincloths as did other attackers. The 800–900-

SPECIAL FORCES CAMP

This illustration provides a basic conceptual layout of a triangular-shaped strike force camp with a counterposed inner perimeter. Regardless of a given camp's shape, the same facilities and defensive considerations would be incorporated.

KEY:

A. Concertina and barbed wire barriers.
B. Area sewn with tanglefoot wire, Claymore mines, and trip flares.
C. Open area wider than grenade range between inner wire barrier and outer perimeter.
D. Guard hut.
E. Gates. Additional concertina coils block the road between gates.
F. Fuel dump (protected by berm).
G. Trench line with fighting position, either at ground level or atop an earth berm.
H. Helicopter pad.
I. Parade ground.
J. Outer perimeter wall .30-cal M1919A6 machine gun bunkers (one gun).
K. Outer perimeter corner .30-cal M1919A6 machine gun bunkers (two guns).

L. Inner perimeter .30-cal M1919A6 machine gun bunkers (one gun).
M. Inner perimeter berm faced with concertina wire.
N. Lateral compartmentalization wire barriers.
O. 60mm M19 mortar positions.
P. 81mm M29 mortar positions.
Q. .50-cal M2 machine gun positions (atop bunker).
R. 57mm M18A1 recoilless rifle position (atop bunker).
S. Schoolhouse.
T. Vehicle maintenance shop.
U. Dispensary.
V. Co Lac Bo.
W. Strikers' and dependants' quarters.
1. USSF team house.
2. USSF quarters.
3. LLDB team house and quarters.
4. Supply and arms rooms with interpreters' quarters attached.
5. Communications bunker with radio antenna tower.
6. Power generators.
7. Emergency medical bunker.
8. Ammunition bunkers.
(Chris Taylor © Osprey Publishing)

211

Montagnard mountain tribesmen patrol the hills near their outpost in the Republic of Vietnam. Trained for three months by American Special Forces men they were, at the time the photograph was taken, eager to face the Viet Cong in combat. (NARA)

man assault force – two VC Main Force battalions (these units were never identified) – positioned one 81mm and three 60mm mortars, a 57mm recoilless rifle, and machine guns on ridges to the north, northwest, and southwest of the camp. The six-man outpost outside the camp had their throats cut in their sleep.

The first mortar rounds impacted at 0226hrs, hitting the USSF mess hall and team house and setting them on fire. Rounds were landing continuously and grenades were being thrown from the wire. The Americans at first thought another fight had broken out between the Nungs and Vietnamese. The team communications NCO immediately alerted the B Team by radio and called for a flare ship, but it was unable to take off because the airfield from which it operated had no runway lights. The communications room was hit as the commo man darted out and soon the supply room and most of the inner perimeter buildings were ablaze. Camp Nam Dong now had no means of communication with the outside world.

Americans and Nungs were manning the mortar pits while other Nungs were firing from the inner perimeter. Some VC sappers were shot inside the inner perimeter. Mortar and 57mm rounds were landing inside the inner perimeter and most of the Americans were soon wounded. The Australian warrant officer was killed. To make matters worse, the US 57mm recoilless rifle proved to be defective. (From the description of the 57mm's loading problem, the author believes the fiberboard canister rounds may have swollen in the humidity, preventing them from being chambered.)

A demolition team was killed attempting to blow the main gate. Small infiltration attacks came from the south, southeast, west, and north, but the main attack struck from the southeast. Over 100 VC attacked in waves, their progress being halted by three Americans and a few Nungs whose efforts ensured that none of the attackers made it over the fence. On the east side, Marine Corps Security Force Company 122 was completely overrun. The assistant communications NCO was killed fighting off VC who had penetrated near the "swimming pool."

The American and Nung defense was centered on their mortar pits, continuously firing two HE, then two WP, then one illumination round. Individual VC and sympathizers were making it through from all directions and being shot at the edge of the pits. The defenders of the 60mm mortar pit by the main gate were forced to withdraw under a continuous barrage of grenades, their team sergeant having been killed and the team commander left for dead. In fact the team commander regained consciousness and vacated the mortar pit, taking the mortar with him. Despite having been wounded several times, he set up the mortar behind a stack of blocks and directed a group of wounded Nungs to fire it while he continued to rally other defenders. The fight continued at close range, but the mortar positions were now down to less than a dozen rounds.

By 0600hrs the VC fire was dwindling and the flare ship finally arrived, allowing the mortars to concentrate on firing HE. The VC

Rangers of Company D, 151st Infantry of the Indiana Army National Guard, the only National Guard infantry unit deployed to Vietnam. They wear woodland camouflage uniforms and olive green boonie hats or sweat bands. Note the CIB on the nearest man's turned-up hat brim. (US Army)

began withdrawing and a transport airdropped ammunition, radios, batteries, and medical supplies by parachute to the defenders. Pre-packaged emergency resupply bundles were kept on hand by B-teams for such contingencies. VC snipers and rear guards continued to harass the smoldering camp as the main body withdrew to Laos. A Civil Guard company arrived at 0800hrs, having been ambushed twice en route. Two hours later, a 100-man relief force of USSF and CIDG arrived in US Marine Corps helicopters from the B-team.

Two USSF and the Australian warrant officer were dead and seven Americans wounded. The Strike Force lost 55 dead and 65 wounded; many others had fled or joined with the VC. The LLDB had done little if anything to defend the camp, adding weight

Exterior view of a 57mm M18A1 recoilless rifle position atop a special forces machine-gun bunker. The M18A1 recoilless rifle was developed at the end of World War II, but was no longer in use by conventional US forces during the Vietnam conflict. It had an effective range of 1,400yd (1,260m) for point targets (Chris Taylor © Osprey Publishing)

to the belief that the LLDB commander was in league with the VC. The bodies of 62 VC attackers were left behind, but as many as three times that number were believed killed and a large number of others wounded. Virtually every building in the camp was burned and the VC managed to make off with over 13,000 carbine rounds from one of the ammunition bunkers. A crater analysis team counted approximately 1,000 mortar craters.

The two dead Americans were each awarded the Distinguished Service Cross, the second highest American award. The other team members received Silver and Bronze Stars. Captain Roger H. C. Donlon, commanding A-726, became the first soldier to be awarded the Medal of Honor in Vietnam. Detachment A-224, arrived from Camp An Diem, which was closed, replaced A-726 and completely rebuilt Camp Nam Dong in a

Interior view of an 81mm M29 mortar position and ammunition bunker in Vietnam, 1960s. Special forces camps generally had three or four 81mm mortar "pits," usually located within the inner perimeter. This helped ensure their protection and being deep within the camp their 230ft (70m) minimum range allowed them to fire into the outer wire barriers. (Chris Taylor © Osprey Publishing)

triangular shape prior to turning it over to the Civil Guard in September 1964. The reconstituted A-726, with five original members, opened Camp Ta Co in September 1964 as planned.

Camp Nam Dong had held out despite its poor defenses, the large number of turncoats, and the poor performance of the remaining strikers and LLDB. It held because of the vigilance and loyalty of the Nungs, a strong centralized inner perimeter capable of holding out when the rest of the camp was overrun, sufficient ammunition stowed in the mortar positions, and the resoluteness and cohesion of the USSF team.

RETURNING HOME

SF NCOs examine captured German World War I 7.9mm MG08 water-cooled machine guns recovered from a cache. Such weapons were provided to the VC by the USSR from captured German World War II stocks. (US Government)

With his year in Vietnam coming to an end and the SF soldier looking forward to DEROS (Date Eligible for Return from Overseas), he frequently endured conflicting emotions. The desire for home, family, and friends was of course overwhelming, but many felt they were leaving an important part of themselves behind. It is a curious paradox in the soldier's heart that makes one yearn for the camaraderie, adventure, and excitement experienced, regardless of the dangers, strife, and boredom. Curious too are the feelings

Walking wounded of 1st Battalion, 3rd MSF, are led into a CH-47A Chinook helicopter for mass medevac near Duc Phong Strike Force Camp, September 1969. Both the 1st and 3rd Battalions took heavy casualties. (US Government)

of closeness to those, in this case the stalwart strikers, who have been a care and often a trouble. The thought of leaving those forlorn soldiers and their families brought as much sorrow to many as the thought of going home did joy. While the job had its perils, challenges, and demands, most SF soldiers viewed camp strike force duty with a strong fondness. Most of all, they would never forget their fellow team members and the strikers.

LRRPS

The USSF were not the only elite Army troops in action during the Vietnam War. Another force that achieved great respect was the Long-Range Reconnaissance Patrol (LRRP) units. Like many other elites of the 1960s, the LRRPs were born from the unique conditions of the conflict itself. For Vietnam proved to be an entirely different kind of war. Seizing and holding terrain seldom accomplished much: the enemy had no need to seize and hold terrain. It wanted to seize and control the population. To destroy the enemy, the enemy had to be found – found while he was moving to attack US-allied forces, exploiting the civilian population, or withdrawing after doing so. The enemy's scattered base areas, weapons caches, infiltration trails, and troop concentrations also had to be found to keep him off balance. Once the enemy was located he could then be engaged with overwhelming firepower, and air mobility ensured that troops could be rapidly deployed at any time and from unexpected directions. But first the enemy had to be found.

This proved to be a much more difficult task than imagined. Traditional reconnaissance and surveillance assets, including fixed and rotary-wing aircraft, satellite surveillance, radio intercept and direction finding, ground surveillance radar, armored cavalry units, and other conventional means were of only limited value. The Army soon began reverting to less conventional means to locate the enemy. Acoustic motion sensors were dropped from aircraft and monitored, scout and tracker dog teams were utilized, defecting enemy soldiers were employed as scouts and guides, and a "people-sniffer" was even developed to detect human scents from helicopters.

In dense terrain where the enemy could easily hide, scouts could also move about comparatively undetected. It was found that "putting eyes on the ground" in the form of small reconnaissance teams, using extreme caution to avoid detection, sometimes

Members of an LRP team open fire against the enemy. While the man in the foreground reloads his M16 rifle, his comrade behind him sprays the jungle foliage with an M60 machine gun. (NARA)

SFGA HALO parachutists, 1973–82. The High Altitude, Low Opening concept was developed by the 77th SFGA in 1957–58, and involves the principles of sport skydiving modified to meet the requirements of military freefall. Its purpose is to provide a means of parachute insertion into the area of operations, while making it difficult to detect and/or destroy the aircraft due to its extremely high altitude of up to 40,000ft (12,192m). (Ron Volstad © Osprey Publishing)

achieved success in locating the enemy. General Westmoreland realized the need for Long Range Patrol (LRP) units soon after taking over MACV in June 1964, although their formation was not officially approved for another two years.

The concept of and the doctrine for such units already existed, but it was intended for operations behind enemy lines on a conventional European linear-front battlefield. However, units were not available for deployment to Vietnam, and instead they had to be created. The situation in Vietnam called for dedicated specialized infantry units that were organized, trained, and equipped to conduct intelligence collection and surveillance in small teams within enemy-controlled territory.

An understanding of the designation of these units is necessary. From the early 1960s they were called Long-Range Reconnaissance Patrol (LRRP) units but in the mid-1960s they were commonly known as Long-Range Patrol (LRP). "Reconnaissance" was dropped because the units were sometimes assigned other missions and, according to some, as a way of simplifying the designation. Through the 1960s the terms LRP and LRRP were used interchangeably, and both were even used in the same official reports. Both terms are pronounced "Lurp." It is incorrect, however, to use the word "Lurp" in text to identify these units (even though it is written that way in some books). Officially, they were identified as an Infantry Airborne Company (Long-Range Patrol). On January 1, 1969, they were redesignated an Infantry Airborne Company (Ranger), but their mission did not change. No Ranger units had existed since 1951, and the redesignation as Ranger was simply to restore a traditional title. In World War II and the Korean War, Ranger units were primarily raider or strike units. LRP units, while they might undertake occasional small-scale direct-action missions, were chiefly passive reconnaissance units and not "commandos."

The earliest US Army unit that could be considered LRP was the Alamo Scouts, who served in the Southwest Pacific in World War II. They mainly conducted passive reconnaissance missions, operated in six-man teams, and used a peer evaluation system in training that was later adopted by the Ranger Course. In 1961 two provisional LRP companies were formed in West Germany to support V and VII US Corps. These units were formalized in 1965, being assigned a table of organization and equipment (TO&E).

US military histories seldom mention that US LRP doctrine is an offspring of the LRP concept developed by NATO in 1960. Largely based on British SAS concepts of deploying small patrols behind enemy lines, units reported enemy movements and rear area targets via long-range radios. The patrols would be inserted by foot, helicopter, or parachute, or left as stay-behind elements as the Soviets advanced into Germany. They also provided targeting for air and missile strikes on Soviet follow-on echelons. Each NATO country formed LRP units of one or more companies, and battalions in some cases. The operational concept of most of these units was to dig completely concealed hides overlooking main avenues of approach. They reported intelligence using single-sideband radios transmitting in Morse code to rear area base stations. For the most part these units were under corps control, as were the early US units. However, the Americans never fully embraced the hide concept and preferred more active patrolling – perhaps because the US military tends not to have the necessary patience for such techniques and prefers to be more proactive.

The existence of the two-corps LRP companies and a couple of provisional platoon-sized units within the US Army prior to Vietnam was not widely known. They trained hard, participating in major exercises, exchanged lessons learned with NATO LRPs, and pioneered operational techniques. The volunteers for these early LRP units were paratroopers with service in the 82nd and 101st Airborne Divisions. Some had served in Special Forces and would return to the Green Berets while others later volunteered for SF. These LRPs often undertook the Ranger Course or the Pathfinder Course, as well as training with NATO LRRP units. Many of these soldiers wound up in LRP units in Vietnam and were invaluable, passing on their skills to the new units being raised to operate in the jungles and rice paddies of Southeast Asia.

Volunteers assigned to a LRP company or detachment found a unit very different from the infantry rifle company, known colloquially as a "line company." A line company possessed a ten-man headquarters, three 41-man rifle platoons with three rifle squads and a weapons squad, and a weapons platoon (the latter usually deleted in Vietnam).

A LRP company was organized along very different lines. They were more self-contained, although they were normally attached to another unit for administrative, mess, and military justice support. They were often attached to the divisional armored or air cavalry squadron or a brigade armored cavalry troop. The division/brigade retained operational control. An advantage of attaching LRPs to cavalry squadrons was that they had organic helicopter support for insertion and extraction, easing coordination. Additionally, the squadron's aero rifle platoon could be used as a reaction force.

The company HQ varied in size. The HQ section contained a captain company CO, a first lieutenant executive officer (XO), a first sergeant, a supply sergeant, an armorer, a clerk or two, a couple of drivers, and perhaps a medic or two. A mess team with a mess sergeant and two to four cooks may or may not have been assigned, depending on the messing arrangements of the unit they were attached to. The operations and intelligence (O&I) section was assigned a captain or lieutenant operations officer, a lieutenant intelligence officer, operations and intelligence sergeants, an assistant operations sergeant, and a few enlisted operations assistants, intelligence analysts, and order of battle specialists. The transportation and maintenance section provided drivers and mechanics. Most units lacked this element, relying on their parent unit for their minimal transportation needs. Most companies possessed two to four ¼-ton M151A1 utility trucks ("jeeps"), perhaps

A five-member team from Company D, 151st (Ranger) Infantry, Long Range Patrol conduct an operation in the Rang Rang area near Long Binh in 1969. Members of the team board a Huey helicopter which will take them to their landing zone. (NARA)

a ¾-ton M37B1 cargo truck, and one or two 2½-ton M35A1 cargo trucks. Brigade detachments/companies likely had only one to three vehicles.

Ideally a LRP company had a communications platoon with a large HQ manning the message center and containing radio repairmen, plus three base radio stations. These were intended to operate widely scattered stations, with all three monitoring all teams' frequencies. Very high frequency (VHF) amplitude-modulated (AM) radios were used that transmitted by skipping radio waves off the ionosphere. One or all stations might receive team messages depending on atmospheric conditions. The messages were transmitted by high-speed data burst and recorded by the base stations, which slowed down the recordings, transcribed them, and transmitted them to the company message center by radio teletype. The message center decrypted the messages and passed them to the O&I section. Intelligence information was then passed to the LRP company's division/brigade G2/S2 section where the information was analyzed, processed, and disseminated.

However, in Vietnam this advanced communications system was not used. The equipment was not available, and there was no time for the lengthy training of Morse code radio operators. For the most part, only line-of-sight frequency-modulated (FM) voice radios were used, although their range was greatly limited. This resulted in companies having only an eight- to 12-man communications section to transmit and receive voice traffic to and from teams and to operate the message center.

The number of patrol platoons varied. The 61-man brigade LRP detachments (called companies from 1969) had one platoon. The 118-man divisional companies had two platoons while the 1st Cavalry Division's 198-man company had three. The two corps-level 230-man field force companies had four platoons.

The platoon HQ typically possessed only a lieutenant, a platoon sergeant, and an enlisted man described as a radio-telephone operator/driver, although he usually did neither; he was simply an assistant. The standard called for eight five-man patrols or teams per platoon. In reality there could be five to nine patrols/teams, with six to eight being common. The number of teams varied over time in any given unit owing to available

Sergeant Curtis Hester, an LRRP assistant patrol leader, inserts a blasting cap into a Claymore antipersonnel mine. LRRP soldiers were as inventive as their enemies in the manner of delivering ambushes and setting booby traps. (NARA)

personnel and reductions forced by casualties, illness, rotations, and personnel attending training or on leave.

A team, sometimes called a "recon team" (RT), was officially a "patrol." It was actually a squad echelon unit, but it would have been misleading to call it such because of its small size. "Squad" denoted an offensive maneuver unit. The term "patrol" had its origins with the British SAS and was adopted by NATO LRPs including those of the United States. "Team" was a more familiar term to Americans, implying a small, close-knit group cooperating with one another. Officially a patrol was comprised of five men: patrol leader (staff sergeant), assistant patrol leader (sergeant), senior scout/observer (specialist 4), senior radio operator (specialist 4), and scout/observer (private first class). More commonly in Vietnam a sixth man was added, either another radio operator or a scout/observer (private first class). Patrol leaders were commonly called team leaders (TL). Six men gave the team another weapon, another pair of eyes, and a body to share watch. The Ranger Course concept of always having two men work as "Ranger buddies" was a strong inducement for even-number-strength teams. They were to watch out for one another and share the burdens. While five- or six-man teams were common, three- and four-man teams were sometimes employed. For ambushes, prisoner snatches, recovery, and other offensive

Recondo School students practice calling for and directing artillery fire on Hon Tri Island off the coast from Nha Trang. They also learned to direct close air support strikes. (US Army)

operations, teams as large as 12 men might be employed as a "heavy team." This might be achieved by combining two "light teams" under the senior or more capable leader, or pulling selected individuals with specific expertise from other teams. On occasion a platoon leader or sergeant might lead a heavy team. The 9th Infantry Division's LRP company, operating in the canal-crisscrossed Mekong Delta, used eight-man teams with four going into each of its two 16ft (4.9m) plastic assault boats. Teams were usually designated by two-digit numbers, the first identifying the platoon and the second identifying the team within the platoon (11 = 1st Platoon, Patrol 1; 36 = 3rd Platoon, Patrol 6). Other numbering systems were used, and some were designated by state or other names.

In 1966–67 the 4th Infantry Division employed three brigade LRRP detachments of eight five-man Recondo teams and three Hawkeye teams. The latter were composed of two Americans and two Montagnards who had undergone a ten-day training program. Recondo teams performed as normal LRPs while the Hawkeyes intercepted enemy couriers and hampered enemy scouting and surveillance efforts. A division Recondo Detachment of the same organization was assigned to the cavalry squadron. Other divisions sometimes attached their company's platoons directly to brigades.

Ideally, patrols developed into tight-knit teams that developed a deep trust in one another, anticipated their teammates' actions, knew their capabilities and limitations, and shared a hooch and off-duty hours. They could recognize one another's silhouettes in the dim jungle and even the gait of their walk from a distance. Assembling new teams after suffering casualties or the turnover of personnel was a slow process. New members had to be trained and accepted. Sometimes a man did not fit into a team – each team had its own personality – and was tried out by others.

It is worth noting that the early provisional LRP units were much smaller and possessed the bare minimum of support personnel. Often they were of platoon size with three to nine patrols. Provisional units were formed from assets drawn from other units of the parent command. That means every man, weapon, vehicle, radio, typewriter, and rucksack was given up by another unit. The provisional unit commander may have had command authority, but the troops' accountability, ration allocation, military justice, and pay were the responsibility of the individual's original assigned unit.

The first small provisional LRP units bore names such as 173rd Airborne Brigade LRRP Platoon and Detachment A (LRP) (Provisional), 196th Infantry Brigade. MACV authorized the formation of such units on July 8, 1966. On December 20, 1967, the Army authorized the establishment of permanent LRP field force and divisional companies and brigade detachments with assigned lineages. This is when the units were provided formal TO&Es and given the lineages of infantry units. On February 1, 1969, these companies and detachments were redesignated as Ranger companies and assigned the lineage of the 75th Infantry.

While it can be said that the primary mission of LRPs was intelligence collection, with combat patrols being a secondary mission, a great variety of operations were conducted. The various kinds of missions are detailed below.

RECONNAISSANCE MISSIONS

- Covert reconnaissance of specified points, areas, and routes
- Surveillance of enemy infiltration routes and base areas
- Terrain analysis and map corrections
- Canal and river reconnaissance
- Locating and plotting trail systems
- Confirming sightings of enemy forces reported by aerial reconnaissance
- Reconnaissance of potential landing zones (LZs) for larger forces
- Prolonged surveillance of planned LZ for larger forces
- Luring enemy forces to a particular point followed by extraction and replacement by larger forces
- Conducting bomb damage assessment of areas struck by B-52s
- Searching for enemy rocket-launching sites outside bases
- Recovering dead, weapons, radios, etc. from downed aircraft
- Emplacing unattended ground movement sensors
- Operating radio relay sites for other teams.

COMBAT MISSIONS

- Reaction teams for downed helicopters
- Rapid reinforcement of outposts
- Local ambush patrols for base security
- Countering enemy patrols near US bases
- Conducting prisoner snatches
- Executing small-scale raids on enemy sites
- Screening the flanks and rear of larger moving units to counter enemy patrols
- Direct air and artillery strikes on discovered enemy forces/facilities
- Security for sniper teams
- Security for underwater demolition and explosive ordnance disposal teams
- Emplacing antipersonnel or antivehicle mines on roads and trails.

It must be emphasized that specific LRP units conducted different types of missions at different times. This was affected by the nature of the enemy, the civilian population, terrain, and the preferences of commanders. Some commanders used their LRPs solely for covert reconnaissance while others focused on small-scale combat and reaction force missions. This focus changed as commanders changed. However, it was realized that to ensure success a team was assigned either a reconnaissance or a combat mission, not both.

If at all possible teams were allowed at least a 36-hour stand-down between missions. Continuous back-to-back missions with inadequate rest wore down a team and led to mistakes and inefficiency. Occasionally, operational tempo did not allow this luxury, but during lulls in missions, teams undertook individual and team training, reinforcing or learning new skills.

No two missions were the same: units operated differently, and the terrain, weather, and enemy and civilian situations caused even more variation. The pre-infiltration phase was extremely important. Effective planning and preparation went a long way to achieving mission success. LRPs' primary mission was to collect and report battlefield intelligence information. The most successful LRP missions were those on which not a single shot was fired. They searched

for, located, and reported the enemy. They might direct artillery or air strikes on him, move into the target area, conduct a battle damage assessment, and report the results. Thus, a six-man patrol had the potential to kill more of the enemy than a rifle company could.

Missions were assigned by the division/brigade G2/S2 specifying the AO, purpose, and dates. Many other details were required, including insertion time, means of delivery, enemy and friendly forces in the area, fire support, weather forecast, exactly what information was to be collected, extraction date/time/means, and more. Many details had to be worked out during the planning process involving the O&I section, division/brigade G2/S2 and G2/S3, LRP communications element, supporting aviation and artillery units, and the team itself. Missions were from one to six days and AOs might be 1½ square miles (4 square kilometers) or smaller. AOs were designated "No fire, no fly zones" where no artillery could be fired and no helicopters allowed to overfly unless supporting the mission. Teams were not resupplied to extend missions as this would compromise their location. If it was necessary to keep a team in the AO, the current

Reconnaissance teams sometimes used the STABO harness for extraction, invented in 1968 by Major Robert L. Stevens, Captain John D. H. Knabb, and Sergeant Firth Class Clifford L. Roberts of the Recondo School. The harness was incorporated in web gear. The UH-1H extraction helicopter dropped a 120ft (36.5m) rope for each man, the rolled-up leg straps were fastened, and the rope's snaphook fastened to the harness. A disadvantage was that roadrunner teams could not use it, as they had to wear VC equipment. (US Government) team was extracted and a fresh one inserted at the same time – "direct exchange" (DX) – either there or elsewhere in the AO.

The LRP team received a warning order 24–48 hours prior to insertion. Teams had well-developed SOPs and preparations were fairly routine. When alerted the team would not bathe or use scented soap, shampoo, or aftershave lotion. Such alien scents were easily detected by the VC/NVA. The team leader and sometimes his assistant or even the entire team were briefed either by representatives of the division/brigade G2/S2 and G2/S3 section or by the LRP operations and intelligence officers. Weapons were cleaned and test-fired, then cleaned without disassembly. Ammunition, grenades, pyrotechnics, rations, radio batteries, expendable supplies (medical items, water purification tablets, insect repellent), and any special items of equipment were drawn. The radio operators did a communications check and received call signs and frequencies (primary, alternate, aviation, artillery). Everything was carefully checked and packed. Coordination was continuous as the plan developed and the inevitable changes were made.

Much attention was given to the insertion plan. LRPs did not conduct local patrols, as infantry units could handle that. LRPs operated in remote, denied areas. It was not a matter of merely walking out of a firebase, although that sometimes occurred if a remote base was situated in the right area. Stay-behind insertions were also conducted. The team might accompany a rifle company that was air-assaulted into an LZ. The team could break off and move in another direction or the company would be extracted after just hours on the ground, to be reinserted elsewhere, and the team would remain. The same was done during airmobile artillery raids. A howitzer battery was inserted on a hilltop, fired on preplotted targets, and departed, leaving the team behind. A team might also ride into an area aboard a mechanized unit's armored personnel carriers or on riverine craft in the Delta, and be dropped off as the unit moved on.

Helicopter was by far the most common means of insertion. A primary LZ and one or two alternatives were selected. This was difficult in some areas due to the scarcity of viable LZs. A danger in such areas was that the enemy could easily place surveillance, often just a village boy who would alert the local VC. When LZs were unavailable or could be under surveillance, a team might rappel in through sparse tree growth, using ropes from as high as 100ft (30m). More commonly the team would disembark from a landed or hovering helicopter a few feet off the ground, carefully avoiding flooding and rocks, stumps, and logs hidden in vegetation.

Once briefed, team preparations continued, which included practicing movement formations, immediate action drills, and disembarking the helicopter, especially if rappelling. Even if they had just completed a mission, such rehearsals served to put LRPs in the necessary frame of mind. The team studied the AO map and aerial photographs, identified LZs, plotted artillery target reference points, and their route and objectives. If

Two Special Forces soldiers in Thailand in 1972 prepare to use the STABO (Stabilized body) rapid airborne extraction system, which was developed by Special Forces instructors at the MACV Recondo School. It was intended to extract one to four men from a site where a helicopter couldn't land. (Ron Volstad © Osprey Publishing)

at all possible the team leader and a unit officer conducted a reconnaissance overflight of the AO, identifying the LZs and route. Such flights did not orbit or hover over points of interest, but merely overflew the area. Their findings might result in further changes.

The team would then present a briefback of all aspects of their mission to the company commander and operations officer. Questions were asked to ensure the team was fully prepared to accomplish the mission and deal with unforeseen situations. The team leader would conduct a final inspection ensuring all weapons and equipment were on hand and ready, that equipment was properly secured and silenced, and that all camouflage measures taken.

Noise discipline was critical, and all gear with the potential of making noise was taped or padded – "taping up" – especially buckles and snaps. Rifle sling swivels were removed along with the unnecessary sling. No metal-on-metal contact was permitted when packing equipment. Small items might be padded by placing them in a sock. Rations were "broken down:" the meal components were removed from the outer packaging and undesired items discarded to reduce weight and bulk. LRP rations were not always available, and C-rations were often substituted. These canned rations were heavier, made more noise when opening, and caused stronger food odors, plus the cans had to be disposed of. Usually only the meat and fruit cans were retained and packed in socks, while the B units (cookies, "John Wayne crackers," cocoa powder) were discarded.

It was also essential to waterproof items from rain, sweat, and wading streams. Plastic sandwich bags had been introduced in 1957 but were scarce in Vietnam and the ziplock bag, introduced in 1968, was even rarer. Soldiers made do with the plastic, foil, or cellophane bags from rations and batteries. The only documentation they carried, if any, was their ID and Geneva Convention cards. A small notebook was carried for recording information with a pencil, as pen ink became illegible if the paper got wet. A Signal Operating Instruction (SOI) extract was carried. This included radio call signs, frequencies, and encryption codes. Radio handsets were plastic-bagged to protect from water and dust; a spare handset was sometimes carried. Maps were covered with "combat acetate" or "sticky acetate" on both sides. This was a thinner, more flexible plastic than the heavier, nonsticking acetate used as map overlays in command posts. It had adhesive on one side, allowing it to be applied to a map sheet. This was more to protect the map from water than for grease pencil marking. No mission data was marked on maps, to deny the enemy information if captured. Yet maps might be annotated with updated information discovered by the team along with enemy information. Each man carried a map in the event that he became separated from the rest of the team.

Each round of ammunition was cleaned and carefully loaded, with 18 per magazine to prevent straining the spring. The third round from the bottom might be tracer to alert the firer that he was almost empty. Some men carried a magazine or two of all tracers (this

OPPOSITE: Reconnaissance troops climb 80ft (24m) wire ladders with aluminum-tube rungs into a UH-1H Huey. These allowed reconnaissance teams to be extracted from pick-up zones on which helicopters could not touch down. The ladders were carried rolled up on the skids and dropped with sandbags attached, to carry them through vegetation. (US Government)

GREEN
BERET
MAY 1970

Helicopters were used extensively to insert LRP units into the field. Here troopers prepare an 80ft (24m) aluminum rung extraction ladder to rig it into a Huey. The rope woven through the center of the rungs is used to pull the ladder back up. (US Army)

does not harm the weapon as some claim) or every other round a tracer. This was carried by the pointman and used to break contact, making it appear to the enemy they were under heavier fire. Magazines were inserted in pouches mouth down and bullets pointing away from the body, with a tape tab affixed to the magazines' bottoms to aid extraction from the pouch. A second magazine was often taped to the magazine in the weapon for quick change. Grenade levers were taped prior to the introduction of safety clips, or arming rings were taped to prevent them from snagging on vegetation. Trip flares and "pop-ups" were removed from packaging, and Claymores were rigged with short delay fuzes and packed in the tops of rucksacks for quick access to leave on the backtrail.

The team loaded aboard the Huey with the team leader on the side they planned to disembark from. They would sit down on the LZ close to a wood line for them to rush into. Normal rules were for weapons to be empty, but a LRP team went in locked and loaded with weapons on "safe." With the seats removed they sat on the floor without seatbelts, with muzzles down and hats in pockets to prevent them from being blown away. Ideally the team riding in the insertion chopper was accompanied by a rescue chopper in the event that their ship went down. A second team might be carried in the other bird with the two teams to be inserted in different AOs. One or two gunships would escort them and provide fire support if the team ran into trouble upon insertion. A C&C bird with a company officer controlled the insertion, made certain the team was inserted on the correct LZ, and coordinated fire support. The team's radios were tuned to the C&C chopper's frequency. Radio antennas were bent down to prevent rotor strikes.

Small, inconspicuous LZs were selected far enough from suspected enemy areas so as not to attract attention, preferably with a terrain feature, such as a ridge, hill mass, or

Rappelling from a UH-1D Huey was used to insert teams when LZs were unavailable, or simply to avoid using the few LZs in an area as they might be under surveillance. It was a less-than-desirable means of insertion as it required special rigging of the helicopter and preparatory training for the team, and exposed the helicopter in a hover at between 50ft (15m) and over 100ft (32m) for several minutes. (Ron Volstad © Osprey Publishing)

belt of forest, separating the LZ from the enemy area. Often this could not be done, and LZs might be in close proximity to the enemy. As a deception, the insertion and rescue choppers made multiple landings on scattered LZs, dropping the team on one. Another method was for several choppers to fly in a trail, or column, at treetop level, and the insertion chopper landed, dropped the team, and rejoined the rear of the trail as the other choppers continued on.

Insertion was the most intense moment of any mission. Each man was lost in his thoughts, but this was where discipline and training paid off. Troops had to focus and be prepared for any eventuality. The crew chief alerted them a few minutes out from the LZ. The team leader leaned out the door, straining to confirm it was the right LZ. Landing on the wrong LZ, even a few hundred yards away, would make it extremely difficult to determine the team's actual location in the dense forest with scarce identifiable landmarks. The team's survival and ability to report accurate locations depended on it knowing its location precisely at all times, and unfortunately it was all too common for pilots to insert on the wrong LZ.

The chopper came in fast, flared, and went into ground effect a few feet off the red dirt. The team might all go out the same side and rush into the trees without slowing. Alternatively, they could also go out both doors, hit the ground, and move out once the chopper departed. This took only seconds. If they were fired upon they knew not to fire from within the helicopter for danger of hitting the chopper, a crewman, or their own men. If only one man was out the door and fire was received they all exited. It was a dash to the nearest concealment, and they halted after 330–1,000ft (100–300m) in a tight circle, kneeling, alert, and weapons ready. After the chopper departed it was startlingly quiet, and the team listened for sounds of movement and signal shots, and accustomed themselves to the natural sounds. The team leader had the radio handset to his ear. Once assured they were safe he gave an all-clear to the C&C bird and a communications check was made with the other radio. The C&C and gunships would orbit nearby on standby. Noses were counted and equipment checked to ensure nothing had been dropped. Satisfied, the team leader reported his direction of movement and then moved out in a file formation.

The most experienced scout was the pointman with his weapon set on full automatic. The team leader followed with the radio operators behind him, then a scout. The assistant patrol leader brought up the rear as the "tail gunner." A wedge or diamond formation might be used in sparse vegetation, but the file was faster (when necessary), quieter, easier to control, and less tiring in dense vegetation as only one trail was busted. It created a less detectable trail than an extended formation, which made a wider path. The interval depended on vegetation, but it was typically close. Each man was assigned a sector of observation and he carried his weapon ready, moving with his eyes. Troops were alert for any unnatural sounds or disruption of normal sounds, the least flicker of movement, and anything that appeared out of place or man-made.

Their pace was deliberate and painstakingly slow, sometimes with only a couple of hundred yards covered per hour. Each toe-heel step was made with caution, the toe feeling for twigs, crackling dead leaves, and loose rocks before firmly planting the heel. They followed the terrain contour, keeping to the most densely vegetated areas and zigzagging through the AO. Map corrections, water points, LZs, and trails were marked. Arm and hand signals were used to relay actions and warnings. When it was necessary to speak, the message was whispered into an ear and relayed man to man.

Extra precautions were used to cross danger areas. Efforts were taken to prevent scuffing the sides of stream banks and gullies, while roads and trails might be crossed in single file – each man stepping in the footprints of the others to minimize tracks and to prevent the team's strength from being determined. Another technique was for the team members to position themselves along the trail and to all cross at once, minimizing their exposure and preventing the team from being split if engaged. The first individuals crossing a gully or other rough terrain learned to slow their pace to allow the following men time to get across and not become separated. Unless a reconnaissance objective, villages and cultivated areas were avoided and bypassed downwind. Crossing a stream meant a short halt to fill canteens, with halazone purification tablets added at the next break.

It was difficult for many commanders to comprehend the slow movement rate necessary for LRPs to remain undetected. They could not always understand the limitations of the team's visibility at ground level in the jungle or that from atop a jungle-covered hill they could see nothing but trees.

Radios were normally turned off to conserve batteries. Batteries burned up quickly and only a limited number of 4.12lb (1.9kg) "bats" could be carried. Radios were only turned on if it appeared enemy contact was imminent. Required contacts were made at specified times three or four times a day to report the team's location,

Two LRPs wearing XM29 tear gas protection masks. They have sewn skirt pockets from their woodlands pattern jungle fatigues on the shoulders. They use 1qt canteen carriers for their XM177E2 submachine gun magazines, which could hold five magazines. (US Army)

movement direction, and status. In AOs out of radio range a helicopter would overfly the area several times a day to make contact. When reporting enemy activity a SALUTE report was made.

Grid coordinates were transmitted by a "shackle code." This was a simple low-level code for encrypting grid coordinates. It consisted of a predetermined ten-letter word with no two letters the same; BLACKNIGHT for example. It was a simple substitution code with the letters assigned 1–0. When transmitting a six-digit coordinate the radio operator would say, "I shackle, Charlie, November, Kilo, Bravo, Alpha, Lima. How copy? Over." Using BLACKNIGHT as the code word, the base station would repeat the phonetic letters; in this case standing for "465132." Another means was a "KAC code," a pocket-sized "wiz-wheel" for converting numbers to letters.

Many missions were a so-called "dry hole" with nothing found. This was of value as it was important to know where the enemy were not located or whether they had moved out of an area. Patrols might also find indications of the size of the force that had occupied a base camp and in what direction it departed. It was common for a team to be extracted from such an AO in a day or so or even hours; sometimes to be reinserted in a nearby AO.

A team would move until dusk, with just enough light remaining to see by. The leader would select a RON position, discreetly point it out, and continue past. The team hooked back to the designated RON and immediately took up position covering their backtrail in case they were being followed. A RON was often compared to a miniskirt: it offered minimal cover and concealment, all-around security, and could be defended for a short time. LRPs might move a short distance after darkness fell to further deceive the enemy. The RON was within dense vegetation well away from trails, streams, lines of drift, and easily traversed terrain. Claymores were emplaced on avenues of approach.

KIT CARSON SCOUTS

This secretive force consisted of VC and NVA defectors, used by the US military as informed sources of information and useful reconnaissance scouts in the field, performing tasks ranging from identifying undercover VC operators to pointing out booby traps. The program was established in late 1966 by the 1st Marine Division, and was named after a famous 19th-century American frontiersman and Indian fighter. During 1967 the program caught the interest of higher authorities, and it expanded beyond the Marine Corps (both the 1st and 3rd Divisions were using such scouts by mid 1967) into the Army, with official endorsement by General William Westmoreland, the commander of the MACV. By 1969, the number of defectors in US service totaled 2,200, and they even served alongside SF units such as the LRRPs. Some 230 of these individuals were killed in action.

September 1967, Mekong Delta, Vietnam. A heavily armed "Mike" boat carrying members of a US Navy SEAL team departs the site of a Viet Cong fortification on the Bassac River which was destroyed by the SEALS during Operation *Crimson Tide*. (US Navy)

Often LRP teams were delivered to a remote temporary firebase and then would depart on foot at dusk or before dawn. To the left a LRP can be seen with a serum albumin can taped to the back shoulder yoke of his suspenders. This was a blood volume expander that saved many lives. (US Army)

The team might assume a "wagon-wheel" formation in the prone, facing outward with their feet in the center. This allowed them to alert one another by tapping boots. An alternative was to sit back-to-back in a tight circle resting on their rucksacks. At rest, weapons and equipment were checked and cleaned without disassembly, and a radio report was made. Troops slept in that position without a bedroll. If the enemy was about, even when it rained, LRPs did not use ponchos as they made noise and glistened. To further minimize the chances of discovery insect repellent was relied upon rather than mosquito nets. Everything was kept packed and ready to move out with only necessary items removed from the rucksacks. Troops did not shave or brush their teeth, and they removed one boot at a time when checking their feet.

Seldom was a situation such that meals could be heated. Issue heat tablets or burning balls of C4 and food odors were too conspicuous. LRP or C-rations were usually eaten cold, and in the case of LRPs dry. On longer missions, especially in the rains, hot meals were prepared well away from possible enemy areas, while tepid drinking water was flavored with presweetened Kool-Aid sent from home.

Night movement was avoided. It made too much noise, was too slow, and there was too much of a chance of running into an enemy camp or ambush. There were no night vision goggles at the time – and there is nothing darker than a jungle floor at night. Moving on trails was suicide.

If contact with the enemy was made, the LRRPS team would hit the opponents fast and hard with every weapon they had, including calling in artillery support from nearby firebases. Following contact, however, the team would usually call in a rapid helicopter extraction, the helicopters adding their own firepower to the support equation. Such missions required men of exceptional nerves and emotional resilience.

SEALS AND OTHER SOF

The US Army was far from the only US military organization to exhibit a new-found enthusiasm for the concept of SOF. The Vietnam War was also the catalyst for the US Navy to develop new SF units, not least the famous US Navy SEALs, the acronym standing for "Sea, Air, Land" – indicating that the force will deploy and fight from every dimension and terrain of combat.

The precedents of the SEALs were the UDTs, Naval Combat Demolition Units, Amphibious Scouts and Raiders, and OSS Operational Swimmers mentioned in the previous chapter. UDTs were reactivated during the Korean War, eventually reaching a strength of 300 personnel, divided into three teams, as part of the Special Operations Group (SOG). The UDTs in Korea were given an expanded operational remit. Not only did they perform all the previous tasks of beach reconnaissance, they also conducted

US Navy SEALS have their rifles ready as they go ashore from whalers into the Rung Sat Special Zone. Once deployed, the SEAL teams could remain deep in VC or NVA territory for days or even weeks. (US Navy)

inshore combat and demolition operations against key coastal positions, such as bridges and power plants. (They even conducted operations against the North Korean fishing industry in Operation *Fishnet* from April to September 1952.) The UDTs received further acclaim in making airborne deployments, which combined with their other talents for demolitions, communications, hydrographic analysis, and the like meant that UDT personnel quickly became some of the most highly trained individuals in the US military.

UDTs would continue to serve into the Vietnam War, but in March 1961 a new elite force emerged to broaden the Navy's special ops capability. Arleigh Burke, the Chief of Naval Operations, recommended to the US President that the Navy establish its own counterinsurgency-capable force of soldiers, a recommendation that fell on Kennedy's receptive ears. So it was that on January 8, 1962, the SEALs were created by Presidential Order. Two SEAL teams were founded: Team 1 at the Naval Amphibious Base (NAB) in Coronado, California, and Team 2 at NAB Little Creek, Virginia. Training was, as expected, extremely rigorous, although it built on the fact that many of the individuals joining the SEALs were ex-UDT. Not only did the soldiers learn the full range of amphibious deployment techniques, but they added the classic SF skills of parachuting, close-quarters combat, demolitions, foreign languages, advanced field first aid, and much more.

SEAL units began their involvement with Vietnam in 1962, although the primary years of operation were between 1966 and 1973. The operational demands placed upon the SEALs expanded from advisory roles to South Vietnamese combat divers through to covert surveillance operations around the North Vietnamese coastline. Yet their greatest

THE PHOENIX PROGRAM

SEAL forces were also used to perform assassination missions as part of the CIA's "Phoenix Program," which ran from 1968 to 1972. The program (initially called the Intelligence Coordination and Exploitation Program) was an intelligence operation designed to identify, apprehend, and, if necessary, kill VC personnel and supporters, particularly those holding influential positions within urban or village life. The two key elements of the program were the Provisional Reconnaissance Units (PRUs), the active intelligence and combat component to which the SEALs sometimes contributed, and the regional interrogation centers. Once identified on the basis of intelligence, suspect individuals were either killed in direct assassination action, or taken for interrogation, where a variety of methods, including torture, might be used to extract information. The program was in many ways highly effective – 81,740 people suspected of Viet Cong membership were "neutralized" between 1968 and 1972, while 26,369 were killed. Yet the cruelty of the methods, and the persistent aggressive searches of villages, helped alienate the Vietnamese population, and the Phoenix Program was largely dissolved by 1972, although some aspects of its operations lingered until 1975.

OPPOSITE: US Navy SEALs ready their weapons as they prepare to conduct an operation from riverine craft, October 1968. (NARA)

contribution was as an elite counterinsurgency force deployed into South Vietnam's labyrinthine waterways, particularly the Rung Sat Special Zone, a huge area of mangrove swamp to the southeast of Saigon, and the similarly challenging Mekong Delta. Small SEAL units would be deployed into the heart of these areas by small shallow-draft boats, often crewed by members of the Boat Support Unit (BSU), an elite unit created in 1964 specifically to provide support to SEAL operations. Once deployed, the SEAL soldiers would blend into the aquatic environment with superb camouflage and perfect endurance, stalking VC units and destroying them with powerful ambushes and raids. It has been noted that an individual SEAL platoon might make 100 such attacks in a six-month period, and the VC respectfully labeled the SEALs "men with green faces," on account of their superb body camouflage. SEAL teams could spend up to and over a week out on their own in the wilderness, the only support coming from their own skill at arms and their exceptional levels of nerve.

Along with the rest of US military forces, the SEALs were officially withdrawn from Vietnam in 1973, as the process of "Vietnamization" (arming and equipping the ARVN

OPPOSITE: March 1968, Mekong Delta, Vietnam. A US Navy SEAL team member sets demolition charges to blow up a Viet Cong bunker on Tan Dinh Island during Operation *Bold Dragon III*. (NARA)

BELOW: Members of a US Navy SEAL team man their weapons as they prepare to come ashore from a river patrol boat at an operation site in Vietnam in October 1968. The Viet Cong came to have a special fear of these elusive, ruthless warriors. (NARA)

for self-sufficiency) was ostensibly nearing completion. The SEALs ended the conflict with literally hundreds of decorations (including three Medals of Honor) and the respect of all who served alongside them.

The US Air Force (USAF) had also developed some of its own elites by the time US forces became embroiled in the Vietnam conflict. Its Pararescue Jumpers (PJs) had laid their foundations in World War II as small, highly trained air rescue units dedicated to recovering downed pilots in the inhospitable China–Burma–India theatre. The medically trained personnel would identify the crash site and make parachute drops, often over enemy-held territory, then find, treat, and rescue the beleaguered aircrew.

In May 1946 the USAF established the Air Rescue Service, of which PJs were an important component part. They were responsible for air rescue missions of pilots and aircrew who had crashed at a substantial distance from their air base, often behind enemy

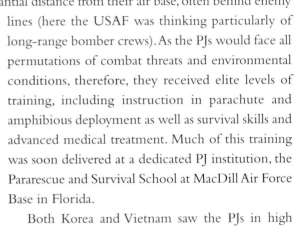

A LRP team returns from a mission. The man in the center carries a 12-gauge pump shotgun, popular with point men, and a Chinese 7.62mm Type 56 (AK-47) assault rifle. It may have been captured or carried by the pointman. (US Army)

lines (here the USAF was thinking particularly of long-range bomber crews). As the PJs would face all permutations of combat threats and environmental conditions, therefore, they received elite levels of training, including instruction in parachute and amphibious deployment as well as survival skills and advanced medical treatment. Much of this training was soon delivered at a dedicated PJ institution, the Pararescue and Survival School at MacDill Air Force Base in Florida.

Both Korea and Vietnam saw the PJs in high demand, during which conflicts they rescued literally thousands of downed airmen. In Vietnam, the new generations of helicopters meant that the PJs had more versatile options for deployment around Vietnam's jungle-covered and mountainous landscape, and even to make low-level incursions across the North Vietnamese border. By the time the conflict ended in 1975, the PJs were an accepted elite with the USAF, and were given the right to wear the revered maroon beret.

The Vietnam conflict ended in failure for the United States. The US armed services were faced with more than a decade of trying to reconcile themselves to what had happened, and hard tactical, strategic, and social questions would haunt their leaders for more than a decade. Yet what the war had proven beyond a shadow of a doubt was that the concept of "elite" soldiers was justified. The war ended with SF troops formalized in the Army, Navy, and Air Force, and the Marine Corps continued with its traditions of elite recon troops and scout-snipers. The challenges to follow the Vietnam War would see special operations expand even further.

POST-VIETNAM
SPECIAL
OPERATIONS
FORCES
1975–2000

LEFT: Three US Army Rangers participate in a training exercise in 1980. By the end of the 1990s, Ranger training was established as one of the toughest programs of military instruction in the world. (NARA)

THE VIETNAM WAR, above all other conflicts, cemented both the idea and practical use of SOF in American military culture. Although many senior commanders and defense analysts would remain wary of the idea of a separate "elite" within the US armed forces – indeed there are such figures to this day – the complex reality of modern warfare necessitated not only the maintenance of SOF, but actually their growth. The 1970s–90s consequently saw the prodigious expansion and increasing diversity of SOF units.

The causes of the growth of SOF in the last three decades of the 20th century are multiple and intertwined. The Cold War was still in progress, and SOF offered a way to prosecute various American foreign policy objectives without the massive cost or political issues of conventional deployments. More importantly, global terrorism was on the rise in a dramatic way, destabilizing governments, threatening international travel, and killing thousands. Indeed, since the 9/11 attacks it is easy to forget how blighted the 1970s and 80s were by terrorism. The 1970s saw a total of 8,114 terrorist incidents worldwide with just under 5,000 people killed; Europe was the most affected, followed by Latin America then the Middle East. In the 1980s, however, the grim tally of incidents rose to no fewer than 31,426 incidents, and the targeting "policy" of the terrorists shifted from property and airlines to people – 70,859 people were killed by terrorism during the decade. Moreover, Europe dropped into second place in the black ranks of worst-affected regions, and Latin America rose to the top spot. Given that Latin America was the US "backyard," it was inevitable that the US military found its force development making an ever-greater investment in elite counterinsurgency forces.

Various disasters also fuelled the American appetite for refining its SOF, most of all the catastrophic failed hostage rescue in Iran in 1980 during Operation *Desert One*, compounded by the mixed outcome of special operations missions during the invasion of Grenada under Operation *Urgent Fury* in 1983 (both missions are discussed below). In an effort to repair the conventional weaknesses so cruelly exposed in Southeast Asia, the US military created a separate branch for its elite units. Policy-makers further recognized the threat of a geo-political shift after the Soviet Union invaded the sovereign state of Afghanistan in 1979 with little international resistance. Since open warfare with the communist bloc was unthinkable, the re-assessment of military strategy led to the creation of an all-encompassing command for US SOF.

The United States Special Operations Command (USSOCOM) was activated on April 16, 1987, and since its inception has been located at MacDill Air Force Base, Florida. USSOCOM promoted the advancement of officers within the special operations field, and allowed well-trained enlisted members to spend the majority of their careers within the elite community. USSOCOM's assets include special operations units and commands from all branches of the American military: the Army, Air Force,

Navy, and the Marine Corps. Now SOF became a fundamental structural component of the US military at the highest level.

THE CHANGING WORLD OF SOF

The years after 1973 brought about major structural changes in existing SOF, plus the birth of many new formations. The immediate aftermath of the Vietnam War, however, saw many cutbacks, and the US Army's SF did not escape intact. The 3rd SFGA, for example, was inactivated on December 1, 1969, followed by the 6th in 1971; the 5th and 7th SFGAs were to assume their African and Middle Eastern responsibilities. The 10th SFGA was moved from Germany to Fort Devens, Massachusetts, in September 1969, but

An 8th SFGA mobile training team member instructs recruits of the El Salvadorian Army at its Sonbonate Recruit Training Center, September 1971. (US Army)

US SOF troops in Panama, 1989–90. 1) "Delta Force" Assault Team operator. 2) Special Forces trooper, A/3/37th SFGA. 3) Navy SEAL Team 4 member. Note how both Delta troops and SEALs wore common uniforms, but were permitted much leeway in equipment selection. (Ron Volstad © Osprey Publishing)

its Company A (redesignated 1st Battalion in 1972) remained at Bad Tölz, and the group as a whole still retained the European mission. Other SF units were also to remain in Germany. SF Detachment Europe had been activated on July 11, 1968, to provide command and control of SF elements there. Another was the 39th SF Detachment (redesignated a company in 1972) which had been activated on September 1, 1965. The 8th SFGA was inactivated on June 30, 1972 and its assets used to form the 3rd Battalion, 7th SFGA, which continued with the former's Latin American mission. The 1st SFGA was inactivated at Fort Bragg on June 28, 1974, leaving only SF Detachment Korea in that part of the world.

Besides the reduction of units, there were substantial manning cuts in the remaining ones. The SF Training Group was reorganized into the Institute for Military Assistance Student Battalion in 1972. SF began to assume a low profile, which it would maintain until the early 1980s. Missions continued, however, with the major emphasis on Latin America, although Europe and Africa were also to see SF teams deployed. SF also began to undertake civic action missions in the States, among them "SPARTAN" (Special Proficiency at Rugged Training and Nation Building) directed towards American Indians.

The US Army responded to the growth of worldwide terrorism by forming Special Forces Operational Detachment-Delta (1st SFOD-D) on July 20, 1978, at Fort Bragg. It had been prompted to do so by one Charles Beckwith, a former SF Vietnam veteran who had also served as an exchange officer with the British SAS during the Malayan Emergency. Against much initial resistance, Beckwith proposed that the US government establish a dedicated counterinsurgency and direct-action force along SAS lines, and eventually received authorization to do so in the mid 1970s. "Delta Force" was, and remains, one of the US armed forces' most shadowy SF units, the presence of its operatives attracting suspicious and often ill-informed speculation from outsiders. In a rather jealous response, another counterterrorist unit – named

March 1985, South Korea. A member of the 1st Special Forces guards the perimeter of the drop zone at Yoju Airfield after an airdrop during exercise Team Spirit '85. (NARA)

The burned-out wreckage of a US aircraft lies in the desert some 300 miles (482km) south of the Iranian capital after the abortive commando-style raid into Iran in April 1980, aimed at freeing the American hostages being held in Tehran. The disaster galvanized the US administration to improve the structure and coordination of special forces. (AP Photo)

"Blue Light" – was formed in 1977 by 5th SFGA and disbanded the following year: it was an hybrid Ranger, psychological operations, and civil affairs unit.

Delta Force would be involved in one of the most disastrous, and subsequently significant, operations in American SOF history – Operation *Eagle Claw*. The action was President Jimmy Carter's attempt to rescue 52 US hostages held captive in the US embassy in Tehran, Iran. The complex rescue plan involved Delta (on their first combat outing), USAF, and Marine Corps assets, but its execution on April 24–25 turned into an unmitigated disaster. The mission was aborted at its initial rendezvous site after only six of eight helicopters made it to the LZ, then a C-130 refueling aircraft crashed into one of the helicopters, resulting in a catastrophic explosion. Five airmen and three Marines died, and the remaining helicopters had to be abandoned at the LZ.

Eagle Claw was not only a tragedy but also a very public embarrassment for the US special ops community, and it prompted a huge amount of soul-searching within the Pentagon. By the end of the year, the Joint Special Operations Command (JSOC) had been established, with responsibility for coordinating inter-service training and operations between what are known as the "Tier 1" Special Mission Units (such as Delta, the Navy Special Warfare Development Group/DEVRGU, and the USAF's 24th Special Tactics Squadron). The USAF rationalized its special ops deployment teams under the

23rd Air Force established on February 10, 1983, which in 1990 evolved to become the Air Force Special Operations Command (AFSOC), responsible for all USAF SOF. Nevertheless, US SOF in their totality were still not placed under a unified command, and this situation made individual SOF forces prey to misuse by regular army commanders. Such was proved to be the case in 1983 during Operation *Urgent Fury*, the US-led invasion of Grenada. Evidence of this misuse fed into the two-year review of US defense structure that led to the Goldwater–Nichols Defense Reorganization Act of 1986. This sweeping change in the organization of the US military command apparatus also led to the creation of USSOCOM in April 1987. Although the birth of a unified SOF command was far from smooth, USSOCOM gave special operations forces a centralization that it had critically lacked at the beginning of the decade. General James Lindsay was to be the first US Commander in Chief Special Operations Command (USCINCSOC).

RANGERS

By the time that USSOCM came into being, the special ops capability of the US military had been expanded by the creation of several new SOF units, not least amongst the US Army Rangers. By the end of the Vietnam War, almost every Ranger company had been deactivated, but in 1974 the Department of the Army decided that the United States needed a force that could rapidly deploy worldwide, and two Ranger units, A and B, 75th

Camouflaged members of the 1/75th Rangers check their parachutes during in-flight rigging aboard a C-141 en route from Hunter Army Airfield to Tocumén/Torrijos Airports, Panama. (DOD)

RANGER BATTALIONS

Ranger regimental headquarters consists of a command group, a signal (communications) detachment (RSD – Regimental Signal Detachment), a fire support element, a reconnaissance detachment (RRD – Regimental Reconnaissance Detachment), a cadre for the Ranger Training Detachment (RTD), and a company headquarters. The RTD is responsible for running the Ranger Indoctrination Program (RIP), a three-week selection course for new recruits; the Ranger Orientation Program (ROP), a two-week program for Rangers returning to the regiment; and lastly, Pre-Ranger, a three-week course to prepare Rangers for the US Army Ranger School. Ranger School is a 58-day leadership course run by the School of Infantry's Ranger Training Brigade (RTB), not the 75th Ranger Regiment.

The three core Ranger battalions are identical in organization. Each battalion consists of three rifle companies and a headquarters and headquarters company (HHC). Each battalion is authorized 580 Rangers, although an additional 15 percent of personnel are allotted to make allowances for Rangers attending military schools. Each battalion must be able to deploy anywhere in the world within 18 hours notice. Ranger battalions are light infantry and have only a few vehicles and crew-served weapons

systems. They operate a minimum of antiaircraft and antiarmor weapons. Rangers can deploy for only a few days at a time as they lack the inherent support needed for longer operations. The three rifle companies are each assigned 152 Rangers. Their organization reflects that of the battalion, each comprising a headquarters and headquarters element, three rifle platoons, and a weapons platoon. The weapons platoon of each rifle company contains a mortar section, an antitank/armor section, and a sniper section.

The battalions alternate as the unit on Ready Reaction Force (RRF) 1, the force able to deploy within 18 hours of notification. RRF1 rotates among the three battalions, normally in 13-week periods. While on RRF1, the designated battalion is prohibited from conducting any off-post training or deployments to ensure that it can meet the required deployment time standards. Additionally, one rifle company with battalion command and control must be able to deploy within nine hours. The regimental headquarters remains on RRF1 at all times. Note that in 2006, the 75th Ranger Regiment added a 75th Special Troops Battalion which performs intelligence and reconnaissance missions previously performed by detachments from within the regular battalions.

Infantry (Ranger), provided the backbone of this force – the 1st and 2nd Battalion (Ranger), 75th Infantry. General Creighton Abrams, Army Chief of Staff and veteran tank commander of World War II, was the impetus behind the creation of the first battalion-sized Ranger units since 1945. He believed a tough and disciplined Ranger unit would set a high standard for the rest of the Army and that its influence would improve the entire Army. The Abrams Charter stipulated, "the Ranger Battalion to be an elite, light, and the most proficient infantry battalion in the world; a battalion that can do things with its hands and weapons better than anyone. The Battalion will contain no hoodlums or brigands and that if the battalion were formed of such, it should be disbanded. Wherever the Ranger Battalion goes, it is apparent that it is the best."

LEFT: RANGER FORCES, 1980S.
1) Specialist 4, Sniper, 1st Battalion (Ranger), 75th Infantry; Egypt, 1984. 2) Specialist 4, Building Clearing Team, 2nd Battalion (Ranger), 75th Infantry; Fort Lewis, Washington, 1981. 3) Private First Class, Squad Automatic Weapon Gunner, 3rd Battalion, 75th Ranger Regiment, Fort Benning, Georgia, 1986. 4) Sergeant First Class, HHC, 75th Ranger Regiment, Fort Benning, Georgia, 1986. (Ron Volstad © Osprey Publishing)

On January 25, 1974, Headquarters, United States Army Forces Command, published General Orders 127, directing the activation of the 1st Battalion (Ranger), 75th Infantry, with an effective date of January 31, 1974. On July 1, 1974, the 1st Battalion (Ranger), 75th Infantry, parachuted into Fort Stewart, Georgia. The 2nd Battalion (Ranger), 75th Infantry was activated shortly thereafter, on October 1, 1974. These units eventually established their headquarters at Hunter Army Airfield, Georgia, and Fort Lewis, Washington, respectively.

The modern Ranger battalions were first called to arms in 1980. Elements of 1st Battalion, 75th Infantry (Ranger) participated in the *Eagle Claw* disaster and in *Urgent Fury*. Despite the varying degree of problems associated with these missions, the exceptional reputation of the Rangers led to the creation of a third battalion and a regimental headquarters, both provisionally designated on July 1, 1984, with an effective date of October 3, 1984 at Fort Benning, Georgia, the Home of the Infantry. By February 2, 1986, the 75th Ranger Regiment was officially awarded the lineage and honors of all previous Ranger units. By the 1990s the 75th Ranger Regiment was composed of a headquarters and headquarters company, as well as three infantry battalions, but held in its ranks fewer than 2,000 Rangers. It was an all-male, homogeneous, strictly hierarchical, and severely disciplined combat unit, complete with its own rituals and idiosyncrasies. The cornerstone of Ranger missions was that of direct action, specifically, airfield seizures and raids. Ranger units conducted training that included movement-to-contact, ambush, reconnaissance, airborne and air assaults, hasty defense, infiltrating and exfiltrating by land, sea, and air, as well as the recovery of personnel and special equipment. A typical Ranger battalion mission involved seizing an airfield for use by follow-on, general-purpose forces (GPF) and conducting raids on key targets of operational or strategic importance.

All members of the 75th Ranger Regiment are given the opportunity to attend Ranger School. Ranger School was developed in the 1950s and although the term "Ranger" is used, the primary purpose of the school is to teach leadership skills. The course was, by the end of the 1990s, 58 days long (it is currently 61 days) and was composed of three phases that had evolved over the years. The description of its 1990s sequence, with some variations, largely holds true today.

THE BENNING PHASE

The Benning Phase had two parts. The first was conducted at Camp Rogers and included a physical fitness test in which the candidate had to complete 49 push-ups, 59 sit-ups, and a 2-mile (3.2km) run in running shoes within 15:12 minutes or less. Also to be completed were six chin-ups (palms facing toward the face), a combat water survival test, a 5-mile (8km) run, several 3-mile (5km) runs with an obstacle course, a 16-mile (26km) foot march, night and day land navigation tests, medical considerations class, rifle bayonet, and pugil stick and combative (hand-to-hand) exercises. Terrain association, demolitions, patrol base/ORP (Objective Rally Point – a location used for last minute procedure prior to the actual attack or mission), and an airborne refresher jump at Fryar Drop Zone completed this phase.

The second part was conducted at nearby Camp William O. Darby. At Camp Darby the emphasis was on squad combat patrol operations. The Ranger had to complete the Darby Queens Obstacle Course and learn the fundamentals of patrolling, the warning order/operations order format, and communications. The fundamental skills of combat patrol operations include battle drills, ambush and reconnaissance patrols, entering/clearing a room, and airborne and air assault operations. The Ranger student had to then demonstrate his expertise through a series of cadre and student-led tactical patrol operations.

Following the Benning Phase, students were transported to Camp Frank D. Merrill in Dahlonega, Georgia for the next step.

Private First Class Art Burgess, a candidate in the Ranger Indoctrination Program (RIP), 2nd Battalion, 75th Infantry (Ranger), fires a Winchester-built combat shotgun during special weapons training at Range 31 in 1982. The 12-gauge shotgun is a useful close-quarters weapon, having decisive take-down power at ranges of under 100yd (90m). (NARA)

THE MOUNTAIN PHASE

During the Mountain Phase, students were instructed in military mountaineering tasks as well as techniques for employing a squad and platoon for continuous combat patrol operations within a mountainous environment. They further developed their ability to command and control a platoon-size patrol through planning, preparing, and executing a variety of combat patrol missions. The Ranger student received five days of training on military mountaineering where he learned about knots, belays, anchor points, rope management, and the basic fundamentals of climbing and rappelling.

Security Team, 2nd Battalion (Ranger), 75th Infantry, Fort Lewis, Washington, 1981. An MI51A2 ¼-ton utility truck was used by security teams to move rapidly to their roadblock sites or other objectives when securing airfields. (Ron Volstad © Osprey Publishing)

At the conclusion of the Mountain Phase, the non–airborne-qualified personnel were taken by bus to the final phase of Ranger training, conducted at Camp Rudder, Florida. The airborne-qualified Rangers took a faster route, parachuting in from military transport.

US Army Rangers, 75th Ranger Battalion. 1) In common with other Rangers, this man wears jungle boots, Vietnam-era hot-weather fatigues, and the all-nylon web gear designated the ALICE System (for All-purpose, Lightweight, Individual Combat Equipment). 2) In addition to his normal ALICE equipment, this 2/75th rifleman wears the unique ammunition vest issued only to this battalion. Developed by a private contractor, who arranged a gratuitous issue to the unit, it was designed to carry various types of magazines and grenades. 3) The little-known 90mm M67 Recoilless Rifle was developed in the early 1960s as a company antitank weapon. A captured Soviet PK machine gun stands in the foreground. (Paul Hannon © Osprey Publishing)

THE FLORIDA PHASE

The objective of this phase was to sharpen the Ranger student's combat arms functional skills. He had to be capable of operating effectively under conditions of extreme mental and physical stress. This was accomplished through practical exercises in extended platoon-level patrol operations in a jungle/swamp environment.

Technique training included: small-boat operations, ship-to-shore operations, expedient stream-crossing techniques, and skills needed to survive and operate in a jungle/swamp environment. Upon completion of the Florida Phase of training, students conducted an airborne insertion into Fort Benning.

The distinct phases of Ranger School would stay with an individual forever, although few would be able to recall the daily events with clarity. Little sleep and even less food ground the Ranger student down over the subsequent eight weeks. Respite was given only a few hours at a time during the course. The rest of the time was spent patrolling, and at some point the Ranger had to lead his unit through a test patrol. One unique aspect of Ranger School was that the squad could "peer" individuals. This process allowed for a squad to eliminate some members who might not be pulling their weight or who stole food, a common occurrence. A number of individuals would quit or recycle because of an injury or inability to perform to the required standard. They would possibly try again when another class came through this particular phase of training.

Finally, the end was near, and the Ranger knew that short of a catastrophe he would graduate. The surviving group fun-jumped into Fort Benning and, finally, graduated from Ranger School. The black and gold tab was pinned onto their shoulders. Roughly 400 soldiers would begin the course and only 200 would make it to graduation. (It is worth mentioning that 99 percent of all battalion Rangers graduated the course.)

Once "tabbed," a Ranger could attend several military courses. These included free-fall parachuting courses teaching HAHO (High Altitude, High Opening) or HALO (High Altitude, Low Opening) techniques or possibly water operations related schools such as SCUBA (Self Contained Underwater Breathing Apparatus) or Scout Swimmer. He might also attend the Army Sniper School.

SEALS

The Rangers have given the Army one of its most potent SOF components, also capable of performing conventional operations when required. For the US Navy, its primary investment in SOF went into the expansion and refinement of the US Navy SEALs, under the control of a new service SOF command, the US Naval Special Warfare Command (NAVSPECWARCOM, NAVSOC), also established in 1987 as part of the system-wide shake-up of US defense.

By the end of the 1990s, the structure of the SEALs broke down as follows, according to the then-current *Special Operations Forces Reference Manual* issued by the US Army Command and General Staff College:

NAVAL SPECIAL WARFARE CENTER

The Naval Special Warfare Center, Naval Amphibious Base Coronado, is commanded by a captain (O-6), and is the schoolhouse for NSW training. The 26-week Basic Underwater Demolition/SEAL (BUD/S) course is held here as well as the nine-week Special Warfare Combatant Crewman (SWCC) course. It is also the venue for advanced maritime special operations training. A detachment is maintained at NAB Little Creek, Virginia, for the training of East Coast personnel.

NAVAL SPECIAL WARFARE DEVELOPMENT GROUP

The Naval Special Warfare Development Group, based at Little Creek, is commanded by a Navy captain (O-6). It tests, evaluates, and develops current and emerging technology, and also develops maritime, ground, and airborne tactics.

NAVAL SPECIAL WARFARE GROUPS

Two Naval Special Warfare (NSW) Groups, One and Two, are based at NABs Coronado and Little Creek, under the command of Echelon 2 captains (O6). Their role is to equip, support, and provide command and control elements. They provide SEAL and SDV (SEAL Delivery Vehicle – a submersible used for special ops) platoons and forces. They are organized into three SEAL teams, each composed of eight 16-man platoons; one SDV team; and small command and control elements outside the continental United States, to support NSW forces during operations.

NAVAL SPECIAL WARFARE COMMAND COMBAT SERVICE SUPPORT TEAMS (CSST)

One CSST is assigned to each NSW Group, and has three main mission elements: (operational) PLAN/CON (tingency) PLAN and crisis-action logistic planning and coordination; in-theater contracting, small purchase and lease actions; and forward operating base support. Additional tasks include force embarkation; load-planning; multi-modal transport co-ordination; combat cargo handling; in-theater logistic coordination; and exercise related construction. Its roles also cover infrastructure support; contingency

engineering; expeditionary camp siting, development, and maintenance; nuclear, biological, chemical (NBC) decontamination; and defensive combat planning and execution. The CSST also deals with military liaison officer/defense attaché officer liaison.

NAVAL SPECIAL WARFARE TASK GROUPS AND TASK UNITS

Naval Special Warfare Task Groups (NSWTG) and Task Units (NSWTU) are tailored to particular missions and can work independently, jointly, or in combined operations. Their missions include providing command and control elements, and administrative and logistical support.

SPECIAL BOAT SQUADRONS (SBS)

These are commanded by Echelon II captains at NABs Coronado and Little Creek, and provide special operations ships and craft. They comprise one or more active-duty or reserve-component Special Boat Units (SBUs) and Cyclone Class Patrol Coastal (PC) ships.

SPECIAL BOAT UNITS (SBUS)

These units are trained and equipped to operate a variety of special operations surface craft in maritime and riverine environments.

SEAL DELIVERY VEHICLE TASK UNIT

This is comprised of one or more SDV or SEAL platoons, and is led by an SDV Team commanding officer or executive officer. It carries out submersible systems operations from specially configured submarines equipped with Dry Deck Shelters (DDS).

SEAL PLATOON

The platoon is commanded by a Navy lieutenant (O-3), and consists of 16 SEALs. It can be divided into two squads or four elements. All SEALs are qualified in diving, parachuting, and demolition.

MOBILE COMMUNICATIONS TEAM

The communications-electronics departments of NSW Groups One and Two provide operational communications in support of NSW forces. They provide new equipment and develop tactics for communications operations and support, and prepare, implement, and review communications plans.

One element of this structure hidden from public gaze was, and remains, the innocuously titled DEVGRU, a Naval Special Warfare Development Group. Previously SEAL Team 6, its title was changed in 1987, and to this day neither the US Navy nor DOD will comment on either its existence or operations. Its exact operational remit,

US Navy BUD/S candidates conduct physical training exercises at the Naval Amphibious Base Coronado, California, April 6, 2011. The aquatic confidence of the candidates is tested to destruction in the BUD/S course. (US Navy)

therefore, is uncertain, but its primary focus is believed to be particularly high-risk counterinsurgency, assassination, and counter-weapons-proliferation operations, with natural specialties in coastal or riverine zones, or aquatic installations such as oil rigs. Its members have also been involved in VIP retrieval and hostage-rescue actions, such as recovering Haitian President Jean-Bertrand Aristide following the coup that deposed him in 1991. DEVGRU personnel were also part of Task Force Ranger during the infamous "Black Hawk Down" battle of Mogadishu in 1993 (see below), and assisted other SOF troops in tracking down war criminals in the fractured former Yugoslavia during the 1990s. Most recently, they have shot to unwelcome prominence via the killing of Osama bin Laden in his Pakistan compound on May 2, 2011.

The SEALs are undoubtedly the US Navy's premier elite, but the US Marine Corps has also kept pace with the rush for special-ops capable troops, particularly in its Marine recon units. The flexibility and aggressive mindset of Marine recon was soon put to good use during the rough decades of the 1970s and 1980s. In 1988 a recon team supporting naval and joint task forces "took down" Iranian oil platforms during the "Tanker War" in the Persian Gulf. Marines were summoned to respond to instability in Central America, when Operation *Just Cause* was launched in Panama in December 1989. By 1990 amphibious and ground reconnaissance units in the Fleet Marine Force included two force reconnaissance companies, with two in reserve. The Marine divisions had three reconnaissance battalions and one in reserve. Also in that year the Iraqi invasion of Kuwait led to the largest movement of Marine Corps forces since World War II, and the Marine recon forces had a major new theater in which to demonstrate their adventurous professionalism.

As we have seen so far in this chapter, special ops were revitalized at both structural and conceptual levels during the later decades of the Cold War and beyond. Nor can this chapter do full justice to the range of new SOF units that came into existence during this period. An overview of some of these units, however, reveals the breadth of special ops capability the United States had gained by the new millennium.

160TH SPECIAL OPERATIONS AVIATION REGIMENT (AIRBORNE)

The 160th Special Operations Aviation Regiment (Airborne), aka the "Night Stalkers," specializes in high-risk aviation deployments, supporting the US military's SOF community. Although its foundations were laid during World War II, the 160th's existence really began in October 1981 with the establishment of 160th Aviation Battalion, which became the 160th Special Operations Aviation Group (Airborne) in 1986, then the 160th SOAR(A) in 1990.

A US Army Night Stalker crew chief mans a M240 7.62mm belt-fed machine gun fitted to a firing port in a MH-47G Chinook helicopter. (US Army)

The regiment consists of a headquarters, four battalions, and a training company, and its pilots are some the best combat aviators in the world. Note that, in a similar manner to the Rangers, the personnel of the 160th are triple volunteers: for the Army, airborne, and the regiment. A recent US Army Special Operations Command (USASOC) update on the battalion describes its aviation composition thus:

> Each battalion also has a strategic composition of light, medium and heavy helicopters, all highly modified in design to meet the unit's unique mission requirements. Regiment reorganization modifying the 160th fleet composition was approved in October 2007 and will be implemented over the next several years. Currently, 1st Bn. has one AH-6 Little Bird helicopter company, one MH-6 Little Bird helicopter company and three companies of MH-60 Black Hawk helicopters; 2nd Bn. has two MH-47 Chinook helicopter companies; and 3rd and 4th Bns. each have two MH-47 Chinook helicopter companies and one MH-60 Black Hawk helicopter company. Each battalion also has a Headquarters and Headquarters Company and a maintenance company.
>
> – http://www.soc.mil/160th/160th%20Overview.html

Given the natural connection between SOF's covert operations and the 160th's night-flying capability, the air unit has been in great demand since its foundation. In Operation

Prime Chance in the Persian Gulf in 1987–89, pilots from the 160th flew sea-skimming nighttime operations to intercept Iranian minelaying vessels, working in cooperation with SEAL teams and Marine units. In one particularly dramatic encounter, on September 21, 1987 the special ops pilots strafed and rocketed an Iranian minelayer, the *Iran Ajr*, an attack that killed five Iranian sailors. Later a SEAL unit successfully boarded and captured the ship, allowing demolitions experts to scuttle the vessel after the remaining Iranian sailors had been taken off to safety. The 160th SOAR was then heavily used during the 1990–91 Gulf War, deploying numerous SOF teams to key targets around Kuwait and Iraq.

AIR FORCE SPECIAL OPERATIONS COMMAND

In 1990, the USAF formed its own SOF unified command, AFSOC, located at the MacDill Air Force Base in Florida. Underneath this umbrella organization has developed an extensive range of units and capabilities, which today have grown to incorporate some 16,000 personnel. These units include the 23rd Air Force, 1st and 27th Special Operations Wings, the 352nd and 353rd Special Operations Groups, 720th and 724th Special Tactics Groups, and various Air National Guard bodies. Tactical capabilities are extremely broad, and include "battlefield air operations; agile combat support; aviation foreign internal defense; information operations; precision aerospace fires; psychological operations; specialized air mobility; specialized refueling; and intelligence, surveillance and reconnaissance" (http://www.afsoc.af.mil/library/factsheets/factsheet.asp?id=13745).

USAF Pararescuemen assigned to the 301st Rescue Squadron (RQS), perform a High Altitude, Low Opening parachute jump over Tallil Air Base, Iraq, during Operation *Iraqi Freedom*. (USAF)

US Army Special Forces troops, 1980s. 1) Staff Sergeant, A Detachment Radio Operator, 10th SFGA, Fort Devens, Massachusetts, 1983. 2) Major, B Detachment Commander, 5th SFGA, Exercise "Bright Star," Egypt, 1982. 3) Sergeant Major, Staff NCO, 1st Special Operations Command, Fort Bragg, North Carolina, 1984. (Ron Volstad © Osprey Publishing)

The aircraft these formations use are equally diverse, from helicopters to AC-130 Spectre gunships, and during the Gulf War they were applied to powerful effect. Sikorsky MH-53 Pave Low helicopters attacked Iraqi radar installations at the beginning of the air campaign, and performed behind the lines rescues of downed Coalition aircrew. More destructively, MC-130 Combat Talon crews dropped enormous 15,000lb (6,800kg) BLU-82 "Daisy Cutter" bombs on hideously exposed Iraqi positions, but also used the same aircraft for "psyops" (psychological operations) leaflet drops over more fortunate troop concentrations. Being both a combat arm and an SOF support organization, AFSOC found itself being used with equal pace in the "War on Terror" following the 9/11 attacks on the United States.

INTELLIGENCE SUPPORT ACTIVITY

SEAL Team 6/DEVGRU and Delta Force, for all their attempted secrecy, are virtually household names. The same cannot be said, however, for the US Army Intelligence Support Activity (USAISA, or just ISA). ISA's place in the SOCOM pantheon was established in 1980, in the form of the Field Operations Group (FOG). FOG was specifically tasked with intelligence gathering, either human intelligence (HUMINT) or signals intelligence (SIGINT) in support of SOF operations. Its initial operations were in Iran following *Eagle Claw*, but when operations there ended in 1981 FOG was actually expanded and became the ISA.

A pair of Force Recon Marines, with the 1st Force Recon Company, wearing closed-circuit rebreathers, exit the water during a training course. (USMC)

ISA personnel were kept busy throughout the 1980s and 1990s, being deployed to Nicaragua and El Salvador to provide counterinsurgency support to indigenous troops; Italy in the early 1980s to help Italian security forces track down the Red Brigades kidnappers of Brigadier General James L. Dozier; and Southeast Asia in an attempt to track down missing Vietnam War POWs. Since 2001, they have been heavily committed to the actions in Iraq, Afghanistan, and Pakistan, including assisting the tracking down of Saddam Hussein in 2003 and Osama bin Laden in 2011.

Note that in 2003, ISA was renamed the Mission Support Activity (MSA), then from 2005 was given a series of changing biannual codenames, such as "Grey Fox" and "Intrepid Spear." The unit is believed to number only a few hundred personnel, and all are trained to the highest degree, not only in all aspects of intelligence gathering, but also in foreign languages and SOF combat tactics.

A platoon of Force Recon team operators (USMC) battle their Combat Rubber Reconnaissance Craft (CRRC) against the surf, a skill they learned during their days in the Basic Recon Course. (USMC)

MARINE UNITS

The Maritime Special Purpose Force (MSPF) was a special-ops capable unit established within the Marine Corps during the 1990s. Rather like the US Navy SEALs, the MSPF was intended for covert amphibious actions and high-risk raids in littoral zones, deploying by various specialist means such as the Diver Propulsion Device (DPD) or airborne infiltration provided by the Marine Air-Ground Task Force's Marine Expeditionary Unit (MEU) Aviation Combat Element. (Note that unlike the self-

Marine Recon troops, 1970s. 1) Division recon, Vietnam, 1970. Uniforms and equipment for recon units were tailored to the task at hand. Improvements resulted from experience, increased funding and availability in Vietnam. 2) Static line parachute pathfinder, Panama, 1974. After Vietnam, reconnaissance units conducted training deployments with a mix of old and new uniforms and equipment that reflected budget constraints and expanding security responsibilities. This force recon Marine is being inspected prior to a pathfinder mission requiring a parachute jump from a C-130 onto the Gatun Drop Zone. 3) Static line parachutist, rough terrain, Arizona, 1975. Rough terrain suits and tree-jumping techniques were developed by the US Forest Service "smoke jumpers," used by the British in Malaya, and adopted by the US Army in Korea and Vietnam. (Paul Hannon © Osprey Publishing)

Marine Recon troops, 1980s. 1) Recon scout, SEATO, 1981. 2) Free-fall parachutist, Direct Action Team, 1988.
3) Closed-circuit combat swimmer, Mediterranean, 1988. (Paul Hannon © Osprey Publishing)

sufficiency of many SOF units, the MSPF cannot operate independently of the conventional MEU.)

The skill sets of the MSPF have expanded with time, and now include capabilities such as forward air controller (FAC), sniper support, SIGINT gathering and electronic warfare. As such, the small number of personnel who join the MSPF receive training comparable to the best of better-known SOF. The MSPF is organized into command, assault, security, and support elements.

Alongside the MSPF, the Marines have also established the Marine Corps Security Force Regiment, another elite added its SOF remit from 1987. The SFR is a dedicated Marine counter-terrorism force, with further responsibilities for protecting high-value maritime installations, such as weapons stations or ships handling nuclear weapons. Sub-divisions of the SFR include the Fleet Antiterrorism Security Team (FAST) and Recapture Tactics Teams (RTTs), the former specializing in the rapid deployment to protect vital installations, while the latter is a SWAT-style combat force already in deployment around vulnerable installations. Both RTTs and FASTs are experts in close-quarters combat, the use of specialist lethal and non-lethal weaponry, marksmanship, and Methods of Entry (MoE) techniques.

It is evident from the units described above – a far from exhaustive list – that the US SOF community has grown prodigiously in scope and rationale in the last 50 years. Today the United States operates SOF with a size and power greater than those of many

ADDITIONAL COURSES AVAILABLE TO MCSF MARINES

Combat Hunter Course	Sergeants Course
Tactical Site Exploitation Course	Staff Academy
HMMWV Driver Course	Mountain Survival Course
BEAR/BEARCAT Driver Course	Mountain Leaders Course
Survival, Evasion, Resistance, Escape School Level B	Basic Jungle Skills Course
Pre-Scout Sniper Course (for Senior DMs in FAST, RTT, and Cadre units)	Jungle Leaders Course
	HRST Master Course
Scout Sniper School (for Senior DMs in FAST, RTT, and Cadre units)	Marine Combat Instructor of Water Survival School
	Formal Marksmanship Training Coaches Course
Infantry Squad Leaders Course	Formal Marksmanship Training Trainers Course
Infantry Unit Leaders Course	Advanced Urban Combat (FAST Company only, equivalent to Close Quarters Battle School)
Martial Arts Instructor Course	
Martial Arts Instructor Trainer School	Urban Leaders Course (MOUT Instructor Course, Convoy Course, Urban Shooting Skills Course, Foreign Weapons Course)
Corporals Course	

national armies. It is also a community that has proven itself in combat time and time again. It would take many volumes to explore and explain all the hundreds of operations that US SOF were involved in during the 1970s to 1990s. Here, however, we will look at some key actions conducted by specific units, using these as illustrations of what remarkable soldiers can achieve, while at the same time acknowledging that oft-forgotten truth – even special forces soldiers are human beings, physically vulnerable and just as capable of making mistakes.

SEALS – GRENADA, 1983

On October 25, 1983, the United States invaded the small Caribbean island of Grenada. The US viewed the ever-increasing presence of Cuban workers and advisers as a threat to its hegemony over the region and invaded under the pretext that American students were in harm's way as civil war was threatening to erupt.

Members of the 82nd Airborne Division aboard a heavily loaded M151 light vehicle prepare to depart for Grenada during Operation *Urgent Fury*. The US invasion of Grenada saw the heavy use of both airborne units and SOF. (US Army)

Navy SEALs conducted four missions during the invasion: the reconnaissance of Point Salines airfield and emplacement of navigational beacons there; the special reconnaissance of Pearls airfield; the assault on the Radio Free Grenada transmitting station; and the assault and hostage rescue at the Governor-General's mansion.

POINT SALINES AIRFIELD RECONNAISSANCE AND BEACON EMPLACEMENT

The SEALs were tasked with two missions on October 23. The first was to acquire timely intelligence on Point Salines airfield. This included a reconnaissance of the airfield tarmac to find out if it was free of any debris or obstacles that could impede the American forces whose job was to seize it. The other was to place navigational beacons to help guide US aircraft carrying two under-strength battalions of the 75th Infantry (Rangers) whose primary mission was to carry out a parachute assault on the airfield, seize it, and secure it.

Sixteen members of SEAL Team 6 were aboard two MC 130 E Combat Talons, each of which carried a 25ft (7.6m) fiberglass Light Patrol Boat. Team 6, which was based at Dam Neck, Virginia, was the US Navy's crack anti-terrorist unit, numbering fewer than 180 personnel. The SEALs were set to conduct a combat waterborne parachute drop, get into their Boston Whalers, and rendezvous with the USS *Clifton Sprague* where the commandos would link up with three additional SEALs and three combat controllers from the Air Force. From that point on the combined special operations team would infiltrate the surrounding beach areas with their boats and carry out their primary mission.

Intelligence at Grenada was spartan at best. Accurate maps did not exist and there hadn't been enough time for proper planning. Initial plans included deploying from a submarine, but, as Major Mark Adkin explained in *Urgent Fury: The Battle for Grenada*, the SEALs in Puerto Rico had not yet been trained to properly deploy from that particular submarine. What would have been considered a standard naval commando infiltration, the insertion of frogmen via submarine, was null and void due to a training shortfall. Therefore, the operation shifted to the waterborne method via parachute jump. This is risky, no matter what sort of conditions it is conducted under. Heavy gear and the unpredictability of the ocean would surely have made this one of the most hazardous ways of getting the SEALs in. As is typical with many special operations forces in combat, rucksacks are overloaded with heavier live ammunition (blank training rounds weigh much less) and other mission-essential war materiel.

The excess gear and equipment, partly the byproduct of the certain sense of invincibility not uncommon in elite troops, had tragic results for some of the men. Despite the recommended weight being no more than 60lb (27kg), the average SEAL probably carried more than 100lb (45kg) for the jump. This phenomenon of packing more than necessary also has its roots in the fact that, like all special operations forces, SEALs tend to be lightly armed and have to be able to sustain a firefight when compromised. Another factor was probably that the Grenadian forces, the People's Revolutionary Army (PRA), around the objective at Point Salines had mechanized units equipped with BTR 60 armored personnel carriers and BRDMs equipped with 12.7mm antiaircraft cannons. The PRA numbered around 5,000 troops. An encounter with any part of such a force could prove fatal if the commandos did not have enough firepower to handle the possible contact.

Although the operation was scheduled to take place during dusk, a delay forced the men into a nighttime jump. Undoubtedly, the excess weight was a handicap. More importantly, weather conditions had deteriorated. The surface wind at sea level was about 25 knots (46km/h), whereas 18-knot (33km/h) gusts were considered the limit for a combat jump. The MC-130s flew below radar at 600ft (182m) until they approached the insertion point. The aircraft climbed to 2,000ft (610m) and, after each aircraft had unloaded its Boston Whaler, the SEALs jumped into the night.

The standard operating procedure for waterborne jumps requires that the paratrooper loosen his parachute harness as he nears the water. This allows him to get clear of the canopy that can easily entangle and snare him. In effect, the paratrooper nearly jumps out of his harness. This is a tricky maneuver and must be practiced regularly. The darkness added to the difficulty of a task where timing is everything. That, along with the unpredictability of the water and the weight of the equipment the men were carrying, led to the deaths of four Navy SEALs. The eight men from the first plane lost three members and had to survive in the open sea until they were picked up by the *Clifton Sprague*. The second team, which lost one man, got on to their boat and made rendezvous with the ship. After linking up, the teams, accompanied by their Air Force controllers, headed for the beach.

A Grenadian patrol boat forced the commandos to retreat. Undeterred, they attempted to infiltrate the area the next night, October 24, but once again encountered an enemy vessel. The SEALs cut their engine and waited. Unable to restart it the men drifted helplessly out to sea where they were picked up 11 hours later by the *Clifton Sprague*.

The mission for the Navy SEALs of Team 6 had ended in utter failure. Everything that could go wrong had done. The airborne Rangers would capture the airfield at Point Salines without any accurate intelligence or navigational aid.

RADIO FREE GRENADA TRANSMITTING STATION

Eight SEALs from Team 6 on board a Black Hawk helicopter were tasked to seize and hold a Soviet-built radio transmitting station at Beausejour on the west coast of Grenada on October 24–25. The intention was to prevent the PRA communicating with the

Rangers in the invasion of Grenada, 1983. During one of the follow-on missions in Grenada, Rangers were airlifted by US Marine Corps CH-46s. As they neared their objective they came under heavy fire, and one helicopter crash-landed. Several Rangers nearly drowned and were ordered to drop rucksacks as they scrambled out of the partially submerged chopper. This man wears the Vietnam-era OG 107 (olive green, Army shade 107) jungle fatigues. His patrol cap was lost and his Ranger "high-and-tight" hair cut is clearly visible. The Ranger carries the M16A1 rifle and the M-67 90mm recoilless rifle. (Michael Welply © Osprey Publishing)

SOF troops in Grenada, 1983. 1) Delta Force, Special Operations Command. 2) US Army Ranger, 2/75th Ranger Battalion.
3) Aircrewman, 16th Special Operations Squadron, USAF. This AC-130 Spectre crewman wears standard CWU-27 flight suit,
steel-toed flying boots, and GR-FRP-1 flying gloves. (Ron Volstad © Osprey Publishing)

civilian population; they had earlier broadcast the news of the American invasion. The SEALs were then to wait for an American relief force. The radio station could then be used by US forces to broadcast information to the local population.

As with most of the operations during *Urgent Fury*, few details existed on enemy troop disposition and strength. Detailed maps of the particular region were not available. Logistical delays meant that the element of surprise was lost. Nonetheless, the eight men went in and secured their objective.

Two security elements were then sent out to engage any enemy reaction forces. Two men secured the road to the north while two others situated themselves along the southern route. They were armed with M60 machine guns and M72 light antitank weapons. Soon a PRA truck was successfully ambushed to the north, and five enemy soldiers were killed. Not long afterwards a PRA reaction force, led by a BTR 60, advanced from Fort Frederick to the south, and the SEAL element engaged it near a bridge. PRA soldiers tried to flank the American position while the armored personnel carrier pinned down the commandos. An experimental rocket, the 66mm RAW, may have been used to destroy the vehicle. Unable to sustain long periods of contact and having no air support to suppress the Grenadians, the SEALs decided to withdraw. The PRA recaptured the transmitting station as the SEALs fought their way through to the beach where they hid in a well-camouflaged site. After another short engagement, the commandos escaped out to sea. Subsequent air strikes launched from the carrier USS *Independence* and an artillery bombardment from the USS *Caron* failed to topple the transmitting mast.

ASSAULT ON THE GOVERNOR-GENERAL'S MANSION

The last SEAL mission during Operation *Urgent Fury* took place simultaneously to the transmitter raid. Two Black Hawks with 23 commandos from SEAL Team 6 were assigned to launch an assault on the British Governor-General's mansion near St George on the west coast of Grenada. The Governor-General, Paul Scoon, was under house arrest along with his staff.

The assault began late and ran straight into trouble when the men were unable to locate the residence due to the density of vegetation, which in turn camouflaged known points. Enemy small arms fire greeted the special forces, but they were soon able to identify their objective. Both elements successfully executed a 90ft (27m) fast-rope insertion. However, one Navy SEAL officer, three State Department officials, and the only satellite radio available to communicate with headquarters on the USS *Guam* were left with the helicopters as small arms fire forced the aircraft to hurriedly withdraw.

The remaining 22 SEALs successfully overwhelmed a few local police officers, secured the staff and the Governor-General, and consolidated their position. Air evacuation proved impossible due to the increasing ground fire. Soon the commandos were surrounded by the PRA as a BTR 60 attempted to punch through the main gate. Although the PRA attack was driven off, it became clear that immediate assistance was needed. Isolated and without the satellite radio, the SEALs still managed to communicate with higher command, and two Marine Corps Cobra gunships came to their aid. Both Cobras were shot down by hostile fire. Subsequently, and from a greater distance, AC-130 gunships started to create a ring of steel around the beleaguered Americans. For over four hours, Spectre gunships would rotate and remain on station, and by night Navy A7 attack aircraft from the *Independence* flew in support of the SEALs. Finally, on October 26, units from the 22nd Marine Amphibious Unit relieved the commandos.

MARINE RECON – GULF WAR, 1990–91

The Gulf War was a conflict of massive SOF activity. Every conceivable type of special-ops unit and soldier swarmed over the battlefields and behind the lines, conducting operations ranging from SIGINT gathering to SCUD missile hunting. The Marine recon forces were part of this activity, as well as part of the thunderous combat resources of the Corps itself. Between August and December 1990, some 24 infantry battalions, 40 air squadrons, and more than 92,000 Marines were deployed to the Persian Gulf as part of the I Marine Expeditionary Force (MEF). Operation *Desert Storm* was launched on January 16, 1991, the same day as the air battle began. The ground attack began on February 24 when the 1st and 2nd Marine Divisions, supported by the 3rd Marine Aircraft Wing, breached defense lines and stormed into Kuwait. At the same time, the hovering threat from two Marine brigades at sea nearby held some 50,000 Iraqis in check along the Kuwaiti coast. By the morning of February 28, 100 hours after the ground battle started, almost the entire Iraqi Army in Kuwait and adjacent areas of Iraq was encircled, with 4,000 tanks destroyed and 42 divisions destroyed or rendered ineffective.

With the I MEF was the 1st Force Reconnaissance Company, reinforced by detachments from the 2nd, 3rd, and 4th Companies. The 1st and 2nd Reconnaissance Battalions, and elements of the 3rd Battalion, served with the two divisions ashore and the two brigades at sea. Initially, observation posts were set up along the Kuwaiti border and motorized patrols were conducted by force and division recon teams. Facilitated by satellite communications, digital terminals, and global positioning systems, these teams were tasked with "scouting the forward edge of enemy lines and division routes." Prior to the ground offensive, reconnaissance patrols took some 238 prisoners.

Probing ahead of main forces, recon units engaged in combat early, and the Iraqi advance into Khafji in January 1991 bypassed several patrols in the town, where they continued to call artillery and air down on Iraqi armor. Division reconnaissance units

A USAF combat controller (CCT) uses his radio to guide an overhead C-130 taking part in a HALO parachute jump. CCTs were used to control US and Coalition air assets during the Gulf War, with devastating effect against Iraqi forces. (USAF)

were assigned to the mechanized task forces formed for the ground offensive, with duties including identifying obstacles and navigating routes through the fortified lines established to defend Kuwait. Army general Norman Schwarzkopf reported to the Joint Chiefs of Staff that for a week Marines "from the reconnaissance units have been crawling through all that stuff. They've been crawling all night and hiding all day and they have penetrated all the way through." Given the Marines' success in passing through minefields, wire, and obstacles to mark lanes for the attack, Schwarzkopf felt that "when the ground war begins it will be like Broadway."

A final note: on February 26, 1991, an advance patrol from 2nd Force Reconnaissance Company drove up to the abandoned US embassy in Kuwaiti city, guided by Kuwaiti resistance fighters, just ahead of the SF assigned to liberate the embassy complex.

Overshadowed by the Gulf War are a number of other events demonstrating the Corps' flexible and rapid response. These included evacuations in Liberia and Somalia to rescue diplomats and civilians, and humanitarian efforts in Bangladesh, the Philippines, and northern Iraq. These actions brought changes and new employment for recon. The differences between the two types of Marine reconnaissance units and their roles were highlighted. Force recon was bolstered, while the division structure was challenged by the need for maneuver regiments to have mobile recon units in direct support. The management advantage of the SR Intelligence Group was inhibited by the mixing of personnel, and by reliance on technical collection of intelligence that neglected ground reconnaissance. The 1990s appeared to be another period of change for Marine recon after their recent war and peacekeeping endeavors.

The 50-year milestone found recon units in a state of transition, and in the position of preparing for the next war with limited budgets – the modern military dilemma. In a reversal of the Vietnam era, when division-level recon was emphasized, the stress is now placed on the force reconnaissance unit and direct-action as a special operations unit. Division recon is undergoing reconsideration, and has yet to find a satisfactory solution. Typically, some commands have changed while others retain the force and division reconnaissance structure that has served for more than 30 years. The patrolling watchword – "Don't believe anything you hear, and only half of what you see" – should also be remembered by recon-watchers trying to follow these evolutions. Recon doctrine, organization, and utilization ultimately depend on the terrain and situation which alone determine what can be accomplished. Such is true of all SOF.

Marine Recon troops, 1990. 1) Recon scout-sniper, North Carolina. The Marine Corps scout-sniper school at Quantico, Virginia, produced the weapons and training needed for an effective "peacetime" sniping program. 2) Direct Action Team, Liberia, dressed and equipped for action during Operation *Sharp Edge*. 3) Recon scout, Persian Gulf. This recon scout exhibits the uniform and equipment worn by force and division units during operations *Desert Shield* and *Desert Storm*. (Paul Hannon © Osprey Publishing)

A team of US Navy SEALs circles the US Embassy compound on February 28, 1991, in Kuwait City in a heavy armored Chenowth LSV dune buggy while Marines secure the embassy grounds. (Christophe Simon/AFP/Getty Images)

RANGERS – MOGADISHU, 1993

Rangers practice Military Operations in Urban Terrain (MOUT) regularly and have provided Delta Force with a security force since 1980. However, as city fighting has become a more common occurrence throughout the world, the Ranger Regiment has built more of this specialized training into its schedule. In Somalia in 1993, Rangers were called into action in the capital, Mogadishu, as part of a combined force tasked to apprehend the Somali warlord, Mohamed Farrah Hassan Aidid. Ranger John Collett recalls in simple and powerful prose the experiences of the Rangers' desperate fight to save the lives of downed crewmen in the heartland of the enemy in Somalia.

It started out as every Sunday had in the four weeks since we arrived in the Mog [Mogadishu]. We woke up when we wanted. There was no first call on Sundays. Everyone was playing volleyball and tanning as usual. All in all, we hadn't hit the ground on a mission for about two weeks. Then word came that we were getting orders to go on a mission. It was October 3, 1993. It didn't occur to anyone until later that the 3rd Ranger Battalion had been formed nine years earlier on this same day.

We got our equipment on as usual, putting on our bullet-proof vests, LCE, K-pot (Kevlar). I carried an M-249 SAW [Squad Automatic Weapon]. This was a day-mission so no night vision devices were taken. I had 950 rounds of 5.56mm ammunition and one frag [fragmentation grenade]. We moved to the aircraft which was already spun up. As usual the Little Birds [helicopters] took off first. The Hardy Boys [Delta Force] gave us the thumbs up as they usually did when they flew by. When the bird takes off is when the adrenaline starts pumping. We had two "brown-outs" where we could see nothing, but the pilot held tight and got us right on target. Tin was blowing off the roofs of buildings; people were getting blown around below us. We got the signal to ready the fast rope. I looked at Sgt Ramaglia and we were both making the Catholic cross at the same time. This was our 7th mission and the first time I made the sign of the cross. It felt different this time. As we hovered over the Somalis, waiting to fast rope down, they were waving to us to come down and play, so we did. I hit the ground, got up against a building and started pulling security up the street. There was sporadic gunfire all around us. We ID'd [identified] our target building, then RPGs [rocket propelled grenades] started going off. I saw one of the birds smoking so I knew it had been hit. PFC Errico and SPC [Specialist] DeJesus were engaging targets down the alley, also saying there were people in the trees and the building windows shooting at us.

The Humvees pulled up about then and Sergeant Strucker got out and started talking to Sergeant First Class Watson. The .50-cal on top of the Humvee started hosing [killing] people that were shooting at us. It's funny that at that time I thought to myself, "shit – another mission I won't get to fire my SAW." I could have never been more wrong. We got word that in fact a bird [helicopter] had gone down about two blocks away and that we were going to have to secure it. The Humvees moved out [to take an injured Ranger back to base]. As we were moving, the fire from the enemy increased. Branches were falling from the trees as gunfire hit them. Bullets have a very distinctive sound when they are being shot at you,

The wreckage of an American helicopter sits in Mogadishu, Somalia on October 14, 1993. This Black Hawk helicopter, which was used to root out ammo caches, was shot down by Somali warlords. It was part of the 160th SOAR. (Photo by Scott Peterson/Liaison/Getty Images)

Ranger, B Company, 3/75th Ranger Regiment, Operation *Desert Storm*, 1991. He is wearing the three-pattern desert camouflage uniform, while his Kevlar camouflage cover is of the six-pattern variety. The M16A2 sling is modified to make it more functional when fast-roping from a Black Hawk helicopter. The Ranger Body Armor (RBA) was specifically manufactured for this mission, and was designed by the US Army Natick Research Center. (Michael Welply © Osprey Publishing)

and not away from you. As we were proceeding up the previous alley, SFC Watson was on the left side of the street and I was on the right. Bullets were hitting above our heads as we were moving out at a trot. He looked over at me, as casual as can be, and said, "This sucks."

We were taking fire from the building from people sticking AK-47s and older weapons around the corner and spraying them in our general direction. I yelled at Sergeant Ramaglia to put a 40mm round [M-203] in the alley. He fired a round and it was short, blowing up about 10 meters in front of our position. I told him it was short. He fired a second round and it hit square into the building, blowing it up. We didn't receive near as much effective fire from that corner after that.

SFC Watson knew we were taking a hell of a crossfire, so he pulled PFC Neathery back and put him in the middle of the road behind a rock, a position I would soon occupy for many hours. They threw a frag at us. I looked up and saw it coming through the trees.

Mogadishu, October 1993. Rangers from B Company, 3/75th Ranger Regiment fight their way through multiple ambushes in the labyrinth of Somalia's capital city, receiving continual heavy small-arms fire. The Humvees are Kevlar armored, and equipped with Mk 19 automatic grenade launchers and .50-cal machine guns. (Michael Welply © Osprey Publishing)

I saw the spoon hit the ground. It landed about 15m in front of our position and exploded. PFC Errico yelled "Frag." We hit the ground as it exploded. Doe caught some shrapnel in the leg. Errico caught some in the ankle. SFC Watson told us to start pulling back so we could defend until night.

We laid down suppressive fire and a Ranger shot a "sammy" [Somali] in the face. A few seconds later he got shot in the right arm and yelled, "I'm hit." I was in the prone position at that time in the middle of the road behind some rocks and a mound of dirt. In this position it was hard for the "sammys" to effectively engage me. I had a great field of fire. I looked back to watch some Rangers and Delta move up the street we were on. Just as I looked back at them one of the D-boys got shot in the head. It rocked his head back and blood went everywhere. The man behind him grabbed him and started pulling him back to cover. He got shot in the neck. When he got shot he put his hands to his face and screamed. I thought, "shit." I knew the shit had hit the fan.

A Ranger asked SFC Watson for some frags. SFC Watson, in his irritated voice, said: "Use the LAW on your back." The Ranger looked back, puzzled, "The LAW, mother [expletive]." He smiled and pulled the LAW off his back, extended it and fired. A few minutes later a "sammy" walked in front of our position, all chilled out, like nothing was going on. He looked at me and our other positions. I guess he was a recon man, well he didn't get to tell much. Someone behind him yelled something, as the "sammy" turned I saw an AK-47 under his shirt. The recon was over. I laid a good burst at him and at the same instant PFC Floyd opened up. The "sammy" staggered and fell behind a building. A few minutes later though, a grenade landed about 2 meters in front of me. I thought, "Oh shit," and put my head behind a K-pot sized rock in from of me. I remember thinking, "This is it." The grenade blew up and knocked me around a bit. I looked up and Specialist Kurth was yelling at me. I couldn't understand what he was saying. I looked over and gave SFC Watson the thumbs up. I was happy that I was still alive. [Shortly thereafter] a Sammy came out of a corridor with an RPG and Floyd and I lit him up. He was gone with a puff of smoke. I guess an RPG exploded when we shot him.

Ammo conservation was a big thing. SFC Watson kept reminding us to keep controlled bursts, which we did. We stayed in this position until dark. When it got dark, we started withdrawing to the buildings behind me where we would set up our defenses for the night. We marked our position with an IR strobe, placing it on the roof of the building we were in. This was done so the Little Birds (helicopters) could start doing their gun runs. I've never felt so much relief as when they started lighting up the buildings around us with 7.62 mini guns and 2½ inch rockets. The decision was made that we would stay here until the reaction forces could get us out.

Several hours later it was decided that we needed to move to the next building. Before making the move, a Black Hawk came in and made an IV and ammo resupply [drop].

[During the short time the bird was hovering, it was] blazing away with the mini guns. They were taking all kinds of fire. Any time a bird came into the area the enemy fire would pick up.

We were told that the reaction forces were on the way. The Little Birds continued to do gun runs and to fire rockets. They kept our spirits up. Floyd and I were pulling guard on the window that we climbed through to enter the courtyard. An RPG was shot at us. The location where the RPG came from was marked with a tracer and blown up with a rocket. After that, the RPG fire tapered off. I kept looking at my watch wondering where the reaction force was. I was praying a lot for all of us. The firing from the enemy lulled a little bit. We found a spigot and we started doing a water resupply by putting canteens on a stick and passing them through the window next door to where the casualties were. This particular water resupply wasn't taught in Ranger School, that's for damn sure.

At about 04:00 the reaction forces finally linked up with us. We gave the Ranger running password. At about 05:45 they had finally recovered the bodies at the crash site. We were told that there wasn't enough room in the APCs [armored personnel carriers] for us. Therefore we would be exfilling by foot, that's when the Mogadishu 500 began. It was a mad dash for our lives. The sun was up and thus began a new day in the Mog. We started to move with the APCs next to us trying to provide cover. Fire was coming from everywhere. The APCs took off and left us – that sucked. Bullets started hitting all around us. I remember I felt something hit my arm and knock me back. I looked over and there was a gash in my BDU, knocking the American flag off my arm. The same bullet that grazed me hit Sgt Ramaglia in the side, taking out a good chunk of meat. I told him he was hit and for him not to worry about it. We crossed the street and continued the Mog 500. Gunfire was coming from everywhere. We passed a 5-ton truck that had been blown up. There was blood all over the streets. We kept pushing on. We turned a corner and there were two tanks sitting in the road, what a sight. We all got under cover near the tanks. Nearby was a tan Humvee that had "security police" written on the side. A guy was in the turret. The guy got shot in the neck. One of the tanks fired a round at the building where the gunfire came from. The entire building was leveled. I thought "holy shit." We started moving again and saw APCs leaving. I thought "here we go again." We yelled at the APCs, but they wouldn't stop. Some of the guys had gotten on the APCs but there were about 25 of us who could not. We were running alongside of the APCs for about another 2 blocks before they stopped. We piled on them and got the hell out of there.

We drove to the Pakistani [controlled] Stadium, got out at the stadium and shook everyone's hands. By the way, the Pakistanis and Malaysians were the ones in the APCs that got us out [the Pakistanis provided 4 tanks during the early part of the relief convoy only]. The casualties were evacuated to the hospitals.

SOF troops, 1970s and 80s. 1) Sergeant First Class, Task Force Ivory Coast, Son Tay Prison, North Vietnam, 1970. The raid on the Son Tay Prison on November 21, 1970 was probably one of the most expertly executed rescue missions in modern history; tragically, however, it proved a "dry hole" – the 65 American prisoners of war being held there had been moved to other prisons shortly before the raid. 2) NCO, Delta Force Operator, "Desert One" Base, Iran, 1983. Delta Force's uniform during the ill-fated hostage rescue attempt was quite different from the usual standards of military dress. This was due to the unit's unique mission requirements and the need to blend into the population, at least from a distance. 3) NCO, SCUBA Diver, 8th SFGA, Panama, 1972. (Ron Volstad © Osprey Publishing)

The training of US military SF has also rubbed off on US law enforcement, not least in the development of the Special Weapons and Tactics (SWAT) units. Here an FBI SWAT team conducts a training exercise. (FBI)

We then found out who had been killed during the mission. The mood was somber. We ate some food and were flown back to our hanger. It had been 18 hours since we had left. Everyone soaked up what had happened.

There was a memorial the next day. Many tears were shed and many more will be for the ones that we lost. I know this event has forever changed my life.

The experiences of the SOF troops outlined above reflect those of numerous other US special forces units during the last decades of the 20th century. Many SOF operations have gone unreported, particularly in Latin America, the drama of these episodes and the human cost known only to those units involved. One thing was certain – the US government was finding no shortage of roles for its special ops personnel. In the early years of the new millennium, indeed, the level of demand would only escalate, and take many US SOF units to breaking point.

NEW WARS

THE HORRIFIC TERRORIST ATTACKS on the United States on September 11, 2001 changed the operational world for US SOF beyond recognition. With the American homeland under direct attack in a way never before witnessed, the US government embarked on two major wars – in Afghanistan and Iraq – covering the full spectrum of combat commitments from COIN to conventional armored warfare, plus actions elsewhere in the world. The "War on Terror" globally and exponentially increased the number of potential targets for SOF operations, particularly throughout the Middle East, Africa, and Central Asia, where terrorist and insurgent groups like al-Qaeda and the Taliban established elusive mobile bases while also prosecuting grim programs of bombings, assassinations, and ambushes directed as much against civilian populations as against foreign troops.

Being a truly international affair, and one with huge defense budget increases behind it, the War on Terror brought a major expansion in both SOF deployments and also in force strength. Special ops soldiers became the tool for aggressive response and pre-emptive action on a global basis, offering the precision targeting capabilities and intelligence-gathering functions so important in conflicts in which enemy combatants are typically indistinguishable from the civilian population. By 2009, US SOF personnel were deployed in 60 countries worldwide, but by 2011 that figure had exceeded 100, if we count those states in which SOF performed training duties for the indigenous armed services.

The pressures of economics and politics will doubtless reduce such commitments, but given the international tensions that prevail they are likely to remain high for decades to come. (The 2013 budget for USSOCOM was $10.4 billion, a 0.6 percent reduction on the previous fiscal year, but still equivalent to the total military expenditure of countries like Greece and Poland.) And when the deployment of conventional forces is not acceptable, SOF will be a stand-by instrument of foreign policy. The greatest challenge will be meeting these demands while also retaining the exceptional levels of skills and expertise amongst its personnel. Already, the US Army SF has taken the significant step of allowing civilians to join the Army specifically for Special Forces service.

In this final chapter, we will look in detail at some American SOF operations in Afghanistan and Iraq. As we shall see, not since Vietnam have SOF been used with such intensity or flexibility. What is quite clear from the study of these operations is that the standards of intelligence and bravery amongst SOF remain as high as ever.

SPECIAL OPS IN AFGHANISTAN

Afghanistan is a land that has rarely known peace. The 19th century saw bloody defeats inflicted on the British and their Indian Army in both the First (1838–42) and Second (1878–80) Anglo-Afghan Wars. During and since the 1979–89 occupation by

Soviet forces in an attempt to shore up a communist regime, Afghanistan has been fought over by rival governments, factions, tribes and warlords. In fact, these particular episodes of widely reported turmoil have differed only in degree, and not in nature, from the pattern of life that that region has known over many centuries: warfare in Afghanistan is essentially based on ethnic or communal rivalries rather than modern ideological quarrels.

The defining moment in the country's modern history, which sowed the seeds for all later events, was the Soviet invasion in 1979. Installing a puppet government under Babrak Karmal in the capital, Kabul, the Soviets boasted that they would eliminate the anti-communist *mujahideen* (fighters) in a few short months. But those local fighters would receive massive covert support from the West, and active reinforcement by Islamic volunteers from many countries. Ten years later the Soviets withdrew, after suffering anything from 35,000 to 50,000 troop deaths and up to three times that number of other casualties. The experience thoroughly demoralized the Soviet Army for a decade thereafter, and released many thousands of physically and psychologically crippled veterans into a society that itself proved to be on the verge of political collapse.

During the 1980s the loosely aligned Afghan *mujahideen* groups were reinforced by the so-called "Afghan Arabs," an eventual 30,000 volunteers from across the Islamic world, fuelled by the Koranic imperative to *jihad*. Amongst these was a man whose name would rise to notorious prominence in later years – Osama bin Laden. The wealthy Saudi son of a construction magnate, bin Laden developed an Islamic charity to support the Afghan Arabs. This organization, centered on a guesthouse for foreign fighters over the Pakistani border in Peshawar, became known as al-Qaeda or "the Base." Blooded in the Soviet–Afghan War, many of these volunteers went on to fight in other conflicts involving Islamic peoples, from Kashmir and Chechnya to Kosovo.

In the vacuum left by the departing Soviets, the *mujahideen* factions fought against the ailing central government before its inevitable collapse in 1992. Hope for a new central government was short-lived, as the seven major *mujahideen* factions descended into a bitter civil war for control of the country. These struggles naturally extended southwards over the political border into and beyond the so-called Tribal Territories along Pakistan's northwest frontier; vast numbers of Afghans had fled across the borders during the Soviet occupation, and the notional powers of the Pakistani government over the Tribal Territories were exercised only covertly.

The Taliban arose in 1994 from a small group of Pashtun religious students (talibs) in southern Afghanistan. Under the leadership of the one-eyed cleric Mullah Muhammad Omar the Taliban became a popular movement, railing against the brutal excesses of the rival warlords and the corruption spread by the ubiquitous opium trade. Their solution, however, was to bring the country under their own Dark-Age

Reconnaissance Marines with the 1st Reconnaissance Battalion (1st Recon) engage Taliban forces during a firefight in Northern Trek Nawa, Afghanistan, August 2010. Note the M14 DMR carried by the rightmost Marine. Battalion Recon, sometimes called Division Recon, carry out division-level ground and amphibious reconnaissance operations in their Marine Air Ground Task Force (MAGTF) Ground Combat Element commander's area of influence in the close/distant battle space. (DOD)

interpretation of *sharia* law; supported by Pakistani intelligence (the ISI), the Taliban movement grew quickly.

Bin Laden returned to Afghanistan in 1996 after being forced to leave his refuge in Sudan. He brought with him a cadre of al-Qaeda fighters, and soon attracted many Afghan Arab veterans. As a gift to Mullah Omar, bin Laden donated vehicles, built roads, and recruited the largest jihadist army of modern times – al-Qaeda's Brigade 055 – which bin Laden deployed against the Shura Nazar or Northern Alliance of anti-Taliban groups.

Everything changed on September 11, 2001. Two days before the terrorist attacks which killed 2,973 people in New York, Virginia, and Pennsylvania, Ahmad Shah Masoud, the leader of the Northern Alliance, was assassinated in his headquarters in the Panjshir Valley in a suicide bombing by two al-Qaeda terrorists posing as journalists. Al-Qaeda had eliminated the United States' closest ally in Afghanistan.

In the aftermath of 9/11 America received pledges of military support from many nations, from the United Kingdom, Australia, New Zealand, and Canada to France. Indeed, on September 12, for the first time in history, NATO invoked Article 5 of its founding charter providing for mutual protection of member states against attack; this paved the way for NATO participation, and the eventual deployment to Afghanistan of the International Security Assistance Force (ISAF).

"JAWBREAKER" AND *ENDURING FREEDOM*

The first US ground forces to set foot inside Afghanistan did so a scant 15 days after 9/11. This small team, codenamed "Jawbreaker," inserted covertly from the former Soviet airbase of Karshi-Khandabad (K2) in Uzbekistan, where a formidable US presence was building, and landed in the Panjshir Valley in a Russian-built but CIA-operated Mi-17 helicopter in the pre-dawn darkness of September 26. These eight men were not members of any military unit, but of the CIA's paramilitary Special Activities Division (SAD) and Counter Terrorist Center (CTC). To the men of the US Special Forces, they would be known colloquially by the acronym OGA – "Other Government Agency."

Consisting of former special operators, plus communications and linguistics experts, the team brought with them satellite communications enabling their "ground truth" intelligence reports to be available instantly to headquarters staff at CIA Langley and Central Command (CENTCOM), the military command responsible for Operation *Enduring Freedom* – the forthcoming US/Coalition operations in Afghanistan. Jawbreaker also carried $3 million dollars in US currency in non-sequential $100 bills, which would be used to shore up Northern Alliance support to *Enduring Freedom*.

The Jawbreaker team facilitated the planned insertion of the first US Army SF detachments with Northern Alliance commanders; assessed potential air targets for CENTCOM; provided an in-country combat search-and-rescue capability; and would provide bomb-damage assessments for the coming air campaign.

Operation *Enduring Freedom* began officially on the evening of October 6, 2001, with Operation *Crescent Wind* – the Coalition air campaign targeting Taliban command-and-control and air defense facilities. Most of the Taliban's ageing SA-2 and SA-3 SAMs, along with their attendant radar and command units, were destroyed on the first night of operations, as were their small fleet of MiG-21 and SU-22 aircraft.

With the threat of high-altitude SAMs negated and total air dominance quickly established, aerial targeting soon focused on Taliban infrastructure, leadership, and troop targets, as well as known

Special forces soldiers watch as a MH-47 Chinook flown by the 160th SOAR takes off from an LZ in Afghanistan. Green Berets in Afghanistan grow their beards out in order to help gain respect from Afghans, who view facial hair as a sign of masculinity. (DOD)

al-Qaeda facilities. These targets were struck by a range of USAF, Navy, and British RAF aircraft types, including the venerable B-52H and the B-1B long- range bombers along with the AC-130 Spectre, operating from bases at K2 and in Pakistan. The way was now clear for deployments on the ground.

The structure of the SOF committed to *Enduring Freedom* was basically as follows. Under the overall leadership of General Tommy Franks, Coalition Forces Commander, CENTCOM, four major task forces were initially dedicated: the Combined Joint Special Operations Task Force (CJSOTF); Combined Joint Task Force-Mountain (CJTF-Mountain); the Joint Interagency Task Force-Counterterrorism (JIATF-CT); and the Coalition Joint Civil-Military Operations Task Force (CJCMOTF). CJSOTF comprised three subordinate task forces: Joint Special Operations Task Force – North (JSOTF-North), known as Task Force Dagger; Joint Special Operations Task Force – South (JSOTF-South), aka Task Force K-Bar; and the secretive Task Force Sword (later Task Force 11).

TASK FORCE DAGGER

JSOTF-North, led by Colonel John Mulholland, was formed around his 5th Special Forces Group, with integral air assets from the 160th SOAR. Dagger was assigned to the north of Afghanistan, and tasked with infiltrating Special Forces Operational Detachment Alpha (ODA) teams to advise and support the warlords of the Northern Alliance. These ODAs were generally composed of a Special Forces A Team supported by an Air Force Special Tactics team, and worked jointly with CIA assets already on the ground.

A US Army Special Forces soldier drives his All-Terrain Vehicle (ATV) across rough ground. SOF have traditionally had the pick of the best military, and relevant civilian, equipment on the market. (US Army)

The Army SF motto *De Oppresso Liber* ("To Liberate the Oppressed") hints at one of the key skills of Army SF – Foreign Internal Defense (FID): infiltrating foreign countries and raising, training, and advising indigenous guerrilla forces. Within the 13-man ODA teams each SF operator has a different primary specialty, from demolitions to communications to engineering, but is cross-trained in others. Several ODAs are supported by an Operational Detachment Bravo (ODB), which provides intelligence, medical, and logistical support to the ODAs. Both the ODB and the ODAs are led by an ODC (Operational Detachment Charlie), generally an SF battalion command element. The ODAs are also supported by integrally attached USAF Special Tactics operators – usually combat controllers (CCTs) trained to guide close air support. Some ODAs, particularly if tasked with direct action missions, may also be supported by USAF Pararescue Jumpers.

TASK FORCE K-BAR

JSOTF-South, TF K-Bar, was led by Navy SEAL Captain Robert Harward, and formed around a core of Navy SEAL Teams 2, 3, and 8 and the Army's 1st Battalion, 3rd SF Group. The SEALs are structured in 16-man platoons, six of which comprise a SEAL Team. Platoons in *Enduring Freedom* were most often deployed in sensitive site exploitation or direct action missions, while four-man sub-elements were assigned to surveillance and reconnaissance (SR) operations. The SEALs are generally considered to be more focused on direct action when compared with the unconventional warfare and FID focus of Army SF. K-Bar nevertheless concentrated on sensitive site exploitation and surveillance and reconnaissance taskings, although some 3rd SF Group ODAs were deployed in the FID role alongside 5th SF Group. K-Bar was additionally the home for several SOF units from other Coalition nations, including the German Kommando Spezialkräfte (KSK), Canada's Joint Task Force 2 (JTF-2), and New Zealand 1st Special Air Service Group (NZSAS).

TASK FORCE SWORD

TF Sword/TF 11 was the JSOC's so-called "hunter-killer" force, with the mission of capturing or killing senior leadership or "high-value targets" (HVTs) in both al-Qaeda and the Taliban. Sword was structured around a two-squadron component of Special Mission Unit operators from the Combat Applications Group (CAG) and the Naval Special Warfare Development Group (DEVGRU), supported by Ranger security teams, and the intelligence specialists of Grey Fox, National Security Agency (NSA), and the CIA.

CAG – 1st SF Operational Detachment-Delta – is modeled on the British 22nd Special Air Service Regiment (22 SAS), and is the US Army's primary direct action, hostage rescue, and special reconnaissance unit. The three Squadrons (A, B, and C) are each divided into three Troops – two dedicated to direct action and one Recce Troop. In *Enduring Freedom* they were often known obliquely as "Task Force Green"; the Rangers who worked in support of Sword were TF Red, DEVGRU were termed TF Blue, Grey Fox were TF Orange, and the 160th SOAR were TF Brown.

Coalition SOF were sometimes attached to Sword to support specific operations; UK Special Forces (UKSF), particularly the Special Boat Service (SBS), were generally integrated and attached for the longer term.

CJTF-MOUNTAIN

CJTF-M also initially comprised three subordinate commands: TF 64 – a special operations task force built around a squadron of the Australian Special Air Service Regiment (SASR); the USMC TF 58, of the 15th MEU – which was replaced in January 2002 by TF Rakkasan (formed of components of the 101st Airborne and 10th Mountain Divisions, along with 3rd Battalion Princess Patricia's Canadian Light Infantry, and TF Jacana, a battle group of 1,700 British personnel built around 45 Commando, Royal Marines.

JIATF-CT

Also known as TF Bowie, the JIATF-CT was an integrated intelligence entity manned by personnel from all *Enduring Freedom* participating units, both US and Coalition, and civilian agencies. Led by Brigadier General Gary Harrell, one of the most experienced special operators in theater, TF Bowie established the Coalition's interrogation facility at Bagram air base and provided intelligence product to the CJSOTFs. At its largest, Bowie numbered 36 US military personnel, 57 from civilian agencies such as the FBI, NSA, and CIA, and officers from Coalition SOF, including UKSF and SASR. Embedded within Bowie, but reporting to TF Sword, was Advanced Force Operations (AFO), a 45-man contingent of CAG recce specialists augmented by SEALs from DEVGRU and supported by Grey Fox. AFO had the mandate of "intelligence preparation of the battlefield"; they conducted covert surveillance and reconnaissance operations for both Bowie and Sword, and would prove instrumental in Operation *Anaconda* (see below).

CJCMOTF

CJCMOTF was eventually headquartered in Kabul but with two geographically divided subordinate commands: Civil-Military Operations Center North, and Civil-Military Operations Center South. They had responsibility for managing *Enduring Freedom* civil support and humanitarian efforts, which evolved in 2002 into the Provincial Reconstruction Team (PRT) concept; some 34 teams are now operational.

AFGHANISTAN OPERATIONS

As the aerial campaign continued, TF Dagger was planning to insert its first teams into Afghanistan from K2. Aviators from the 2nd Battalion of the 160th SOAR maintained their MH-47E Chinooks and MH-60Ls on "strip alert," awaiting a break in the bad weather to allow the helicopters to negotiate safely the notorious Hindu Kush mountains.

After two weeks of preparatory aerial bombardment, the first two SF ODAs were infiltrated into Afghanistan in the evening and early hours of October 19/20, 2001. The first team to touch down was the 12-man ODA 555, who linked up with Jawbreaker in the Panjshir Valley and were taken to a safe house to meet representatives of warlord Fahim Khan, the successor to Masoud as military commander of the Northern Alliance. They began operations alongside Khan's forces the very next day.

The weather that night had been dangerous enough to force the two MH-60L Direct Action Penetrators (DAPs) flying escort for the MH-47E carrying the second SF team, ODA 595, to turn back to K2. As well as a potentially deadly ice build-up on their rotors, and the treacherous 16,000ft (4,900m) peaks, the aviators found they had to contend with a night-time sandstorm on the way into Afghanistan. But despite the appalling conditions, the Chinook crew managed to complete their mission, touching down at 0200hrs local time in the Dari-a-Souf Valley just south of the regional capital of Mazar-e-Sharif. ODA 595 was met at the landing zone by the militia of ethnic Uzbek warlord General Abdur Rashid Dostum, commander of the largest Northern Alliance faction. Dostum held a strong powerbase around Mazar-e-Sharif and was an accomplished political intriguer: he had previously allied himself with, and later betrayed, the Soviets, their Kabul puppet government, and the Taliban.

USAF Pararescue Jumpers maintain security at an helicopter LZ. The HH-60 Pave Hawk features a mid-air refueling probe, and has .50-cal M2s in the door-gunner hatches. (Courtesy USSOCOM)

ODA operators meet with General Tommy Franks in October 2001. Note the *pakol* hats, Mk 11 sniper rifle (left), and M4A1 carbine fitted with a sound suppressor and the ACOG 4x optical sight. (USSOCOM)

Meanwhile, in southern Afghanistan, another special operation was under way. Some 200 Army Rangers from 3rd Battalion/75th Ranger Regiment (3/75th), with airmen from the 23rd Special Tactics Squadron (STS), conducted a combat drop from MC-130P Combat Talons onto a remote airstrip southwest of the city of Kandahar.

Preceded by a small Army Pathfinder team, the Rangers met minimal Taliban resistance and the location, codenamed Objective "Rhino," was quickly secured. The parachute drop and airstrip seizure were filmed, and later some grainy night-vision footage was televised by the Pentagon as proof that US forces could operate in any location within Afghanistan – a strong psychological message to the Taliban. The Ranger mission also paved the way for the later use of the airstrip as Forward Operating Base (FOB) Rhino by the Marines of 15th MEU. No casualties were suffered in the actual operation, but two Rangers assigned to the combat search and rescue (CSAR) element supporting the mission died when their MH-60K crashed in Pakistan (the result of a "brown out" rather than enemy action).

Concurrently, another much less publicized mission was being conducted outside Kandahar; this remains classified, but its aim was to capture or kill Taliban HVTs. It was launched from the USS *Kitty Hawk* (which was serving as a floating SOF base in the Indian Ocean). The ground elements were drawn from JSOC's Combat Applications Group and supported by teams from 23rd STS. The Kandahar target was one of Taliban leader Mullah Omar's residences and, although Omar was absent, intelligence material was recovered. As the CAG team prepared to extract, Taliban forces approached the compound and engaged them with small arms and rocket-propelled grenades. The CAG operators returned fire, breaking contact under suppressive fire from an orbiting AC-130 gunship, and successfully exfiltrated on helicopters from the 160th SOAR.

Officially, casualties were described as "light," but rumors point to multiple casualties amongst the operators. CAG had planned to insert a "stay-behind" SR team in the area, but was frustrated by the Taliban response. A possible piece of evidence for the ferocity of the contact is that a wheel assembly from an MH-47E was torn off as it struck a compound wall during the extraction; the Taliban, unsurprisingly, used the wheel as a propaganda opportunity, claiming it as evidence of a shot-down US helicopter.

All Coalition SOF are trained and equipped for night fighting. The white light and faint line visible above the muzzle of the weapon in this photo taken during a US Army Special Forces nighttime raid is the infrared laser from the PEQ-2 target illuminator. (US Navy)

PREVIOUS PAGE: US Army Special
Forces en route to a target aboard
a Black Hawk helicopter. (US Navy)

THE NORTHERN ALLIANCE

While TF Sword carried out the Kandahar raids, ODA 595 was striking up a productive relationship with General Dostum in the north. The ODA had split into two elements, Alpha and Bravo; Alpha rode on horseback with Dostum to his headquarters, to plan the impending attack on Mazar-e-Sharif, while Bravo, tasked with clearing the Dari-a-Souf Valley, travelled into the Alma Tak mountains to begin preparations.

On October 20 the team guided in the first Joint Direct Attack Munition (JDAM) "smart bomb" from an orbiting B-52H. Dostum was suitably impressed – "You made an aircraft appear and drop bombs. General Dostum is very happy!" Dostum was soon taunting his Taliban opponents over their radio frequencies – a curious aspect of the war between the Taliban and the Northern Alliance, and a crude example of psychological warfare: "This is General Dostum speaking. I am here, and I have brought the Americans with me!"

The US conducted their own psyops, with EC-130E Commando Solo aircraft beaming radio transmissions in both Dari and Pashto dialects to the Afghan civilian population. Aircraft also dropped huge numbers of leaflets decrying the Taliban and al-Qaeda as criminals, and promoting the $25 million reward placed on bin Laden's head.

The ODA 595 Bravo team were coordinating their own airstrikes in the Dari-a-Souf Valley, cutting off and destroying Taliban reinforcements and frustrating their attempts to relieve their embattled forces in the north. Cumulatively, the airstrikes showed increasing results as the Taliban began to withdraw towards Mazar-e-Sharif. Dostum's riders and the ODA 595 Alpha team followed, pausing only to direct further air support. On the Shomali Plains, ODA 555 and an OGA team with Fahim Khan's forces began calling in air support on entrenched Taliban positions at the southeastern end of Bagram air base. The Alpha team set up an observation post (OP) in an air traffic control tower, using it as a base for their AN/PEQ-1 SOFLAM (Special Operations Forces Laser Marker), and guiding in two BLU-82 "Daisy Cutters" that devastated the Taliban lines.

By November 5 the advance of Dostum and his horsemen was stalled at the Taliban-held village of Bai Beche in the strategically vital Dari-a-Souf Valley, where two Northern Alliance attacks had been driven back. While ODA 595 organized close air support, Dostum prepared his men to follow up the bombing with a cavalry charge; this was mistimed, and 250 Uzbek cavalry charged the Taliban lines exactly as the B-52 made its final approach to bomb them. An operator with ODA 595 is quoted in Max Boot's *War Made New*: "Three or four bombs hit right in the middle of the enemy position. Almost immediately after the bombs exploded, the horses swept across the objective – the enemy was so shell-shocked. I could see the horses blasting out the other side. It was the finest sight I ever saw. The men were thrilled; they were so happy. It wasn't done perfectly, but it will never be forgotten." The political fall-out from a serious "friendly fire" tragedy might have severed Dostum's relationship with the Americans – a relationship that was the key to their goals in northern Afghanistan; thankfully, fate dealt a lucky hand and the cavalry charge succeeded, breaking the back of the defense.

Other ODAs were now inserting at regular intervals. On October 23, ODA 585 was infiltrated near Konduz to assist the warlord Burillah Khan. On November 2 the ten-man ODA 553 inserted into the Bamian Valley with General Kareem Kahlili's forces; and ODA 534 got into the Dari-a-Balkh Valley (after being delayed by poor flying conditions) to support General Mohammed Atta, a sometime associate of General Dostum and head of the Jaamat-e-Islami militia. An operator with ODA 534 recalled:

> The team was finally able to infil northern Afghanistan by Chinook on the night of November 2 after several days of bad weather. If the helo insertion failed, an airborne operation was scheduled for the following evening. In addition to the 12-man ODA and two Air Force CCTs, three Agency officers were attached. The Agency team consisted of a case officer/Dari linguist, a former SEAL officer, and a former SF [medical] officer. The team was met on the HLZ by Atta's forces and an Agency CTC officer [from Jawbreaker] who had infiltrated two weeks prior and had been working with Dostum. He now took command of the Agency team, while the rest of his group and another ODA [595] remained with Dostum and his men. The ODA team leader's Russian did come in handy once the RON site was reached and the team split, but the primary [interpreter] between the team and Atta and his men was the Agency case officer.

ODAs 586 and 594 were brought into the country on November 8 in MH-47s, and picked up on the Afghan/Tajik border by CIA Mi-17s; 586 deployed into Konduz with the forces of General Daoud Khan, and 594 into the Panjshir to assist ODA 555.

MAZAR-E-SHARIF

ODA 534 moved through the Dari-a-Souf with Atta's militia, and linked up with Dostum and ODA 595 outside of Mazar-e-Sharif to develop a plan of attack against the Taliban-held city. At the critical Tangi Pass, the gateway from the Balkh Valley to Mazar-e-Sharif, Taliban forces were dug in to halt the Alliance's rapid advance. On November 9 ODAs 595 and 534 positioned themselves in mountainside hides and began calling in airstrikes against these entrenched defenders. The Taliban responded with indirect fires from BM-21 rockets; these were quickly silenced by the B-52H, and Northern Alliance forces – on foot, on horseback, in pickups, and in captured BMP armored personnel carriers – raced toward the gates of the city. On November 10, Mazar-e-Sharif fell to the Alliance, providing the first hint that the war might not be the year-long affair predicted by the Pentagon. Civil Affairs Teams (CAT) from the 96th

Civil Affairs Battalion and Tactical Psyop Teams (TPT) from the 4th Psychological Operations Group, both assigned under TF Dagger, were immediately deployed into Mazar-e-Sharif to assist in winning the hearts and minds of the inhabitants.

In the central northern region, ODA 586 were advising Genreal Daoud Khan outside of Taloqan, and coordinating Coalition airstrikes, when the general launched a surprise infantry assault. Before the first bomb could be dropped, Taloqan fell on November 11.

The Rangers of 3/75th carried out their second combat drop in Afghanistan on the night of November 13, when a platoon-sized element, accompanied by eight men from the 24th STS, dropped into a site southwest of Kandahar codenamed "Bastogne," to secure a Forward Air Refueling Point (FARP). MC-130s soon landed at the improvised strip and deposited four AH-6J Little Birds from the 160th, which launched an attack on targets around Kandahar. With their mission completed the "Little Birds" returned, reloaded onto MC-130s, and the combined team flew off into the night.

KABUL, KONDUZ, AND KANDAHAR

Three days after the fall of Mazar-e-Sharif, Kabul was captured by General Fahim Khan and the men of ODA 555; surviving Taliban and al-Qaeda retreated toward Kandahar and Tora Bora. On November 14, ODA 574 inserted into the southern village of Tarin

JSOTF AND AFGHAN MILITIA FORCE (AMF) FORCE BREACH A TALIBAN COMPOUND, C.2003.

Here, the SOF team have overwatch from a circling AH-64 Apache (1). As the raid goes in, the main gate of the mud-brick compound and its side wall are covered against any escapees by a Soviet PKM machine gun mounted in a Toyota Hilux pickup truck, manned by a member of the AMF directed by a US operator (2); and a US Special Forces Humvee mounting a Mk 19 automatic grenade launcher (3). In the main gateway of the compound, two SF operators are directing about a dozen AMF (4). Once inside, other SF soldiers of this primary entry team disarm a couple of captured black-turbanned Taliban (5) – the aim is to take prisoners, not to kill unless unavoidable. Meanwhile, on the far side of the compound, an SF secondary entry team climb in by means of a ladder, surprising and if necessary engaging the Taliban, who rush out of the houses amidst the startled civilians. Not shown here, but commonly employed, a sniper or designated marksman team on higher ground would be ready to provide precision fire if resistance was met, taking out targets of opportunity. (Ramiro Bujeiro © Osprey Publishing)

Kowt in four MH-60Ks, bringing with them the future President of Afghanistan, the Pashtun leader Hamid Karzai.

As the cities fell in rapid succession, TF Dagger's attention became focused on the last northern Taliban stronghold – Konduz. Daoud Khan and ODA 586 used massive airstrikes to demoralize the Taliban defenders, and after 11 days of continual aerial bombardment Daoud took the traditional Afghan step of opening negotiations with his enemies, successfully securing the Taliban's surrender on November 23.

On November 25 the establishment of FOB Rhino near Kandahar added further pressure on the beleaguered Taliban. A three-man SEAL team conducting a reconnaissance before the Marines landed was mistakenly engaged by orbiting AH-1W Cobras, but thankfully suffered no casualties. The 15th MEU landed a battalion-size force at Rhino, and was soon reinforced by the newly arrived Australian SASR squadron.

Hamid Karzai began moving on Kandahar with ODA 574, gathering fighters among local Pashtuns until his militia eventually numbered some 800. They fought for two days against Taliban dug into ridgelines overlooking the strategic Sayd-Aum-Kalay bridge, before seizing the bridgehead and opening the road to Kandahar. Tragedy struck on December 5 when a 2,000lb (909kg) JDAM landed among this force, killing three members of the ODA and seriously wounding five; more than 20 of Karzai's militiamen were killed and Karzai himself was slightly wounded in the blast. An ODA operator explained that the accident occurred due to unfamiliarity with the PLGR, a precision lightweight GPS receiver widely used for navigation and targeting: "When the PLGR batteries go dead and you put new ones in, it defaults to showing the GPS location of itself. The TACP [tactical air control party] with 574 wasn't trained for that; [he] put new batteries in, looked at the unit, and called the GPS location in to the bird; the bird asked for confirmation because the data had changed since last call, and 574 confirmed that it was correct – at which time they dropped the JDAM." Along with a Marine casevac CH-53, ODB 570 and ODA 524 were deployed by helicopter to assist with evacuating the wounded and to replace the fallen operators of 574. The following day, Karzai successfully negotiated the surrender of both the remaining Taliban forces around Sayd-Aum-Kalay and of the entire city of Kandahar. ODA 524 and ODB 570 mounted up with Karzai's militia and began the final push.

Another SF team was also fighting its way toward Kandahar: ODA 583 had infiltrated into the Shin Narai Valley, southeast of the city, to support Gul Agha Sherzai, its former governor. By November 24 the ODA had established OPs which allowed it to call airstrikes on Taliban positions at Kandahar airport, weakening them every day. On December 7, Sherzai's forces seized the airport and, informed of the surrender of the Taliban in Kandahar, entered the city, soon followed by Karzai.

The campaign had taken just under two months – 49 days – from the insertion of the first ODA teams to the fall of Kandahar. It was accomplished by several hundred SOF and perhaps 100 OGA, supported by their determined allies of the Northern Alliance and the awe-inspiring might of United States air power.

TORA BORA

After the fall of Kabul, al-Qaeda elements – allegedly including bin Laden and other leadership figures – withdrew to the eastern city of Jalalabad, capital of Nangarhar province. Jalalabad was only a short distance from Tora Bora, the network of cave systems and defenses developed by the *mujahideen* during their war against the Soviet occupiers. Tora Bora lies in the White Mountains, only just over 12 miles

US Navy SEALs with Special Operations Task Force-South approach a village during a clearing operation in Panjwai district, Kandahar Province, Afghanistan, April 25, 2011. Afghan National Army Commandos, joined by US service members with Special Operations Task Force-South and members of the Afghan National Civil Order Police, found Taliban propaganda at a site in Panjwai district and removed three suspected insurgents from the area during the operation. (US Army)

(19km) from the border, where a crossing point at Parachinar leads into Pakistan's Northwest Frontier province. The area was familiar to bin Laden; he had spent time there with the *mujahideen* in the 1980s, and knew that the mountain caverns would provide the perfect stronghold – one that the Soviets had never managed to conquer fully.

Coalition signals and human intelligence suggested that significant numbers of al-Qaeda fighters and possible HVTs were moving from Jalalabad to take refuge in Tora Bora. Due to resistance from the higher echelons of both the US government and military to committing conventional forces on the ground (in the misplaced fear of replicating the Soviet experience), a decision was made to attack Tora Bora using SOF supporting local militia. ODA 572 and a small group of SAD operators were deployed to advise Eastern Alliance forces under the control of two warlords – Hazrat Ali and Mohammed Zaman, who nursed a deep-seated mutual dislike. Eventually some 2,500 to 3,000 Afghan Militia Forces (AMF), paid for by the CIA, were recruited for the operation to isolate and destroy al-Qaeda elements using Tora Bora as a sanctuary.

The leader of the CIA Jawbreaker team requested the 3/75th Rangers (who were at that time deployed to Pakistan in support of TF Sword) to act as stop groups along escape routes from Tora Bora, but the JSOC commander denied the request. The logistics, particularly in terms of helicopter lift capability, would have been difficult, although both the Jawbreaker leader and USMC General James Mattis believe that using Rangers to seal the trails might have succeeded. It must also be remembered, however, that up until Tora Bora the use of AMF militias supported by ODAs had been consistently successful.

At the onset of the attack ODA 572, with their attached CCT, called in precision airstrikes including strikes by B-52Hs, while the Afghan militias attacked al-Qaeda positions with varying degrees of enthusiasm. According to ODA members, the militias would gain ground initially, only to relinquish these gains later the same day. At one point ODA 572 was going to be extracted due to the militias' reluctance to press the attack.

With 5th SF Group and Jawbreaker stretched thin across the country, JSOC was tasked to assist, and on December 10, 40 operators from B Squadron CAG arrived at Tora Bora. Small teams attached themselves to local commanders, and took over tactical command from the CIA. Advised by ODA, CAG, and CIA operators, the militias

LEFT: US SOF TROOPS, AFGHANISTAN.
1) Sergeant of an Operational Detachment Alpha, US Army Special Forces. 2) Operative, Special Activities Division, US Central Intelligence Agency. 3) Combat Controller of a Special Tactics Squadron, US Air Force. (Ramiro Bujeiro © Osprey Publishing)

eventually started to make some halting progress; but on December 12, Mohammed Zaman (incredibly) opened negotiations with the al-Qaeda forces in Tora Bora. Much to the frustration of the SOF, a truce was called until 8am the next morning "to allow al-Qaeda forces time to agree a surrender amongst themselves."

This appears to have been a transparent ruse: several hundred al-Qaeda members (some estimate up to 1,000), including men of Brigade 055, escaped during the night along the mountain paths towards Pakistan. It has also been alleged, by both Afghan and US SOF sources, that members of the CIA-funded militias acted as guides for bin Laden's fighters; one rumor indicates a payment of US $6 million made to Hazrat Ali to shepherd the al-Qaeda leadership to safety. Gary Berntsen, leader of the CIA team at Tora Bora, believes that two large al-Qaeda groups escaped: one of 135-odd personnel headed east into Pakistan, while bin Laden, with 200 Saudi and Yemeni jihadists, took the snow-covered route through Parachinar.

Eventually, around December 17, the battle drew to a close. Indications were that several hundred al-Qaeda members had been killed and just under 60 captured at Tora Bora. Across the border, Pakistani Border Scouts, allegedly assisted by members of JSOC and the CIA, captured upward of another 300 foreign fighters. ODA 561 was brought in on December 20 to support 572 in conducting sensitive site exploitations of the cave complexes, and to take DNA samples from the al-Qaeda bodies.

In January 2002 another series of caves used by al-Qaeda were discovered in Zhawar Kili, just south of Tora Bora, and airstrikes were called in before ground elements were infiltrated. A SEAL platoon accompanied by a German KSK and a Norwegian SOF team spent nine days conducting an sensitive site exploitation, clearing the estimated 70 caves and 60 structures in the area and recovering a huge amount of intelligence materials and munitions.

OPERATION *ANACONDA*, 2002

In February 2002 an SF intelligence analyst working for TF Bowie identified patterns in intelligence product that led him to believe that surviving al-Qaeda forces were massing in the Lower Shah-e-Khot Valley, 60 miles (97km) south of Gardez. The Lower Shah-e-Khot bordered the Pakistani Tribal Territories into which many al-Qaeda fighters were believed to have escaped during the battle for Tora Bora. Other personnel within TF Dagger, the AFO, and the OGA were making the same connections. The analysis by TF Bowie, supported by HUMINT from the OGA and SIGINT from NSA, indicated that perhaps 150 to 200 al-Qaeda fighters were harboring in the valley, with the strong possibility of leadership targets also being present. An operation was soon in the planning, to be known as *Anaconda*.

Initially three AFO teams (two from CAG and one from a DEVGRU recce troop) were infiltrated into OPs around the valley to provide real-time "eyes on" intelligence to the planners. The DEVGRU team (callsign Mako 31) discovered an al-Qaeda position, complete with 12.7mm DShK heavy machine gun, nestled in the same location that they had selected for their OP; this was the first of several ominous signs.

The plan evolved around TF Hammer and TF Anvil, an ad hoc grouping of Afghan militia led by three ODAs (394, 372, and 594), and supported by a collection of AFO types and an Australian SASR patrol. Hammer would enter the Shah-e-Khot to flush out the al-Qaeda believed to be hiding in the small villages dotted across the valley floor, while Anvil would act as a blocking force to seal off the escape routes. Several SASR teams from TF 64, along with other Coalition SOF, would also establish outer cordon covert OPs, to call in air on any retreating al-Qaeda.

Conventional forces of TF Rakkasan – 3rd Brigade, 101st Airborne Division, and 1st/87th Infantry of 10th Mountain Division – would be committed in their first major operation, air-assaulting into the valley from Chinooks supported by six AH-64 Apaches. The infantry were to take up blocking positions inside the valley to cut off escape from the villages. Late-breaking CIA HUMINT alleging that the al-Qaeda forces were living on the peaks surrounding the valley rather than down in the villages was apparently overlooked by the planners.

The operation was launched on March 2, 2002, and immediately ran into problems: TF Hammer had difficulty driving their trucks under blackout conditions over the muddy tracks into the Shah-e-Khot. Hammer halted to await the planned preparatory aerial bombardment of the peaks; but a single B-1B dropping six bombs was the sum total of preparatory fires, due to a miscommunication by the planners. The militiamen, expecting massive US air support, were even further demoralized.

A small combined SF/AMF element, led by Chief Warrant Officer Stanley Harriman, broke off from the main convoy to establish a planned OP. Concurrently, the Mako 31 recce team called in an orbiting AC-130 to "service" the al-Qaeda position they had discovered, after the SEALs were spotted and engaged in a short fire-fight with the al-Qaeda gun team. The gunship was then tasked to scan the surrounding area for any enemy forces with their infrared and night vision cameras. Tragically, the AC-130's navigation system was malfunctioning, and the crew identified and plotted Harriman's small column in error. After being cleared to engage, the AC-130 struck. Harriman received a fatal fragmentation wound, two other SF were wounded, and several AMF were killed and many wounded before the AC-130 ceased fire after being informed by AFO of the "blue-on-blue." Soon afterwards, the main element of TF Hammer was engaged by effective mortar fire from al-Qaeda positions on the slopes; this broke their unit cohesion, and the AMF scattered and refused to advance.

With no opportunity to alter timings, the Chinooks of the 101st Airborne began their air assault into the Shah-e-Khot. As the grunts de-bussed they were engaged by heavy mortar and small arms fire, pinning them down. The assigned Apaches attempted to suppress enemy mortar teams, but ran into a wall of RPG and 12.7mm fire, with one gunship losing all its electronics to an RPG hit. It was now estimated that there were between 750 and 1,000 al-Qaeda fighters in and around the Lower Shah-e-Khot – a far cry from the original estimates.

The grunts of TF Rakkasan and the SF operators with Hammer fought all day, while the AFO OPs called in continuous close air on al-Qaeda weapon positions and the Apaches valiantly protected the exposed troops. Only one 120mm mortar had been deployed by the 10th Mountain's troopers and, whilst effective, it soon ran out of ammunition, forcing the grunts to rely on air to suppress the enemy indirect fires. Eventually, at nightfall, the most exposed Rakkasan elements were exfiltrated after suffering numerous wounded.

A US Air Force Special Tactics airman attached to an SOF patrol – close liaison with air assets, and precise control of air support, is essential during special operations. He wears a Com-Tac headset attached to his MBITR; his M4A1 carbine, mounting an Aimpoint sight and PEQ-2 target illuminator, has a hand-painted camouflage finish in sand and brown. (USAFSOC)

A US Army Special Forces soldier engages Taliban positions during a fierce gun battle in Sangin, Helmand Province, Afghanistan, 2007. The intensity of operations in Afghanistan has actually placed a severe strain on SOF personnel, particularly those who have conducted multiple tours. (US Army)

At AFO, alarming news was received from the leadership of TF 11: command of the AFO component of *Anaconda* was to be handed over to the newly arrived DEVGRU element, TF Blue. Apparently more for political than any operational reasons, TF 11 also demanded that two DEVGRU recce teams be inserted into the battle on the evening of March 3 (callsigns Mako 30 and Mako 21).

A hastily drawn plan called for the MH-47 insertion of both these SEAL elements into the valley, with Mako 30 landing on Takur Ghar, a towering peak with commanding views of the Shah-e-Khot. After mechanical difficulties with the first pair of Chinooks, the teams eventually took off in the early hours of March 4. As the 160th SOAR ship callsign "Razor 03" approached Takur Ghar, an AC-130 scanned the peak and reported no hostiles present. The CAG operators at AFO had advised Mako 30 to insert some 1,420yd (1,300m) off-set from the peak, taking into consideration the al-Qaeda OP and gun position already discovered by Mako 31; but the TF Blue element apparently ignored this advice.

As Razor 03 touched down on Takur Ghar, the Chinook was struck by an RPG and 12.7mm fire. A DEVGRU operator, Petty Officer First Class Neil Roberts, fell from the open ramp as the MH-47 attempted to escape. Leaking hydraulic fluid, the crippled Chinook made an emergency landing several kilometers away and awaited rescue. Retrieving the missing PO Roberts was now the pressing objective; Mako 30 were picked up by the now empty Razor 04, which had successfully inserted Mako 21, and lifted onto the peak. The combined DEVGRU/STS team were immediately pinned down, and called for the TF 11 quick-reaction force (QRF) – a team of Rangers and attached STS based at Bagram. Mako 30 broke contact, and withdrew into cover under a rocky overhang.

The QRF launched immediately in two more 160th SOAR Chinooks, Razor 01 and Razor 02. The lead helicopter, Razor 01, was vectored in to land on the peak, unaware of the RPG and DShK threat and of the fact that the SEALs had actually broken contact. Razor 01 was engaged by intense RPG, 12.7mm and small arms fire as soon as it arrived, and was forced to crash-land when an RPG destroyed one of its engines; three Rangers and a crewman were killed immediately by small arms fire. The other Rangers and STS operators broke clear from the stricken aircraft and began engaging entrenched al-Qaeda defenders.

Razor 02 landed its team of Rangers at the off-set LZ, from where they began the arduous climb to the peak. The STS team and Enlisted Terminal Attack Controller (ETAC) attached to the Razor 01 Rangers called in numerous "danger close" airstrikes to keep the enemy at bay until the second half of the Ranger QRF could negotiate the climb and link up. Together they used classic infantry tactics to fight through and kill the al-Qaeda elements on the peak; but the re-united Ranger QRF were soon engaged by al-Qaeda reinforcements who attempted to retake Takur Ghar. An Australian SASR OP

OPPOSITE: Airman First Class James Blair coordinates air cover for Army 10th Mountain Division light-infantry soldiers during recent operations in the Sroghar Mountains. Blair and other tactical air control party airmen are serving with SOF in operations *Enduring Freedom* and *Iraqi Freedom*. (USAF)

A Special Forces soldier looks down the scope of a Mk 12 Special Purpose Rifle (SPR). The SPR is a 5.56mm system fitted with a OPS Inc SPR Muzzle Brake Suppressor, Harris swivel bipod, and Leupold scope. (US Navy)

on a nearby mountain assisted by calling in continuous airstrikes on these reinforcements. Eventually, after 16 hours of pitched combat, the Rangers and Mako 30 were extracted that night. Sadly, efforts to locate and rescue PO Roberts were in vain. The SEAL appears to have died soon after falling from the Chinook; despite putting up a ferocious resistance, he was overcome by sheer weight of numbers.

A new plan was now hatched to relieve the embattled Rakkasan units still in the valley. The 2/187th Infantry air-assaulted into the east of the valley on March 4 and immediately attacked the heights under heavy gunship cover; 3rd Battalion were dropped into the north of the valley, with the objective of clearing through and linking up with the stranded forces. Supported by 16 Apaches, five Marine Cobras, and several USAF A-10 Thunderbolts, the Rakkasans methodically worked their way through the Shah-e-Khot, eventually clearing an estimated 130 caves and 40 buildings.

The exhausted Rakkasans were replaced on March 12 by fresh elements from 10th Mountain Division, who continued to clear the southern end of the valley. Task Force Commando – consisting of units drawn from 10th Mountain and the Canadians of 3rd Battalion/PPCLI – were airlifted in on March 14 to conduct sensitive site exploitation operations. AFO teams reconnoitered into the nearby Naka Valley, hunting for al-Qaeda escapees, but they came up empty-handed. Operation *Anaconda* officially ended on March 19.

PAYBACK

On March 17, TF 11 at Bagram received real-time intelligence from an RQ-1 Predator UAV (unmanned aerial vehicle) showing a group of three vehicles driving at speed in the Lower Shah-e-Khot towards the Pakistan border. The two Toyota 4Runners and a Hilux, travelling in daylight, attracted a mixed team from CAG and DEVGRU

USAF Pararescue Jumper of the 306th Rescue Squadron zeroing weapons at Kandahar; he carries a slung M4A1 while he examines a newly issued 7.62mm Mk 14 Mod 0 Enhanced Battle Rifle (EBR). Built by Troy Industries for the SEALs, the EBR is a shortened development of the trusty old M14, with a collapsible stock and a rail capability for mounting accessories. (USAF)

(along with an attached British SBS operator) in the 160th birds that were kept on strip alert for just such an eventuality.

The three MH-47Es carrying the TF 11 team, and two MH-60Gs carrying a Ranger security team, flew up behind the small convoy at below 50ft (15m), and the lead Chinook leveled out and landed on the road directly in front of it. As the occupants leapt from their vehicles and aimed their weapons, the door-gunner opened up with his 7.62mm minigun, cutting down a number of the al-Qaeda fighters. The second Chinook overshot the column and raked it with minigun and M249 fire from the ramp. The TF 11 operators added their fire to the helicopter's weapons, having earlier gained permission to punch out the Plexiglas side windows to enable them to fire their M4s and SR-25s from inside the fuselage.

As the third Chinook passed overhead, its minigun only managed a short burst before it jammed. A 160th SOAR flight medic and former Ranger took over, firing his M4 while the stoppage was cleared, and killing the driver of one of the SUVs as he tried to reverse out of the kill zone. A fourth vehicle had driven into a wadi some distance behind the convoy; one of the Chinooks hovered over it until positive identification could be made that the occupants were non-combatant civilians. The other Chinooks landed in cover nearby, and the operators took up positions overlooking the convoy while the Rangers orbited nearby in their Pave Hawks. As the al-Qaeda survivors attempted to reach cover they were caught in a devastating ambush by the CAG and DEVGRU operators. It was all over in the space of a couple of minutes: 16 al-Qaeda lay dead or dying in the dust, and two wounded prisoners were taken.

As the TF 11 operators cleared through and examined the bodies for intelligence, they confirmed that all were foreign fighters – Arabs, Chechens, and Uzbeks; one male

Navy SEALs – from Team 2, 3, or 8 – pictured here during a sensitive site exploitation operation to search al-Qaeda caves and buildings at Zhawar Kili in January 2002. (Getty Images)

corpse was disguised in a woman's burkha, and another was wearing a suicide belt device. The Americans also recovered an M4 suppressor and US fragmentation grenades that were subsequently traced to the Ranger QRF which had landed on Takur Ghar, and a Garmin GPS which was confirmed as lost there by a member of the 160th SOAR.

After the collapse of the Taliban and the destruction or expulsion of a large part of al-Qaeda's forces during *Anaconda*, and with the US military then re-aligning to prosecute Operation *Iraqi Freedom*, NATO stepped in to take over the burden of improving security in Afghanistan, establishing the International Security Assistance Force (ISAF) to carry out peacekeeping duties and ensure that the Taliban did not return to power. The remaining Operation *Enduring Freedom* forces were assigned primarily to hunting HVTs and the surviving remnants of al-Qaeda.

IRAQ

"A lot of guys obviously hate the place. But in the early mornings when the sun came up, the temperature got just right and the sky looked lovely. I can't tell you about the people. My only interaction with them is in their house at 2am, usually scared shitless."

– US SOF operator, Iraq

Planning for what was eventually to become Operation *Iraqi Freedom* began in December of 2001, even as Coalition Forces continued to battle Taliban and al-Qaeda elements in Afghanistan under Operation *Enduring Freedom*. Drawing on a pre-existing battle plan, the harried leader of CENTCOM, General Tommy Franks, began to

Iraqi and US Special Forces soldiers post security during an operation in as-Sadiyah September 5, 2008 in search of a suspected al-Qaeda in Iraq financier and facilitator. (US Navy)

develop options for an invasion of Iraq under the orders of then–Defense Secretary Donald Rumsfeld.

The plan soon evolved into a concept of operations that required far fewer resources than the original, and one that called for a concurrent start for both the air and ground components, in contrast with the protracted preliminary bombing campaign for Operation *Desert Storm* in 1991. SOF were an integral part of the plan, and their role would increase in light of the early successes of SOF in Afghanistan.

CENTCOM's Special Operations Command Central (SOCCENT) joined the planning process formally in March 2002 as conventional forces took over command and control of SOF in Afghanistan. Brigadier General Gary "Shooter" Harrell, a leader with an impressive SOF service history, took over command of SOCCENT in June 2002. Harrell had most recently commanded Task Force Bowie during Operation *Enduring Freedom*, and had previously served with 1st SFOD-D, after earlier stints with the 10th and 7th SFG.

Harrell and Franks developed a concept of operations that would see Coalition SOF deployed in three major areas. In the western deserts of Iraq, SOF would hunt down mobile SCUD TEL launchers, while providing special reconnaissance and screening tasks in support of conventional forces. In the north, SOF would work with the local Kurdish Peshmerga guerillas to draw Iraqi forces away from reinforcing Baghdad, while capturing strategic sites to allow conventional follow-on forces to deploy (a task which grew in importance with Turkey's refusal to allow conventional forces to deploy from her soil).

In the south, SOF would seize the national oil production facilities, provide special reconnaissance, and capture key facilities and transport nodes. A fourth covert SOF unit would carry out the hunt for weapons of mass destruction (WMD), and high-value leadership targets within the regime of Saddam Hussein.

Once the plan was signed by President George W. Bush, D-Day for Operation *Iraqi Freedom* was set for March 20, 2003. An air campaign known as "Shock and Awe" would kick off proceedings, while SOF teams quietly infiltrated into Iraq ahead of conventional forces. In reality, the first conventional operation of the war would occur during the early morning of March 19, when intelligence indicated that Saddam Hussein and his sons Uday and Qusay were holding a meeting at a location known as Dora Farms outside Baghdad. Four 2,000lb (909kg) laser-guided bombs struck the Dora Farms complex, dropped from a pair of F-117A Night Hawks, followed immediately by a salvo of Tomahawk land attack missiles (TLAMs) fired from ships in the Gulf. Disappointingly, the targets of this "decapitation strike" were not present.

Iraqi Freedom officially began in the early hours of March 20, after the deadline for Saddam and his sons to leave the country expired. As "Shock and Awe" got underway, conventional forces crossed the Kuwaiti border: the 3rd Infantry Division took the lead for V Corps, across the western desert heading north for Najaf, Karbala and finally Baghdad; the 1st Marine Expeditionary Force (1 MEF) headed up the rough centre of southern Iraq toward Nasiriyah and al Kut; and the British 1st Armoured Division headed up the east of the country bound for Basra. The planned attack from the north by the 4th Infantry Division was stymied by Turkey, and it thus fell to SOF alone to carry out the northern attack.

COMBINED JOINT SPECIAL OPERATIONS TF-WEST

Resurrecting the "Task Force Dagger" moniker from their operations in Afghanistan, the Combined Joint Special Operations Task Force-West (CJSOTF-West) was again led by Colonel John Mulholland and built around his 5th SFG (Airborne). The 5th SFG ODA teams were tasked with two core missions: the first was to counter the SCUD ballistic missile threat by both locating and destroying the SCUD TEL launchers and denying the Iraqi military the use of potential launch sites; the second was to

A US Navy SEAL on joint patrol with Iraqi SOF, carrying an Mk 18 Mod 0 CQBR (Close Quarter Battle Receiver); an EOTech 551 sight is unusually mounted on the forward rail, and note the forward grip with flashlight. The antenna poking over his shoulder shows that he also carries an MBITR radio on the back of his plate-carrier. (US Navy)

provide both an intelligence-gathering and a screening function in support of the conventional forces, to build up an accurate picture of Iraqi force dispositions in the west of the country.

The ODAs of 5th SFG were deployed under the command and control (C2) of ODB teams; the latter operated as advanced operating bases (AOBs), which also provided a mobile resupply function with their modified "War Pig" Light Medium Transport Vehicles. The concept was first developed by 5th SFG in the mid-1990s, based on the use of Unimog forward resupply "motherships" to resupply their mobility patrols by UK Special Forces during Operation *Desert Storm*. The 5th SFG were assigned responsibility for two sectors of western Iraq – the western and southern Joint Special Operations Areas (JSOAs). One element, termed FOB 51 and commanded by AOB 520 and AOB 530, was composed of the ODAs of 1st Battalion staged out of H-5 airfield in Jordan, and was responsible for the western zone. The group's 2nd and 3rd Battalions deployed from Ali al Salim Air Base in Kuwait as FOB 52 and 53 respectively, dedicated to the southern JSOA. Assigned to all teams were Special Tactics airmen from the 23rd STS, trained to guide in close air support and manage the airspace above the ODA teams.

A company element from the 19th SFG was attached to Dagger, as were several regular Army and National Guard infantry companies to provide FOB security and act as a QRF – a role previously provided in Afghanistan by the Rangers, but these were otherwise tasked in Operation *Iraqi Freedom*. As the prospect of war grew, the ODAs of Company A, 1st Battalion, 19th SFG were tasked with liaison roles supporting conventional forces: ODA 911 and 913 were to support 1 MEF; 914 was divided into two sub-teams, one being assigned to 3rd Infantry Division alongside ODA 916, and the other to the British 1st Armoured Division; while ODA 915 was attached to 101st Airborne Division following 3rd Infantry Division across the western desert. A final 19th Group ODA, 912, was tasked with providing the Personal Security Detail (PSD) for General Harrell, commander of the Combined Forces Special Operations Component Command (CFSOCC).

The aviators of 3rd Battalion, 160th SOAR deployed alongside TF Dagger, as the Joint Special Operations Air Detachment-West (JSOAD-West), with eight MH-47D heavy lift Chinooks, four MH-60L Direct Action Penetrators (DAP), and two MH-60K Black Hawk helicopters. In addition, a flight of Air National Guard (ANG) A-10 Warthogs and a flight of USAF F-16Cs were deployed to H-5 to serve as dedicated SOF close air support. Task Force 7 also had their own dedicated close air support at H-5 from two flights of RAF GR7 Harriers that had trained with the UKSF elements, and heavy lift in the form of CH-47 Chinooks from 7 Squadron and C-130s from the RAF Special Forces Flight from 47 Squadron.

COMBINED JOINT SPECIAL OPERATIONS TF-NORTH

Responsibility for special operations in the north was assigned to Combined Special Operations Task Force-North (CJSOTF-North), known as TF Viking. Its core component, the 10th SFGA, was the obvious choice, having extensive experience between 1991 and 1996 in Kurdistan during Operation *Provide Comfort*, a United Nations-led operation to save the Kurds living in northern Iraq from persecution by Saddam. Working alongside the 10th SFGA would be the men of 3rd Battalion, 3rd SFG who had recently returned from Afghanistan; 20th SFG (NG) and 2nd Battalion 7th SFG had assumed the role of CJSOTF-Afghanistan in September 2002, freeing up 3/3rd SFG to contribute to Viking. The 123rd STS, an ANG Air Force Special Operations Command unit, were slated to support the Viking ODAs on the ground. Conventional infantry units attached to Viking were the 173rd Airborne Brigade and several companies from 2nd Battalion, 14th Infantry Regiment, of 10th Mountain Division.

Originally, the war plan called for TF Viking to support 4th Infantry Division's march south toward Baghdad from Turkey. With Turkey denying staging rights to US forces and the 4th Infantry Division's mission consequently scrubbed, Viking was assigned the task of keeping Iraqi forces in the north from reinforcing Baghdad. The men of Viking began to look for other infiltration routes bypassing Turkish airspace. As the official Army Special Operations History account *All Roads Lead To Baghdad* succinctly explains, after Turkey denied permission "CJSOTF-North transitioned from being a supporting element to being a supported command. Without a strong infantry presence in the north, it fell to the 10th SFG to organize the Kurdish Peshmerga and keep 13 Iraqi infantry and armored divisions north of Baghdad busy" – a tall order for the lightly equipped SOF.

In late 2002 several covert teams of mixed 10th SFG and OGA personnel from the CIA SAD (SAD) had been infiltrated into Kurdistan. They were based in the Harir Valley outside the Kurdish capital, Arbil, to develop "ground truth" intelligence and organize and train the Peshmerga. These teams now paved the way for the eventual insertion of the Viking ODAs, in much the same way as had the CIA Jawbreaker teams in Afghanistan in 2001.

The 10th SFG were not equipped with the Ground Mobility Vehicles (GMVs) of the 5th Group, and civilian vehicles therefore had to be procured. (Actually, 5th SFG had left many of their vehicles in Afghanistan with 3rd SFG, and consequently they had to embark on a hasty and extensive program of refitting standard HMMWVs to GMV specifications before deployment.) Some 230 non-standard tactical vehicles (NTVs) – the majority white Land Rover Defenders, along with some 30 Toyota Tacomas – were purchased and modified to SF requirements. These vehicles had to be driven covertly from warehouses in Turkey, under continual petty interference from the Turkish

The urban battlefield: a US Army SF operator covers the advance of an Iraqi Army ambulance and HMMWV. (DOD)

authorities, until they finally crossed the border into Kurdish territory. However, when the first ground operations of the war began in the pre-dawn hours of March 19, 2003, TF Viking was still trying to find a way into northern Iraq.

TASK FORCE 20

Assigned to the western desert along with Dagger was another special operations element known as Task Force 20. TF-20 was based on the concept of Task Force 11/Task Force Sword in Afghanistan, and was structured around similar units primarily drawn from JSOC. TF-20 was commanded by Major General Dell Dailey, a former commander of the 160th SOAR.

For Iraq, TF-20 was initially composed of C Squadron from 1st Special Forces Operational Detachment-Delta (1st SFOD-D), commonly known by their cover designation Combat Applications Group (CAG) or simply as Delta. Alongside the special operators of Delta were all three battalions of the 75th Ranger Regiment; a battalion-strength element from the 82nd Airborne Division, serving as both a heavier infantry punch and a QRF; and a truck-mounted High Mobility Artillery Rocket System battery to provide mobile indirect fire. (Later in the campaign, another Delta squadron and even a company of Abrams MBTs (main battle tanks) were added to TF-20.) A squadron from DEVGRU also operated under TF-20, although their mission set was principally around heliborne direct action raids. OGA SAD operators worked alongside the TF-20 operators, as did members of Grey Fox, JSOC's intelligence-gathering unit – previously known as the Intelligence Support Activity, amongst numerous other code names. Dedicated aviation was provided by 1st Battalion, 160th SOAR with their MH-60K Black Hawks, MH-60L Direct Action Penetrators, MH-6M transport, and AH-6M gunship Little Birds.

TF-20 were covertly based at an airbase at Ar'ar in western Saudi Arabia; they were tasked with seizing key targets including airfields deep in Iraq, capturing high value targets, and providing long-range special reconnaissance. One of the primary targets in prewar planning was the seizure of Baghdad International Airport, an operation for which two full-scale dress rehearsals were carried out but which was never mounted; conventional forces eventually seized the airport.

NAVAL SPECIAL OPERATIONS TASK GROUP

More commonly known simply as the Naval Task Group (NTG), this was the fourth and final special operations task force. It was built around a core component of US Navy SEAL Teams 8 and 10; the Polish special operators of GROM (Grupa Reagowania Operacyjno Mobilneho or Operational Reserve Group); the British Royal Marines of 40 and 42 Commandos under the command of HQ 3 Commando Brigade, and a small element from M Squadron, SBS; and attached US Psyop and Civil Affairs teams.

The NTG was principally tasked with the capture of Umm Qasr, Iraq's only deep-water port; the oil pipeline facilities of the Al Faw Peninsula; and the two off-shore platforms that these pipelines fed. Once these initial targets were secured, the NTG was tasked with supporting conventional forces in the south. Aviation was provided by both Marine Air of 15th MEU and the USAF's 20th Special Operations Squadron.

FIRST SHOTS

First blood in Operation *Iraqi Freedom* went to the aviators of the 160th SOAR. A flight of two MH-60L DAPs and four "Black Swarm" flights – each comprising a pair of AH-6 armed Little Birds and an MH-6 equipped with forward-looking infrared radar (FLIR) to identify and laser the targets for the AH-6s. Additionally, each Black Swarm was assigned a pair of A-10s to deliver Maverick air-to-ground missiles (ATGM) against

Joint operations by US Army Special Forces in up-armored M1114 "Humvees" and Iraqi Police Commandos in GM pickup trucks – the latter have home-made armor shields round the rear beds and mount PKM machine guns over the cabs. (US Navy)

any hardened targets the AH-6s couldn't handle with their .50-cal machine guns and 2.75in rockets.

At 2100hrs local on March 19, the DAPs and Little Bird flights engaged their first targets – Iraqi visual observation posts along the country's western and southern borders. The DAPs hit their targets with Hellfire ATGMs and followed up with bursts from their 30mm cannons. The Black Swarm teams relied on their MH-6 flight leads, who guided in the strikes or called in the orbiting A-10s. In the space of seven hours of darkness, 70-plus sites were destroyed, effectively depriving the Iraqi military of any early warning mechanism.

As the sites were eliminated, air corridors were opened and the first heliborne SOF teams were launched from H-5 in Jordan, including vehicle-mounted patrols from the British and Australian SOF components transported by the MH-47Ds of 3/160th. In the early morning hours, ground teams from Dagger, TF 20, and Coalition SOF breached the sand-berms along the borders with Jordan, Saudi Arabia, and Kuwait and drove into Iraq.

For TF Viking, the delay in infiltrating all of its ODAs into theater was becoming increasingly frustrating. Planners finally developed a punishing route from 10th SFG's forward staging area in Constanta, Romania, to northern Iraq via two undisclosed countries, and this was codenamed "Ugly Baby" – allegedly from a flippant description of the air route by an SF officer. March 22 saw this epic lift completed, with the majority of 2nd and 3rd Battalions landing near Arbil on board six MC-130H Combat Talons. The lift was not without its perils; several MC-130s were engaged by Iraqi air defense, and one airframe was sufficiently damaged by antiaircraft fire to make an emergency landing at – ironically enough – Incirlik Air Base in Turkey.

The initial lift had deployed a total of 19 ODAs and four ODBs from 10th SFG into northern Iraq. On March 23, Turkey allowed over-flights, and three final MC-130s flew in to Bashur outside the Kurdish capital of Arbil to reinforce the new arrivals. Eventually TF Viking numbered 51 ODAs and ODBs, alongside some 60,000 Kurdish Peshmerga militia of the Patriotic Union of Kurdistan (PUK). The SF had to make do with locally procured civilian transport as the first of their NSVs were still several days away. On March 26 the 173rd Airborne Brigade conducted a successful combat jump from C-17s into Bashur airfield, which was already secured by SF and Peshmerga; the 173rd were assigned the task of securing the Kirkuk oilfields.

Viking deployed initially to the Green Line, a north/south demarcation of the boundary of Kurdish territory. Their initial objectives were threefold: to prevent the reinforcement of Baghdad by tying up the estimated 13 Iraqi Army divisions operating in the north; to advance on the cities of Kirkuk and Mosul; and to carry out a direct action operation against an Ansar al Islam terrorist training camp along the border with Iran – this to be known as Operation *Viking Hammer*. Ansar al Islam was a Sunni terrorist group which counted among its founding members Abu Musab al Zarqawi, a Jordanian international terrorist who would later rise to prominence as the self-appointed head of al-Qaeda in Iraq (AQI). According to surveillance, around 700 Ansar members inhabited the valley, along with a Kurdish splinter faction. They had developed prepared defensive positions, including antiaircraft machine guns, and maintained a facility where intelligence suspected biological or chemical agents might have been developed or stored.

The operation was scheduled to launch on March 21, but the ground component was set back by several days due to the issues around infiltrating the majority of 3rd Battalion, 10th SFG into the country. A Tomahawk missile strike was set for midnight on the 21st as a preparatory barrage, and the strike could not be delayed because of the high tempo of operations elsewhere in theater. In the early hours, 64 Tomahawks struck the Ansar al Islam camp and surrounding sites, while SF members maintained surveillance to carry out a bomb damage assessment.

The ground attack was finally launched on March 28 with a six-pronged advance into the valley, each prong being composed of several ODAs from the 3rd Battalion and upwards of 1,000 Peshmerga fighters. The main advance set off toward Sargat, the location of the suspected chemical/biological site, but became pinned down by 12.7mm heavy machine gun fire from the surrounding hills. A pair of Navy F/A-18s responded to an urgent close air support request and delivered two 500lb (227kg) JDAMs against the Ansar machine gun nests; the pilots then obligingly strafed the positions with 20mm cannon before exiting the valley, low on fuel. The advance resumed, only to be halted repeatedly by hidden DShK and PKM positions. ODA 081 deployed a Mk19 automatic

grenade launcher from an NSV and suppressed the gun positions, allowing the PUK to assault and wipe out the Ansar defenders. The PUK captured the town of Gulp and attacked their primary target, the village of Sargat, which was heavily defended by fortified fighting positions, DShKs, and mortars along with several BM-21 MLRS firing in support. Unable to call in "fast air" (jet close air support) due to the location of the PUK, the ODAs used a dismounted .50-cal M2 to suppress the entrenched Ansar; this allowed the Peshmerga to bring up their own mortars and BM-21s, which eventually forced the Ansar to retreat.

TF Viking advanced to secure the Daramar Gorge, which was surrounded by caves in the rock walls. The Peshmerga were again engaged by small arms and RPG fire, which they and the ODAs enthusiastically returned with .50 and 40mm grenades; however, it soon became obvious that they could advance no further without air support. Covering their withdrawal again with the dismounted .50-cal, the ODAs called in fast air, and six 500lb (227kg) JDAMs shut down any further resistance. During the night of the 28/29th four AC-130 gunships maintained the pressure on the retreating Ansar as they moved toward the Iranian border. On the 29th, TF Viking seized the high ground and pushed through the valley, killing small pockets of diehards. With *Viking Hammer* successfully completed, 3rd Battalion and their Peshmerga returned to the Green Line to assist in the push on Kirkuk and Mosul.

A specialist sensitive site exploitation team was brought in to document the finds at Sargat. The team recovered traces of several chemicals including Ricin, along with stocks of NBC suits, atropine injectors (used to counteract the effects of chemical weapon exposure), and Arabic-language manuals on chemical weapons and improvised explosive device (IED) construction. Examination of the bodies at the site showed many of the Ansar al Islam to be foreign fighters from a variety of countries. Estimates of enemy dead numbered over 300; 22 Peshmerga had been killed, with no US losses.

TF Viking regrouped before launching an operation to seize the town of Ayn Sifni, which straddles the main highway into Mosul and was thus of strategic importance. Following the lead from their brother teams in the west, the 10th and 3rd SFG ODAs called in fast air on the Iraqi garrison, resulting in many retreating. By April 5 there appeared to be only two Iraqi platoons left in Ayn Sifni. On the 6th, the attack was launched with three ODAs – 051, 055, and 056. The 051 would lead the actual assault

LEFT: US ARMY SPECIAL FORCES IN IRAQ.
1) US Army 10th Special Forces Group. He is firing a .50-cal M107 Barrett sniper rifle mounting a Leupold scope and PEQ-2 IR laser; the weapon next to him is a 7.62 x 51mm M14 Designated Marksman Rifle (DMR). 2) US Army 5th Special Forces Group. Another member of an ODA, wearing three-color Desert Combat Uniform and SPEAR body armor. 3) USAF 24th Special Tactics Squadron. This combat controller has a rare Integrated Ballistic Communications Helmet (IBCH) (Richard Hook © Osprey Publishing)

An HH-60G Pave Hawk casevac helicopter lands in a stony riverbed to evacuate a casualty, while a Special Forces GMV provides security at the landing zone. (DOD)

with some 300 Peshmerga, while 055 and 056 would act as fire support groups (FSGs) along with Peshmerga heavy weapons teams. As 051 advanced toward the village they came under intense fire – the "two platoons" of defenders turned out to be closer to battalion strength, and equipped with 82mm mortars, antiaircraft artillery, and even an artillery piece. After four hours of air support and fire from the two FSGs, the assault elements finally entered Ayn Sifni. Soon afterwards an Iraqi infantry counterattack supported by several mortars attempted to retake the town, but was beaten back by 051 and the Kurds. On the same day, southeast of Ayn Sifni, another action was occurring which would go down in Special Forces history – the battle of the Debecka crossroads.

THE BATTLE OF THE DEBECKA CROSSROADS

The Debecka crossroads cut both the main roads leading to Kirkuk and Mosul, and seizing the road junction would effectively eliminate Iraqi capabilities to reinforce the north. Overlooking this strategic crossroads was the Zurqah Ziraw Dagh ridge, which was occupied by Iraqi forces protecting the crossroads.

The operation commenced with B-52 strikes against the Iraqi defenders on the ridge. In the wake of the bombing, ODA 044 with 150 Peshmerga advanced toward Objective Rock, a T-junction leading to the crossroads and to the town of Debecka itself.

Supporting 044 were two 3rd SFG ODAs – 391 and 392 – providing fire support from their GMVs. To their north, two groups of Peshmerga fighters, some 500 strong in all, advanced on the ridgeline. Further north, ODA 043 – again with 150 Kurds, and with ODAs 394 and 395 acting as FSGs – attacked Objective Stone, a commanding hilltop occupied by Iraqi forces.

The central columns of Peshmerga reached their objectives first, and ran into only token resistance, successfully seizing their sector of the ridgeline. ODAs 394 and 395 began suppressing the defenders of Objective Stone after a scheduled airstrike failed to soften up the defenses (only four JDAMs were dropped, and only one hit). The two ODAs were engaged by DShK and 120mm mortar fire, and due to the poor results of the air strike 043's Peshmerga refused to move forward. 043 finally managed to procure additional close air support, which covered the withdrawal of the fire-support ODAs back out of mortar range and suppressed Stone's defenders. ODAs 394 and 395 quickly re-supplied from the FOB and raced forward once again, but were not yet in place when 043 and their Peshmerga closed on the objective. Thankfully, the SF and the militia speedily routed the Iraqis and captured the hilltop.

To the south, ODAs 044, 391, and 392 ran into a dirt berm that the Iraqis had built across the road toward Objective Rock, with mines scattered over the roadway. While the Peshmerga attempted to clear the mines, the ODAs went cross-country to bypass the roadblock. As the teams crested the ridge they contacted Iraqi infantry in prepared positions and bunkers, who soon surrendered under the guns of the GMVs. One of the prisoners, an Iraqi colonel, related that an armored unit that had been supporting them had withdrawn to the south. The teams returned to breach the dirt berm on the road behind them with demolitions in case a hasty retreat was required, and moved up onto a ridge (known later as Press Hill) overlooking the concealed southern approach. The ODAs then advanced down to the Debecka crossroads; 392 pursued several 60mm mortar teams at the edge of Debecka until they were engaged at long range by a ZSU-57-2, while 391 destroyed fire several trucks and "technicals" (armed pickups) heading from Debecka with Javelin ATGM and .50-cal.

Soon afterwards, the ODAs saw several Iraqi MTLB APCs appear out of the haze, moving toward the crossroads and using smoke generators to lay down a smoke screen behind them. Engaging with the .50s and Mk 19 automatic grenade launchers on their GMVs in an attempt to suppress them, the SF raced to ready their Javelins. At that moment, four Iraqi T-55 MBTs pulled out from behind the MTLBs' smoke screen, which had been cannily used to cover their approach.

The T-55s began firing their 100mm main guns directly at the ODAs. Abandoning a plan to engage with Javelins, since the Command Launch Units (CLU) required too long to warm up, the ODAs mounted their GMVs and pulled back to a ridgeline some

1

2

1,000yd (900m) from the crossroads, which they quickly dubbed "Alamo" – in SOF parlance, a site for a last-ditch defense while awaiting reinforcement. The ODAs quickly requested air, only to be told it would take 30 minutes to arrive. They began killing MTLBs with their Javelins; they soon ran low on rounds, but the onslaught of missiles temporarily halted the Iraqi armored attack and bought the SF time. The T-55s used the cover of a berm to approach the crossroads, effectively shielding them from a "lock on" from the Javelins.

Finally, some 35 minutes after the initial request was made, two Navy F-14s arrived. After the SOF talked in the first bombing run on the T-55s, the unthinkable happened: the first 2,000lb (909kg) bomb was dropped amongst friendly forces, including the AOB now located back at Objective Rock. The pilot had somehow become confused and targeted the rusted hulk of an old T-55 at Rock rather than the four tanks engaging the ODAs. The bomb killed a dozen Peshmerga, and wounded both the four AOB members and a BBC camera crew accompanying the Peshmerga; veteran BBC correspondent John Simpson was among those injured. A half-team from 391 immediately drove to the scene and began treating casualties.

The rest of the ODAs were forced to pull back from Alamo to Press Hill as Iraqi artillery began to bracket them. One of the ODA members managed to destroy with a Javelin a T-55 that attempted to advance toward them; F/A-18s arrived and soon drove off the remaining armor. With the battle over, the results were tallied: 26 Army SF had managed to blunt an attack by a reinforced company of Iraqi mechanized infantry in APCs, supported by a platoon of tanks and artillery. Ironically, a day after the battle, Task Force 1-63 Armor arrived in Arbil with its company of M1A1 MBTs and Bradley infantry fighting vehicles (IFVs) – a force that would have been ideally suited to assist at Debecka.

THE FALL OF KIRKUK AND MOSUL

The Peshmerga and the nine ODAs from FOB 103 encircled Kirkuk on April 9, after fierce fighting to capture ridges overlooking the approaches to the city. The earlier capture of the nearby city of Tuz had broken the will of the Iraqi Army, and primarily only *fedeyeen* (militiamen) remained in Kirkuk. The first ODA units entered the city on

LEFT: SPECIAL FORCES VEHICLES, IRAQ.
1) M1078 LMTV "War Pig," US 5th SFG. The modified LMTV was developed by 5th Special Forces Group to act as both a mobile resupply and a command-and-control vehicle, crewed by ODB teams. 2) Ground Mobility Vehicle, US 5th SFG. This GMV is typical of the modified "Hummers" used by 5th SFG for their operations in western Iraq in spring 2003. Doors and windows have been removed to allow firing from inside the vehicle and to make rapid "de-bussing" easier. (Richard Hook © Osprey Publishing)

April 10, to a Normandy-like reception from the Kurdish inhabitants. By April 18 the 173rd Airborne Brigade had taken over responsibility for Kirkuk and the city was firmly in Coalition hands.

A day after the first teams entered Kirkuk, an advance element from FOB 102 numbering no fewer than 30 operators – including the 2nd Battalion commander himself – drove unopposed through abandoned Iraqi lines and into Mosul; this advance followed several days of heavy airstrikes on three Iraqi divisions defending the city. On April 13 the 3rd Battalion of 3rd SFG, a battalion from the 10th Mountain and the 26th MEU (who had infiltrated into Arbil only days earlier) were ordered into Mosul to take over responsibility from the 10th SFG and their loyal Peshmerga.

In the west, Bravo and Charlie Companies of 1st Battalion, 5th SFG crossed the Kuwaiti border with ODA 531 using breaching demolition charges to clear a path through the berms for its "War Pigs" and GMVs. Charlie's seven ODAs, in some 35 vehicles, took to the southeastern half of the western desert, heading toward the towns of Nukyab, Habbariya, and Mudyasis. ODA 534 headed for the area surrounding Nukyab to search for SCUD launch sites. Bravo set out for the central western town of Ar Rutba and the Iraqi airbase west of it, code-named H-3, with six ODAs and an ODB in the resupply War Pigs. ODAs 523 and 524 searched a suspected SCUD storage facility, while ODAs 521 and 525 were tasked with clearing several abandoned airfields. With no sign of SCUDs, ODA 525 was re-tasked on March 21 with deploying a special reconnaissance team to conduct surveillance on the town of Ar Rutba itself. A two-man team was inserted onto a hill overlooking the town, and almost immediately called in a pair of nearby F-16s to destroy a radar facility they identified.

ODA 525 had deployed a second special reconnaissance team covering the two highways leading to Ar Rutba; this team was soon compromised by Bedouins who reported their location to the Ar Rutba garrison. A pickup truck leading four technicals, each mounting a DShK and carrying members of the Saddam Fedeyeen, appeared looking for the team. The SF soldiers pulled out in their GMVs, quickly using the FalconView mapping software on their Toshiba Toughbook laptops to establish a hasty ambush. As the *fedeyeen* drove into range they were engaged by the M2 .50-cal and Mk 19 40mm advanced grenade launcher mounted on the GMVs, and retreated rapidly. Quickly realizing that the hilltop team could be compromised and overrun, the ODA 525 GMVs attempted to exfiltrate them; but before they could, Iraqi vehicles began driving out of Ar Rutba, pulled into prepared defensive positions around the southwest of the city, and then began advancing up the hill. The ODA team leader recognized the danger and broadcast the emergency brevity code "Sprint" on the Guard Net emergency channel, which is heard by all nearby Coalition aircraft. The brevity code is only used when friendly ground callsigns are in imminent danger of being overrun, and it is not used lightly. An Airborne Warning and Control System (AWACS) immediately responded and an urgent request was made for close air support.

While the ODA awaited the arrival of the fast air, the special reconnaissance team began taking out individuals among the *fedeyeen* force at the base of the hill with their sound-suppressed Mk 12 sniper rifle. The team leader meanwhile managed to contact 521, which was clearing suspect sites east of Ar Rutba, and they raced to reinforce 525. Within minutes, the first F-16Cs swooped in and engaged the enemy vehicles. The response to the brevity code emergency call was heartening. Speaking directly with the AWACS, the ODA's attached ETAC stacked arriving fast air as it arrived. He then assigned flights, which were called in to their targets by the reconnaissance team, with one man operating the Multi Band Inter Team Radio (MBITR) and the other firing the Mk 12. At one point there were as many as four flights stacked – so many that mid-air refueling was needed. Finally, after four hours of punishing air strikes on the *fedeyeen*, the eight GMVs of 525 and 521 managed to extract the team under the air cover of a B1B bomber, which shadowed them back to ODB 520's location in a dry wadi bed south of Ar Rutba. Conservative bomb damage assessment pointed to over 100 *fedeyeen* killed.

The other ODAs had also had their hands full. A *fedeyeen* convoy attempting to flank 525 ran into the weapons systems of 524's GMVs. In the resulting three-hour contact, four technicals were destroyed and 524 repelled an assault by a company of infantry, with 525 vectoring fast air to 524 as and when required. To the west, ODA 523 had moved to reinforce 524 but ran into a pair of technicals on the highway, which they engaged and destroyed with the GMVs and small arms; 523 ceased fire as a civilian station wagon packed with Iraqi children drove – incredibly – straight through the middle of the action. 522 had identified two *fedeyeen* technicals proceeding down the highway toward 523 and set a hasty vehicular ambush that caught the Iraqi militia unawares; both technicals were disabled and 15 *fedeyeen* were killed.

The intent of the ODAs was to shut down the main supply routes and to secure sites around Ar Rutba and the strategically important H-3 airfield, before slowly tightening the noose around both. H-3 appeared to be defended by around a battalion of Iraqi troops and significant amounts of both mobile and static antiaircraft firepower. From March 24 the surrounding ODAs (and elements from Task Force 20, the UK Task Force 7, and Australian Task Force 64, who supported the operation) called in a solid 24 hours of precision airstrikes on H-3, using their SOFLAM laser designators. The bombardment seemed to do the trick: on the 25th, two long columns of military vehicles left H-3 at speed, heading east toward Baghdad during a respite in the bombing. ODA 521 managed to set an ambush and destroyed the lead vehicle in the first convoy, a truck-mounted ZPU-23, with a Javelin antitank missile shot. With the convoy halted in disarray, 521 made an urgent call for fast air, but as luck would have it a sudden sandstorm swept

A US Army Special Forces soldier, wearing night vision goggles, provides cover for a joint US Special Forces/Iraqi SOF night raid. (US Army)

across the desert, forcing an abandonment of the close air support; under cover of the sandstorm, the convoys scattered and escaped in all directions.

Airfield H-3 now looked unoccupied, and on March 27, Bravo Company and the Coalition SOF patrols moved in. They found a French Roland SAM, around 80 assorted AA guns including a ZSU-23-4, SA-7 MANPAD SAMs, and an enormous amount of ammunition. H-3 became Bravo's patrol base, with ODAs returning for resupply delivered by C-130s and MH-47s. ODA 581 captured the Iraqi three-star general formerly in command of H-3, trying to escape dressed in civilian clothes in the back of a taxi. He was quickly secured and flown out by a 160th SOAR MH-6 for further interrogation. Additionally, 523 discovered chemical weapons samples in a lab on H-3.

BASRA AND NAJAF

In the south, 2nd Battalion of the 5th SFG was given two key tasks: Charlie Company would support the Marines and the UK Battle Group around Basra, while Bravo would work targets around Najaf. ODA 554 crossed the border on March 21 with the USMC, tasked with supporting the seizure of the Rumaylah oilfields which would later be secured by UK forces. A half-team from 554 drove to the outskirts of Basra to pick up four Iraqi oil industry technicians who had earlier been recruited by the OGA to assist in safeguarding the oilfields. The half-team successfully contacted the technicians, who were passed to the Marines, and 554 rejoined the other half of their team after several gunfights with *fedeyeen*.

Their new mission was to infiltrate undercover with an OGA-recruited local sheikh to assist the UK forces in identifying targets around Basra, during which task they encountered a surprising amount of resistance from militia in the city. ODA 554 ran an informer network, with the sheikh's assistance and supported by a hand-held mini-UAV called the AeroVironment Pointer; they eventually assisted the British in rounding up some 170 *fedeyeen* and Baathist leadership targets in and around Basra.

ODA 544 was infiltrated into Wadi al Khirr airfield by MC-130 and drove the 50 miles (80km) to Najaf. Upon arrival they began setting up temporary vehicle check points to gather local intelligence. (They were not the first ODA into Najaf; 572 had accidentally driven into the city after being given an incorrect grid reference, but quickly withdrew under mortar fire.) Once targets were identified, 544 would call in fast air to destroy them. The 3rd Infantry Division had bypassed Najaf on its way to Karbala, and 544 linked up with the follow-on forces, General Petraeus's 101st Airborne Division, who entered the city on March 30.

The 101st secured the city, leaving a brigade to clear up militia and Baath Party remnants; ODA 544 assisted by setting up a local security force to act as de facto police, and worked on developing a local civilian government. They ran into a character whose name would later become synonymous with violence in the south – Moqtada al Sadr, who organized the killing of a moderate cleric supported by the ODA. Meanwhile, ODA 563 worked in support of the USMC around Diwaniyah. Again working with local sheikhs and their militias, and supported by Marine Air, 563 managed to capture a whole city by itself – Qwam al Hamza. The next day 563, their local sheikhs' militiamen, and a Marine Force Recon team captured the bridge leading to Diwaniyah. The sheikhs' militias entered the city to pinpoint enemy positions, which were then engaged by Marine Air using 500lb (227kg) JDAMs to limit collateral damage. The surgical bombing worked, and the Iraqi Army and *fedeyeen* withdrew from the city toward Baghdad, chased by Marine aviators all the way.

ODA 563 then went into reconstruction mode – setting up a police service, restoring 80 percent of the city's electricity within a fortnight, reopening schools and hospitals, and even foiling a bank robbery. ODA 563's efforts in Diwaniyah were the fastest return of civil services anywhere in Iraq – again, a template that should have been followed.

ODA 553 attempted to infiltrate into Nasiriyah, but west of the city the left front tire of their MH-53J struck a sand dune, flipping the helicopter. A CSAR team landed and recovered the team members, several of whom were injured, before placing charges to destroy the stricken bird. The CSAR then ferried 553 back to Kuwait, where they reconfigured their loads; they later successfully inserted to conduct a special reconnaissance on the bridges leading into Nasiriyah. They had several contacts with *fedeyeen* before linking up with and escorting Army and Marine units into the city. They then went to work setting up an informer network and operating undercover to track local Baathists and *fedeyeen*, gradually building up a comprehensive intelligence picture. ODAs 565, 546, 543, and 542 were busy training the so-called Free Iraqi Forces, who had been ferried into Kurdistan and flown into the recently captured Tallil airfield outside Nasiriyah. The results were mixed; some units performed well, but others proved a liability.

TF-20 ACTIONS

On March 19 the men of C Squadron, 1st SFOD-D, attached to TF-20 became the first US SOF unit to enter Iraq, as they rolled across the border from Ar'ar in western Saudi Arabia in some 15 Pinzgauer 6x6 special operations vehicles and several armed NSVs. Accompanying the squadron of operators were Special Tactics CCTs, an intelligence team, several K-9 teams, and a pair of American Iraqis serving as interpreters. Delta was tasked with conducting selected high priority sensitive site exploitations on suspected chemical weapon facilities, before heading for the Haditha dam complex. Along the way, Delta supported the 5th Group ODAs and Coalition SOF at Ar Rutba, and in seizing the H-3 airfield. Meanwhile, on March 24, Rangers from 3rd Battalion conducted a combat drop into H-1 airfield located between Haditha and Ar Rutba, securing the site as a staging area for operations in the west.

For several nights, operators drove through Iraqi lines around Haditha dam on their custom "stealth" ATVs, marking targets for Coalition fast air; this resulted in the destruction of a large number of armored vehicles and antiaircraft systems. Delta's reconnaissance of the dam indicated that a much bigger force would be needed to seize it, and a request was made and approved for a second Delta squadron from Fort Bragg to be dispatched along with a battalion of Rangers and a company of M1A1 Abrams MBTs from Company C, 2/70th Armor. The tanks, soon to be termed "Team Tank," were flown in C-17s from Tallil to H-1 and on to Mission Support Site Grizzly, a desert strip established by Delta located between the dam and Tikrit. The additional Delta squadron – remarkably – flew directly into Grizzly from the US.

The evening of April 1 saw the Delta squadron and 3/75th Rangers conduct a ground assault in Pinzgauers and GMVs against the Haditha dam complex. Supported by a pair of AH-6Ms, they seized the dam's main administrative buildings with little initial opposition. Soon after daybreak a Ranger sniper killed three Iraqis with RPGs on the western side of the dam, and Rangers on the eastern side engaged a truck carrying infantry, which led to an hour-long contact. South of the dam itself, another Ranger platoon was busy securing the power station and electricity transformer, while yet another established blocking positions on the main road into the Haditha complex. The blocking positions came under mortar fire, resulting in the AH-6s flying multiple gun runs to silence the mortars; when another mortar opened fire from a small island it was quickly engaged and silenced by a Ranger Javelin team.

For five days after the seizure of Haditha dam Iraqi forces continued to harass the Rangers. The harassment principally consisted of artillery and mortar fire, but included several infantry assaults. Three Rangers were tragically killed on April 3 by a suicide car-bomber at one of the blocking positions; the car was driven by a distressed pregnant Iraqi woman, who asked the Rangers for water before detonating the car and killing herself, another female in the vehicle, and the three Rangers. At one point an Iraqi forward observer took to the waters of the dam in a kayak; this was sunk by .50-cal fire and the spotter was captured with sketch maps of the Ranger positions. Another, more pressing problem occurred when an artillery round struck a transformer, shutting down electricity to the dam. After the transformer was repaired it was discovered that only one of the five turbines at the dam was operating, and that the dam's seals were leaking. A former SF engineer with Civil Affairs flew in by MH-47E, and, assisted by the Iraqi civilian staff, managed to jury-rig fixes that would stop the dam bursting. An Army Engineer unit was later brought in to stabilize the facility. Ironically, it appeared that the

Iraqis had not been planning to destroy the dam, flooding the 3rd Infantry Division advancing through Karbala, but that the SOF mission to prevent it almost resulted in that unintended catastrophe.

Delta had handed over to the Rangers on April 1 and headed north to conduct ambushes along the highway north of Tikrit, tying up Iraqi forces in the region and attempting to capture HVTs trying to escape into Syria. In a contact with half a dozen *fedeyeen* technicals near Tikrit on April 2, two Delta operators were wounded, one seriously. C Squadron, still in contact, requested an urgent casevac and close air support as Iraqi reinforcements in the form of a company of infantry arrived. Two MH-60Ks and two MH-60L DAPs from 1/160th lifted off immediately and were over the beleaguered operators' positions 90 minutes later. The DAPs began engaging ground targets, allowing the Delta operators to move their casualties to an LZ where the MH-60Ks could land. One of the operators had died from blood loss and was loaded onto the second MH-60 wrapped in a US flag; the MH-60s raced back toward H-1 escorted by a pair of A-10s.

The DAPs stayed on station and destroyed a truck carrying a mortar team and several infantry teams; as they passed by the target, Iraqis began firing small arms up at the retreating DAPs until they were silenced by Delta snipers. Another pair of A-10s soon arrived and were guided onto their targets by the DAPs. One airburst 500lb (227kg) bomb sprayed fragments within 22yd (20m) of Delta positions, but killed a large number of infantry gathering in a ravine. The DAPs handed over to the A-10s to cover the Delta squadron as they prepared to advance further north. Low on fuel, they flew ahead of the ground callsigns and spotted several enemy mortar and infantry teams which they quickly engaged with 30mm cannon and minigun before they finally turned back for H-1.

Staging out of Grizzly, Delta mounted operations to interdict avenues of escape for Baath HVTs on Highway 1 (Highways 2 and 4 through the western desert were secured by UK and Australian SAS teams). On April 9 the combined team seized another airfield near Tikrit. During the night attack an M1A1 had driven into a deep hole, flipping the tank and injuring the loader. The Abrams was later destroyed by two 120mm rounds from one of its brother tanks, since it was judged as non-recoverable. In mid April, Delta moved into Baghdad and Team Tank returned to their parent unit.

HUNTING HVTS

In the early post-invasion operations, TF-20 concentrated on the hunt for the 55 HVTs featured in the infamous "HVT deck of cards"; carrying out sensitive site exploitations at facilities suspected of being used to store or process WMDs; and hunting down both Baathist targets escaping the country, and foreign jihadists

TASK FORCE 20 – HIGH-VALUE TARGET RAID

This generic scenario depicts a raid to capture or eliminate high-value AQI personnel reported hiding out in a suburban villa. Most such operations have top cover, here provided by an AH-6M Little Bird from the USAF's 160th SOAR (1). Ranger security teams (2, 3) are deployed along the access roads to intercept "squirters" leaving the location and any external attempts to interfere; they wear Army Combat Uniforms and are armed with M4A1s, M203s, and Mk46 Mod 0s. Their GMV (4) is parked opposite the main gate, covering the approach with a mounted M240B; a Ranger NCO orders curious civilians to keep clear (5). Inside, the Joint Special Operations Task Force assault team, composed of Delta operators, are in position in two four-man "stacks" each side of the main door (6). The lead man in the left stack is about to blow the door with a frame charge; the men behind him cover the door, upper windows and roof lines, and the team's rear. The operators wear a mix of Army Combat Uniforms, Desert Combat Uniforms, and commercial Multicam, and cutaway MICH helmets with Peltor headsets; their primary weapon is the Heckler & Koch 416 mounted with a mixture of sights – EOTech 553s and Schmidt & Bender Short Dots, and the lead man on the right also has a Remington 12-gauge to take care of any internal door locks. (Richard Hook © Osprey Publishing) attempting to enter it. They also carried out several unusual one-off missions, including the recovery of a Mi-17 Hip helicopter to use for later covert operations. The Task Force chalked up several early successes, including the capture of Palestinian terrorist leader Mohammed Abbas in Baghdad on April 19, 2003, and of the Iraqi deputy Prime Minister, Tariq Aziz, on April 25.

Notoriously, the hunt for WMDs went less successfully, with only the operation against the Ansar al Islam terrorist group in Sargat in northern Iraq by the 10th SFG recovering any evidence of chemical or biological weapons. TF-20 continued to conduct sensitive site exploitations throughout April 2003, sometimes only hours ahead of the "official" Army WMD sensitive site exploitation team – the 75th Exploitation Task Force – but with disappointing results.

Their third broad mission set, the interdiction of fleeing Baathists, notched up some notable successes. On the night of June 18, 2003, near the Syrian border, AC-130

July 22, 2003: a mixture of 101st Airborne and Delta personnel watch TOW missiles strike the villa during the last stand of Uday and Qusay Hussein. The Delta operators are those standing near the front in olive drab and black helmets; just visible are their SATCOM units resting on the HMMWVs and – under magnification – IR strobes attached to the rear of their helmets. (DOD)

Spectres guided by TF-20 operators struck a convoy of high-value Baath Party members escaping to Syria. Intelligence indicated that the convoy might include Saddam Hussein or his sons; other reports claimed that the convoy consisted only of oil-smugglers. Once the convoy was destroyed by the AC-130s, TF-20 conducted a heliborne assault into a nearby compound which proved to be a Baathist safe-house for ferrying former regime elements across the border. TF-20 also came under fire from Syrian border guards; in the uneven firefight that ensued, several Syrians were killed, 17 were captured and immediately released, and five were wounded and treated by Coalition forces before repatriation.

One of TF-20's next public HVT successes was the killing of Saddam's murderous sons, Uday and Qusay. With a $15 million reward on each of their heads, it did not take long for a former regime member to sell them out. The information was initially passed by the informer to the 101st Airborne, who consequently passed it to their divisional Special Forces liaison, who contacted TF-20. Uday and Qusay were hiding out in the informer's home in the Mosul suburb of Al Falah, along with Qusay's 14-year-old son and a bodyguard. According to several sources, a 12-man team of 22 SAS operators working in Mosul for TF-20 conducted an initial close target reconnaissance, and reported to the TF-20 leadership that they felt confident of covertly entering the premises at night and killing or capturing the targets. The US Army disagreed, however, and a plan was launched to attempt a daytime capture of the Hussein sons.

On July 22, elements of 101st Airborne set up a perimeter around the target house, and a Delta entry element made ready as the occupants were called upon via loudspeaker to surrender. The offer was met with silence; the operators rapidly breached the front door and deployed "flash-bangs" (stun grenades) before entering. They were immediately engaged with small arms fire, one man reportedly receiving a gunshot wound to the hip and several others being lightly wounded by grenade fragments as they withdrew to cover. A second Delta entry attempt was again met with gunfire, and the team discovered that the interior stairs to the second floor where the brothers were holed up were blocked with furniture and other obstacles. Another element of operators fast-roped to the roof of the building from an MH-6 to examine the possibility of an explosive entry point through the roof (and were almost accidentally engaged by orbiting OH-58 Kiowas). Finally the decision was made to soften up the target, and the 101st cordon engaged the building with .50-cal and AT-3 rockets. A third Delta entry was attempted, but was again driven back by gunfire. The Airborne were asked to deploy their TOW II-equipped HMMWVs, which proceeded to launch perhaps ten of these missiles into the house while from overhead Kiowas also hosed the premises with .50-cal and 2.75in rockets. After the TOW strikes, Delta successfully made entry on their fourth attempt. Qusay and the bodyguard had already died under the barrage; Uday was discovered

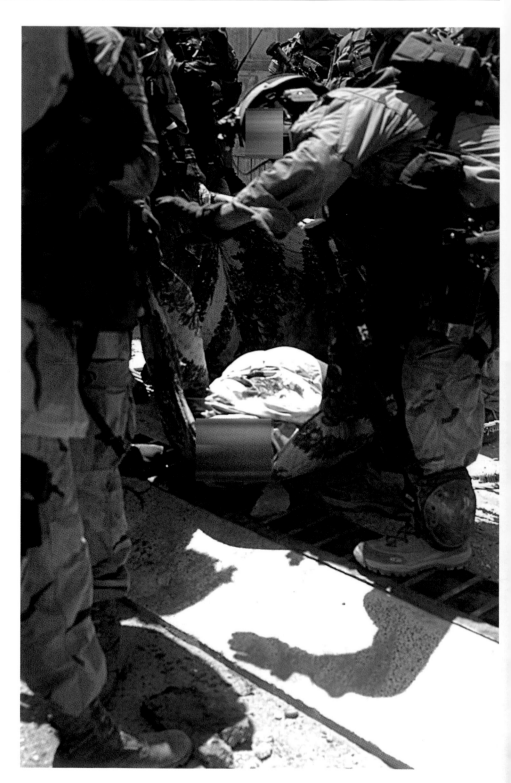

Delta operators carry the body of Uday Hussein from the rubble of the villa where he was cornered. The big sidearm just visible strapped to the thigh of the operator at right is a custom .45 ACP 1911 with an extended magazine, apparently with a tactical flashlight mounted under the barrel. (Photographer unknown)

gravely wounded but still armed and moving in the bathroom, and was shot and killed by a Delta operator. Qusay's teenage son Mustapha was hiding under a bed and opened fire as the operators entered; they had no choice but to return fire.

"RED DAWN"

Although they continued to successfully target former regime members, one of the Task Force's "Tier One HVTs" eluded capture – Saddam Hussein himself. Intelligence from former members of the Baath Party, supported by signals intelligence, finally pinpointed the fugitive dictator in a farm compound outside Al Dawr south of Tikrit, in the heartland of his clan. On the evening of December 14, 2003, Operation *Red Dawn* was launched (apparently named after the 1980s action film).

The 1st Brigade Combat Team of the 4th Infantry Division provided the cordon, while operators from C Squadron, Delta attached to the then-TF-121 searched two locations in the area codenamed Wolverine 1 and 2. An initial sweep found nothing, but as the operators were preparing to exfiltrate one noticed a piece of flooring material,

This Ranger on operations in Baghdad is armed with a 7.62mm Mk 48 Mod 0 machine gun, fitted with an M68 Aimpoint sight and Surefire light. His helmet mounts the AN/PVS-18 NOD, and note the combination of ECWCS jacket and Army Combat Uniform camouflage trousers. (Courtesy US Army Ranger Regimentt/USSOCOM)

which he kicked to one side, exposing a spider-hole dug in the ground. A Delta operator was preparing to drop a fragmentation grenade into the hole to clear it when Hussein popped up. Hussein was disarmed of his handgun and an AK-47 concealed in the hole

Marines with Bravo Company, 4th Reconnaissance Battalion (Marine Division Recon), wait to disembark the amphibious assault ship USS *Bonhomme Richard* during an exercise, June 2008. (US Navy)

with him; he was also carrying $750,000 in US dollars. The capture of the dictator was somewhat anti-climactic after the months Task Force 121 had spent searching for him; Hussein surrendered rather meekly, and was exfiltrated on a 160th SOAR MH-6 and taken into formal US custody.

ZARQAWI

The Task Force's most high profile target after Hussein was the Jordanian terrorist Abu Musab al Zarqawi. Zarqawi graduated from Palestinian terrorist organizations through Ansar al Islam, and finally became the nominal leader of AQI. He was responsible for numerous mass atrocities against Iraqi civilians in an attempt to incite a full-scale civil war between Sunni and Shia, and for beginning the barbaric practice of slowly beheading hostages on camera and releasing videotapes of these murders to jihadist websites. He made the top of the Task Force's hit list early in his brutal career with AQI, but it took the-then-TF-145 almost three years to kill him, despite several very near misses – including an operation in May 2006 where Zarqawi ran a Ranger roadblock to escape the Task Force. In fact, intelligence gathered and exploited (by the Grey Fox/Task Force Orange cell) from a series of raids that April and May eventually led directly to their principal target. These raids resulted in the killing or capture of over 100 AQI members including at least eight HVTs. A special operator described how many of these raids were conducted:

Marines from the 26th Marine Expeditionary Unit (SOC), Force Reconnaissance Detachment move quickly to their objective during a *Visit Board* search-and-seizure exercise in the Mediterranean in 2009. (USMC)

You have what they call landing on the X, the Y, and then an offset landing. Landing on the X is literally right on top of the target; the Y is within 500 meters or so; and an offset is a hike, say 3 to 6km typically, to mask the presence of helicopters. You'll usually post

The Deep Reconnaissance Platoon (DRP) with the 31st Marine Expeditionary Unit perform pistol and rifle drills aboard the USS *Essex*, 2006. Note the MEU(SOC) .45-cal pistols wielded by the Marines. The Deep Reconnaissance Platoon is focused on ground and amphibious reconnaissance, typically in the deep battle space. (USMC)

some sort of overwatch, rear security, and then a squad will clear the actual house.

It's not a loud thing. We have ICOM radios as well as MBITRs for everybody, so we've cleared entire houses and not awakened the occupants. No need for "sounding off" and yelling. We call it "softknock"; but you pan across the doorway and peak through windows before entering the room, to clear as much as possible before you even go in. After that, it's like typical CQB where you clear corners and such. My guys were pretty big on this, but others are bigger on the door breaches and flash-bangs.

After you clear it, you'll have security out to isolate the target, probably get machine guns on the roof top, and then start SSEing the house, interrogating occupants, etc. After that you'll call the birds, move to exfil with prisoners and evidence, and take off. We do both helo and ground insertions. We almost always have air overwatch – usually a DAP, sometimes AH-6s, and on occasion, if they're expecting something big, a Spectre gunship.

On April 16, 2006, a DEVGRU assault team supported by the Rangers assaulted an AQI safe house in Yusifiyah southwest of Baghdad, capturing five terrorists and killing five foreign fighters. On May 2 another operation in the same area resulted in ten foreign fighters killed, including three actually wearing suicide-bomb vests. On June 2, an AQI HVT was killed outside Balad. Each operation netted additional valuable intelligence, but the Task Force's successes did not come without casualties. An operation in Yusifiyah on May 14 saw an AH-6M gunship from B Company, 1/160th SOAR shot down by small arms, tragically killing both pilots while they supported operators from Delta; this battle raged around several AQI safe houses, resulting in 25 AQI killed and four captured.

On June 7, 2006, this intense series of raids finally culminated at an isolated compound outside Baqubah. US Army Major General Bill Caldwell said the operation crowned "a very long, painstaking, deliberate exploitation of intelligence, information-gathering, human sources, electronic and signal intelligence." It is believed that the captured HVTs provided information leading TF-145 to Sheikh Abd al Rahman, Zarqawi's personal "spiritual adviser"; Rahman was tracked electronically and by covert UAVs, and eventually he led the hunters to Zarqawi. A decision was taken that a ground operation might allow Zarqawi to escape, as he had done several times in the past. The uninhabited rural area around the identified safe house offered a reduced risk of collateral damage, allowing the Task Force to look at the option of a precision air strike. A special reconnaissance team from B Squadron of Delta was infiltrated covertly into the area to provide real-time surveillance, along with an RQ-1 Predator UAV which transmitted live imagery to the headquarters. Two orbiting F-16C Fighting Falcons flying a routine patrol out of Balad were tasked with the mission, and at 1815hrs local time the lead F-16 dropped a 500lb laser-guided bomb with a delayed fuse to allow the bomb to penetrate the house before detonation. A quick bomb damage assessment led to a second bomb, this time a GPS-guided 500lb (227kg) JDAM, which leveled what remained of the target. Zarqawi, Rahman, a bodyguard and three unknown women had been killed in the strike. Iraqi Army and regular US military arrived while the reconnaissance team covertly exfiltrated. Zarqawi was actually still alive when US forces arrived; they attempted to revive him, but he died almost at once.

The actions described above constitute just a small percentage of the totality of US SOF operations in Afghanistan and Iraq. They convey, however, not only the technical and tactical brilliance of these men in action, but also the confusion, horror, and general "friction" experienced by all soldiers in combat – SOF are not excluded from these. The accounts also illustrate how on many occasions US SOF work together with equivalent units from the foreign special ops community. Such cooperation is of enormous benefit to all parties involved. It not only facilitates the sharing of tactical information and relevant intelligence, but also provides insights into different ways of approaching the same problems, and into the various bits of equipment and weaponry out there on the international market. (All SOF personnel are invariably interested in new tools that will increase both their survivability and operational success rates.) Yet from a purely US perspective, we see the SOF operations since September 2001 not only as breaking new ground in unconventional warfare, but also as building upon lessons first laid in the woodlands of eastern North America back in the 18th century.

CONCLUSION

ON MAY 2, 2011, IN THE EARLY HOURS of the morning, two modified Black Hawk helicopters flown by aircrew of the 160th SOAR deployed two teams of US Navy SEALs from DEVGRU in and around a compound in Abbottabad, Pakistan, the known whereabouts of Osama bin Laden. The deployment itself did not go entirely smoothly – one helicopter was forced to make an emergency crash-landing (although without injury to any of the occupants) – but within seconds of touching ground the SEALs were racing through the compound rooms, scanning for targets with their night-vision goggles and HK 416 suppressed carbines. Shots were soon ringing out across the compound, splitting the night air. Several men and a woman were shot and killed before the SEALs then spotted their target, the man that the US SOF and the CIA had been searching for for more than a decade.

Corned in an upstairs room, bin Laden took shelter behind two of his wives. Both were brutally shoved out the way, one of them being shot in the leg to encourage her. Then SEAL operatives killed bin Laden with shots to the chest, before radioing "For God and country – Geronimo, Geronimo, Geronimo," and then, "Geronimo EKIA" (Enemy Killed in Action). Thousands of miles away in Washington DC, the US National Security Team alongside President Barack Obama watched the action unfold via real-time video link. At that point Obama said simply, "We got him."

The killing of Osama bin Laden once again shone the light on the US SOF. Such a bright light was not entirely welcome for the soldiers and staff of DEVGRU, who prefer anonymity to public identification, but there was no doubt that the mission illustrated the powerful international reach of US Special Forces. In his address to the nation, Obama acknowledged those who did service to the nation:

So Americans understand the costs of war. Yet as a country, we will never tolerate our security being threatened, nor stand idly by when our people have been killed. We will be relentless in defense of our citizens and our friends and allies. We will be true to the values that make us who we are. And on nights like this one, we can say to those families who have lost loved ones to al Qaeda's terror: Justice has been done.

Tonight, we give thanks to the countless intelligence and counterterrorism professionals who've worked tirelessly to achieve this outcome. The American people do not see their work, nor know their names. But tonight, they feel the satisfaction of their work and the result of their pursuit of justice.

We give thanks for the men who carried out this operation, for they exemplify the professionalism, patriotism, and unparalleled courage of those who serve our country. And they are part of a generation that has borne the heaviest share of the burden since that September day.

The operation against bin Laden illustrates perfectly the thinking behind the creation of and investment in SOF. The strike involved a mix of top-secret intelligence gathering on the part of the CIA, plus the specialist troops who were capable of making a nighttime incursion across national borders to take out a high-value target, and with the minimum of "collateral damage." The soldiers demonstrated the same planning and operational focus we have seen on many occasions in this book, from the assault on the Cabanatuan prison camp raid in 1945 through the LRRP actions against the VC in Vietnam through to actions by US SF in the mountains of Afghanistan. On account of such operations, there is always the danger of making SOF appear superhuman, and capable of anything – SOF are exposed to terrible misuse by ignorant commanders and politicians. Yet there is the undoubted truth that the limits of military action are stretched by this unique breed of soldiers.

A US airman with a special tactics training squadron prepares to conduct a HALO mission during exercise Emerald Warrior 2010 on March 16, 2010, near Fort Walton Beach, Florida. (USAF)

GLOSSARY

AEF	American Expeditionary Force
AFO	Advanced Force Operations
AFSOC	Air Force Special Operations Command
AGFRTS	Air and Ground Forces Resources and Technical Staff
AIT	Advanced Individual Training
AMF	Afghan Militia Forces
ANG	Air National Guard
AO	area of operations
AOB	advanced operating base
APC	armored personnel carrier
AQI	al-Qaeda in Iraq
ARCT	Airborne Regimental Combat Team
ARVN	Army of the Republic of Vietnam
ASTC	Alamo Scouts Training Center
ATGM	air-to-ground missiles
AWACS	Air Warning and Control System
BAR	Browning automatic rifle
BCT	basic combat training
BIS	Bureau of Investigation and Statistics
BSU	Boat Support Unit
BUD/S	Basic Underwater Demolition/SEAL
CAG	Combat Applications Group
CBI	China–Burma–India (theater)
C&C, CCT	combat controller

CENTCOM	Central Command
CIA	Central Intelligence Agency
CIC	Counterintelligence Corps
CIDG	Civilian Irregular Defense Group
CJCMOTF	Coalition Joint Civil-Military Operations Task Force
CJSOTF	Combined Joint Special Operations Task Force
CJTF-Mountain	Combined Joint Task Force-Mountain
COC	Combat Orientation Course
COI	Coordinator of Information
COIN	counterinsurgency
CRT	Command Readiness Team
CSAR	combat search and rescue
CTC	Counter Terrorist Center (CIA)
CTR	close target reconnaissance
CTZ	Corps Tactical Zone
DA	direct action
DAP	MH-60L Direct Action Penetrator
DEVRGU	Navy Special Warfare Development Group
DOD	Department of Defense
DSC	Distinguished Service Cross
ETAC	Enlisted Terminal Attack Controller
FBI	Federal Bureau of Investigation
FID	Foreign Internal Defense
FIS	Foreign Information Service
FLIR	forward-looking infrared radar
FOB	forward operating base
FOG	Field Operations Group
FSG	fire support group
FTX	field training exercise
GMV	Ground Mobility Vehicle
HAHO	High Altitude, High Opening
HALO	High Altitude, Low Opening (parachute team)
HMMWV	High-Mobility Multi-Purpose Wheeled Vehicle
EOU	Enemy Objectives Unit
HUMINT	human intelligence
HVT	high-value target
ISAF	International Security Assistance Force
JCS	Joint Chiefs of Staff

JDAM	Joint Direct Attack Munition
JIATF-CT	Joint Interagency Task Force-Counterterrorism
JSOA	Joint Special Operations Area
JSOAD-West	Joint Special Operations Air Detachment-West
JSOC	Joint Special Operations Command
JSOTF	Joint Special Operations Task Force
JTF-2	Joint Task Force 2
KSK	Kommando Spezialkräfte (German)
LLDB	Lac Luong Dac Biet
LRP	Long Range Patrol
LRRP	Long-Range Reconnaissance Patrol
LZ	Landing Zone
MACV-SOG	Military Assistance Command Vietnam, Studies and Observation Group
MBT	main battle tank
MCSF	Marine Corps Security Force
MEDCAP	Medical/Civic Action Program
MEF	Marine Expeditionary Force
MEU	Marine Expeditionary Unit
MGF	Mobile Guerrilla Force
MO	Morale Operations
MOS	military occupation specialty
MPC	Military Payment Certificate
MSPF	Maritime Special Purpose Force
MU	Maritime Unit
NAB	Naval Amphibious Base
NBC	Nuclear, Biological, Chemical
NSA	National Security Agency
NSW	Naval Special Warfare (Group)
NSWTG	Naval Special Warfare Task Groups
NSWTU	Naval Special Warfare Task Units
NTG	Naval Task Group
NTV	non-standard tactical vehicle
NVA	North Vietnamese Army
NZSAS	New Zealand 1st Special Air Service Group
ODA	Operational Detachment Alpha
ODB	Operational Detachment Bravo
ODC	Operational Detachment Charlie

OG	Operational Group
O&I	operations and intelligence
OP	observation post
OSS	Office of Strategic Services
OWI	Office of War Information
PJ	Pararescue Jumper
PRA	People's Revolutionary Army
PRT	Provincial Reconstruction Team
PRU	Provisional Reconnaissance Units
PWE	Political Warfare Executive
PX	post exchange
QRF	quick-reaction force
R&A	Research & Analysis (branch)
R&D	Research & Development (branch)
RON	remain overnight (position)
RRF	Ready Reaction Force
RTO	radio-telephone operator
SAD	Special Activities Division (CIA)
SAS	Special Air Service (British)
SASR	Australian Special Air Service Regiment
SAW	M249 Squad Automatic Weapon
SCI	Special Counterintelligence
SDV	SEAL Delivery Vehicle
SEAL	Sea, Air, Land (US Navy)
SFGA	Special Forces Group (Airborne)
SFHQ	Special Forces Headquarters
SFOB	Special Forces Operations Base
SFOC	Special Forces Officer Course
SFOD	Special Forces Operational Detachment
SFOD-D	Special Forces Operational Detachment-Delta
SFR	Security Force Regiment
SI	Secret Intelligence (branch)
SIGINT	signals intelligence
SIS	Secret Intelligence Service
SO	Special Operations (branch)
SOAR(A)	160th Special Operations Aviation Regiment (Airborne)
SOCENT	Special Operations Command Central
SOCOM	US Special Operations Command

SOE	Special Operations Executive
SOF	Special Operations Forces
SOFLAM	Special Operations Forces Laser Marker
SOG	Special Operations Group
SOI	Signal Operating Instruction
SOU	Ship Observer Unit
SR	surveillance and reconnaissance
SSE	sensitive site exploitation
SSTR-1	Special Services Transmitter Receiver Model No.1
STS	Special Tactics Squadron
TAOR	tactical area of responsibility
TF	Task Force
TO&E	table of organization and equipment
UAV	unmanned aerial vehicle
UDT	Underwater Demolition Team
UITG	US Army Vietnam Individual Training Group
UKSF	UK Special Forces
USAAF	US Army Air Force
USAF	US Air Force
USAISA	US Army Intelligence Support Activity (ISA)
USASFV	US Army Special Forces Vietnam
USASOC	US Army Special Operations Command
USCINCSOC	US Commander in Chief Special Operations Command
USMC	US Marine Corps
USNR	US Naval Reserve
USSF	US Special Forces
USSOCOM	US Special Operations Command
USSS	US Sharpshooters
UW	unconventional warfare
VC	Viet Cong
WMD	weapons of mass destruction

BIBLIOGRAPHY AND FURTHER READING

OSPREY TITLES

Badsey, Stephen, *Normandy 1944*, CAM 1 (Oxford, Osprey, 1990)

Bahmanyar, Mir, *Darby's Rangers 1942–45*, WAR 69 (Oxford, Osprey, 2003)

Bahmanyar, Mir, *US Army Ranger 1983–2002*, WAR 65 (Oxford, Osprey, 2003)

Bahmanyar, Mir, *US Navy Seals*, ELI 113 (Oxford, Osprey, 2005)

Chartrand, René, *Colonial American Troops 1610–1774 (2)*, MAA 372 (Oxford, Osprey, 2002)

Chartrand, René, *Colonial American Troops 1610–1774 (3)*, MAA 383 (Oxford, Osprey, 2003)

Foster, Randy E. M., *Vietnam Firebases 1965–73*, FOR 58 (Oxford, Osprey, 2007)

Gilbert, Ed, *US Marine Corps Raider 1942–43*, WAR 109 (Oxford, Osprey, 2006)

Henry, Mark R., *US Marine Corps in World War I 1917–18*, MAA 327 (Oxford, Osprey, 1999)

Katcher, Philip, *American Civil War Armies (3)*, MAA 179 (Oxford, Osprey, 1987)

Katcher, Philip, *Sharpshooters of the American Civil War 1861–65*, WAR 60 (Oxford, Osprey, 2002)

McLachan, Sean, *American Civil War Guerrilla Tactics*, ELI 174 (Oxford, Osprey, 2009)

Melson, Charles D., *Marine Recon 1940–90*, ELI 55 (Oxford, Osprey, 1994)

Neville, Leigh, *Special Operations Forces in Afghanistan*, ELI 163 (Oxford, Osprey, 2008)

Neville, Leigh, *Special Operations Forces in Iraq*, ELI 170 (Oxford, Osprey, 2008)

Rottman, Gordan L., *Green Beret in Vietnam 1957–73*, WAR 28 (Oxford, Osprey, 2002)

Rottman, Gordon L., *Mobile Strike Forces in Vietnam 1966–70*, BTO 30 (Oxford, Osprey, 2007)

Rottman, Gordon L., *Panama 1989–90*, ELI 37 (Oxford, Osprey, 1991)

Rottman, Gordon L., *Special Forces Camps in Vietnam 1961–70*, FOR 33 (Oxford, Osprey, 2005)

Rottman, Gordon L., *The Cabanatuan Prison Raid: The Philippines 1945*, RAID 3 (Oxford, Osprey, 2009)

Rottman, Gordon L., *The Los Baños Prison Camp Raid: The Philippines 1945*, RAID 14 (Oxford, Osprey, 2010)

Rottman, Gordon L., *US Army Airborne 1940–90*, ELI 31 (Oxford, Osprey, 1990)

Rottman, Gordan L., *US Army Long-Range Patrol Scout in Vietnam*, 1965–71, WAR 132 (Oxford, Osprey, 2008)

Rottman, Gordon L., *US Army Rangers and LRRP Units 1942–87*, ELI 13 (Oxford, Osprey, 1987)

Rottman, Gordon L., *US Army Special Forces 1952–84*, ELI 4 (Oxford, Osprey, 1985)

Russell Lee E. & Mendez, M. Albert, *Grenada 1983*, MAA 159 (Oxford, Osprey, 1985)

Smith, Carl, *US Paratrooper 1941–45*, WAR 26 (Oxford, Osprey, 2000)

Votaw, John F., *The American Expeditionary Forces in World War I*, BTO 6 (Oxford, Osprey, 2005)

Wiest, Andrew, *The Vietnam War 1956–74*, ESS 38 (Oxford, Osprey, 2002)

Zaloga, Steven J., *D-Day 1944 (1): Omaha Beach*, CAM 100 (Oxford, Osprey, 2003)

OTHER WORKS

Adkin, Mark Major, *Urgent Fury: The Battle for Grenada* (New York, Lexington Books, 1989)

Alexander, Joseph H., *Edson's Raiders* (Annapolis, MD, Naval Institute Press, 2001)

Alexander, Larry, *Shadows in the Jungle: The Alamo Scouts Behind Japanese Lines in World War II* (New York, New American Library, 2009)

Benson, Susan Williams (ed.), *Confederate Scout-Sniper, The Civil War Memoirs of Barry Benson* (Athens, GA, University of Georgia Press, 1992)

Berntsen Gary & Ralph Pezzullo, *Jawbreaker: The Attack on Bin Laden and Al-Qaeda: A Personal Account by the CIA's Key Field Commander* (New York, Three Rivers Press, 2006)

Black, Robert W., *Rangers in Korea* (New York, Ivy Books, 1989)

Black, Robert W., *Rangers in World War II* (New York, Ivy Books, 1992)

Bowden, Mark, *Black Hawk Down* (New York, Atlantic Monthly Press, 1999)

Breuer, William, *The Great Raid on Cabanatuan* (New York, John Wiley & Sons, 1994)

Cuneo, John R., *Robert Rogers of the Rangers* (New York, Richardson & Steirmna, 1987)

Darby, William & William Baumer, *We Led the Way: Darby's Rangers* (San Rafael, CA, Presidio Press, 1980)

Dockery, Kevin, *SEALs in Action* (New York, Avon Books, 1991)

Donahue, James C., *Blackjack-33: With Special Forces in the Viet Cong Forbidden Zone* (Novato, CA, Presidio Press, 1999)

Dunlop, Major W.S., *Lee's Sharpshooters; or, The Forefront of Battle* (Dayton, OH, Morningside, 1988)

Flanagan, Edward M. Lieutenant General., *Battle for Panama: Inside Operation Just Cause* (New York, Brassey's US Inc., 1993)

Foley, Dennis, *Special Men, A LRP's Recollection* (New York, Ivy Books, 1994)

Halberstadt, Hans, *US Navy SEALs in Action* (Osceola, FLA, MBI, 1995)

Hoffman, Jon T., *From Makin to Bougainville: Marine Raiders in The Pacific War* (Washington, DC, Headquarters Marine Corps, 1995)

Hoffman, Jon T., *Once A Legend – Red Mike Edson of the Raiders* (Novato, CA, Presidio Press, 1994)

Hogan, Jr., David W., *Raiders or Elite Infantry? The Changing Role of the US Army Rangers from Dieppe to Grenada* (Westport, CT, Greenwood Press, 1992)

Hopkins, James E.T. & John M. Jones, *Spearhead A Complete History of Merrill's Marauder Rangers* (London, Galahad Press, 2000)

Johnson, Forrest B., *Hour of Redemption: The Ranger Raid on Cabanatuan* (New York, Manor Books, 1978)

Kelly, Francis J., *US Army Special Forces, 1961–1971*, Vietnam Studies series (Washington, DC, Department of the Army, 1973)

Ladd, James, *Commandos and Rangers of World War II* (New York, St Martins Press, 1978)

Lanning, Michael Lee, *Inside the LRRPs: Rangers in Vietnam* (New York, Ivy Books, 1988)

Maloney, Sean, *Enduring the Freedom: A Rogue Historian in Afghanistan* (Dulles, VA, Potomac Books Inc., 2006)

Montgomery, George, Jr., *Georgia Sharpshooter, The Civil War Diary and Letters of William Rhadamanthus Montgomery* (Macon, GA, Mercer University Press, 1997)

Simpson, Charles M., *Inside the Green Berets* (Novato, CA, Presidio Press, 1983)

Smith, George W., *Carlson's Raid* (Novato, CA, Presidio Press, 2001)

Stanton, Shelby, *Green Berets at War: US Army Special Forces in Southeast Asia 1956–1975* (Novato, CA, Presidio Press, 1985)

Updegraph, Charles L. Jr., *U.S. Marine Corps Special Units of World War II* (Washington, DC, Headquarters Marine Corps, 1977)

INDEX

References to illustrations and plates are shown in **bold**. Captions to plates are shown in brackets.

coalition forces 295, 297, 298, 306, 311, 312, 313, 324, 330, 341
Coalition Joint Civil-Military Operations Task Force (CJCMOTF) 296, 298
coded messages 121, **131** (130), 152, 153, **181**, 236
code talkers **60–1**
Cold War 157, 160, 171, 248
collateral damage 342, 352–3, 357
Collett, John 282–3
Collins, General J. Lawton 160, 165
Combat Applications Group (CAG) 297, 298, 301, 311, 313, 317, 319, 328
combat controllers (CCT) **280**, 297, 311, 342
combat missions 226–7
Combat Orientation Course (COC) 199, 202
combat search and rescue (CSAR) 300, 342
Combat Service Support Teams (CSST) 261–2
Combat Water Survival Test (CWST) 193
Combined Forces Special Operations Component Command (CFSOCC) 326
Combined Joint Special Operations Task Force (CJSOTF) 296, 325, 327–8
Combined Joint Task Force-Mountain (CJTF-Mountain) 296, 298
Command and Control (CC) 184
Command Launch Units (CLU) 335
Command Readiness Teams (CRTs) **192**
Commando Training Center (Vietnam) 172
communications 132, 197; *see also* radio communications
communism 75, 168, 248, 293
and China 97, 98, 144–5
and Vietnam 141, 172
Communist National Liberation Front 172
Confederate Army 36, 45, 46–7, 50–1, 52, 53–4, 56
Confederate Ordnance Department 51
Connecticut Mohegan Indians 21
Connecticut Rangers 21, 24
Connecticut River 18
conscription 62
Continental Army 32
conventional forces 292, 311, 324, 325, 326, 327, 329
Cooper, Sergeant First Class Johnny F. **173**
Coordinator of Information (COI) 117, 118

Corps Tactical Zones (CTZs) 180
Counter Terrorist Center (CTC) 295
counterespionage 125–7
counterfeiting 130, 153
counterinsurgency (COIN) 94, 130, 132, 160, 169, 171, 176, 204, 243, 248, 264, 269, 292
Counterintelligence Corps (CIC) 127
counterterrorism 272
covert operations 63–4, 78
Cresap, Captai Thomas 21
Crown Point 22, 27
currency 133, 200–1
cyanide 156
Czechoslovakia 124

Dailey, Major General Dell 328
Dammer, Captain Herman 70–1
Darby, Lieutenant-Colonel William 70–3
Dari-a-Balkh valley 305
Daria-a-Souf valley 304
Davis, Jefferson 36
Debecka crossroads 334–5, 337
Delta Force *see* Special Forces Operational Detachment–Delta (1st SFOD–D)
demolitions 100, 116, **207**, 335, 338; *see also* Underwater Demolitions Team
Department of Defense (DOD) 165, 263
DEVGRU *see* US Navy: Special Warfare Development Group
Dickert, D. Augustus 54
Diver Propulsion Device (DPD) 269
Diwaniyah 342
Dixie Mission 144, 145
documentaries 130, 132
dogs **99**, 196, **199**, 218
Donlon, Captain Roger H.C. 215
Donovan, Major General William J. "Wild Bill" 95, 116–17, 118, **122**, 128, 130, 142
Doolittle raid (1942) 109
Dostum, General Abdur Rashid 299, 304, 305
Dozier, Brigadier General James L. 269
Dunlop, Captain W.S. 54, 56
Dunn, Captain Hezekiah 21, 24

Eastern Alliance 311
economics 128, 133, 292
Edson, Lieutenant-Colonel Merritt Austin "Red Mike" 94–5, 96, **97**
Eglin Field (Florida) 161
Eisenhower, Dwight D. **64**, 137–8, 165
El Salvador **249**, 269

Eleanor system 150, 152
elite troops 160
Civil War 36, 37, 58–9
and Vietnam 217, 239, 244, 245, 248
and World War II 67, 110–11, 116, 157
Enemy Objectives Unit (EOU) 129
enemy territory 62–3, 67, 118, 119, 120, **132**
and Vietnam 217–18
Engineer Course 196
Enlisted Terminal Attack Controller (ETAC) 317, 339
equipment **16** (17), **29**, 129–30, **259**
gas masks **235**
sharpshooter **49** (48), **57**
STABO harness **227**
and Vietnam **183**, 206–8, 230
World War II **65** (64), 154, 156–7
espionage 116, 118, 138; *see also* counterespionage
ethnic groups 176, 178, 204
Europe 119, 126, 128, 248, 251
Evans, Warren 70–1
extraction systems **229**

Far East 119, 121, 124–5, 126, 127, 128, 169; *see also* Southeast Asia
Far East Command 168
Fascism 120
Al Faw Peninsula 329
Federal Bureau of Investigation (FBI) 117, **289**, 298
fedeyeen 337, 338, 339, 341, 342, 344
Fertig, Colonel Wendell 164
fictitious organizations 121, 122, 124
Field Operations Group (FOG) 268
Field Photography Division 117–18, 130, 132, **146**
Field Training Exercise (FTX) 196
fire support groups (FSG) 334, 335
first aid 240
flags **57**
Fleet Antiterrorism Security Team (FAST) 272
Fleet Marine Force 264
Florida Phase 260
Flying Tigers 144
food 26–8, 206–7, 230, 238
Forbes, John 24
Forces Armées Nationales Khmer Training Command (FANK) 184
Ford, John 130
Foreign Information Service (FIS) 117, 118